OXFORD ENGLISH MONOGRAPHS

Committed Styles

Modernism, Politics, and Left-Wing Literature in the 1930s

BENJAMIN KOHLMANN

OXFORD
UNIVERSITY PRESS

Great Clarendon Street, Oxford, OX2 6DP,
United Kingdom

Oxford University Press is a department of the University of Oxford. It furthers the University's objective of excellence in research, scholarship, and education by publishing worldwide. Oxford is a registered trade mark of Oxford University Press in the UK and in certain other countries

First Edition published in 2014

Impression: 3

Published in the United States of America by Oxford University Press
198 Madison Avenue, New York, NY 10016, United States of America

British Library Cataloguing in Publication Data
Data available

Library of Congress Control Number: 2013956947

ISBN 978–0–19–871546–7

Printed and bound by
CPI Group (UK) Ltd, Croydon, CR0 4YY

Acknowledgments

Many people have read and commented on parts of this book. Above all I am grateful to Valentine Cunningham for his intellectual generosity and encouragement, both of which extended well beyond the time I spent working on my doctoral thesis at Oxford. I also owe special thanks to Laura Marcus, Matthew Beaumont, and Peter Stansky for their incisive comments on the whole manuscript—their perceptive advice greatly improved this book. At the University of Freiburg I am very grateful to Monika Fludernik who offered important feedback and was supportive of the project from its inception. A number of people have read individual chapters or parts of chapters: Susan Wolfson, my panel chair at the MLA, gave extremely helpful feedback as I began to work on William Empson; the conversations and email exchanges with Kate Bucknell (on Edward Upward) and with Nick Hubble (on Mass-Observation) have been invaluable. I am also grateful to Nick Jenkins, Peter Stansky, and Alex Woloch for inviting me to present my work at Stanford as I was revising the book manuscript for publication—their comments came at exactly the right moment and helped me to articulate the argumentative framework of this book. Finally, I want to thank Daniel Brückenhaus, Kirsty Martin, and Piers Pennington for reading and discussing central portions of this book with me and for spotting many major and minor mistakes.

Every attempt has been made to contact copyright holders, and thanks are due to several persons and institutions for granting me permission to reprint archival material from their collections. Materials by Empson are reprinted by permission of the Master and Fellows of Magdalene College, Cambridge; archival material relating to Hugh Sykes Davies is reprinted by permission of John Kerrigan and the Master and Fellows of St John's College, Cambridge. Permission to quote from David Gascoyne's unpublished notebooks was kindly granted by Stephen Stuart Smith at Enitharmon Press. Curtis Brown granted copyright to quote from materials in the Mass Observation Archives and the Charles Madge Archive at the University of Sussex. The two photographs by Humphrey Jennings are reprinted with permission of Dr Mary-Louise Jennings and the Bolton Museum and Archive Service. The permission to reprint Eugène Atget's photograph was granted by the Musée Carnavalet and Roger-Viollet. It is a special pleasure to acknowledge the help and advice offered by Edward Upward's daughter Kathy Allinson and her son Dave Allinson, who kindly granted permission to quote from Upward's letters, notebooks, and diaries. Parts of the chapter on William Empson first appeared in *ELH*, 80, 1, Spring 2013, pp. 221–49, and I am grateful to Johns Hopkins University Press for permission to reprint these passages here.

At OUP, I would like to express my gratitude to Jacqueline Baker for taking on this project and to Ariane Petit and Rachel Platt for their editorial advice. Thanks are also due to Marina MacKay and the anonymous reader for OUP for their incisive and very helpful comments on the full manuscript.

In terms of financial support I owe a great debt of gratitude to the German Academic Exchange Service, as well as to the University of Oxford for generously awarding me its Michael Foster Scholarship. I am also grateful to the FAZIT foundation (Frankfurter Allgemeine Zeitung) for funding my doctoral work during its earliest stages. The manuscript of this book was completed while I was a postdoctoral researcher at the Department of English and Comparative Literature at Columbia University. I want to take this opportunity to thank Bruce Robbins for inviting me to Columbia, and the Alexander von Humboldt Foundation for awarding me a Feodor Lynen fellowship that made this stay possible.

Thanks of a very different kind are due to my parents. I am more grateful to them than I can say.

Thanks of yet a different sort are due to Katharina. I would not have begun this book without her. Mit Dir fällt mir alles leicht.

Contents

List of Illustrations

List of Abbreviations

CIP	San Marino, Huntington Library, Christopher Isherwood Papers
CMA	Brighton, University of Sussex Special Collections, Charles Madge Archive, SxMs 71
DGC	New Haven, Yale University, Beinecke Rare Book and Manuscript Library, David Gascoyne Collection, GEN MSS 529
DGP	London, British Library, David Gascoyne Papers
EUP	London, British Library, Edward Upward Papers
JTA	University of Cambridge, Trinity College, Julian Otto Trevelyan Archive
MOA	Brighton, University of Sussex Special Collections, Mass Observation Archives
PSD	University of Cambridge, St John's College, Papers of Hugh Sykes Davies
RA	University of Cambridge, Magdalene College, I. A. Richards Archive

Introduction

In the winter of 1932, T. S. Eliot delivered the Charles Eliot Norton Lectures at Harvard University. The lectures, published in 1933 as *The Use of Poetry and the Use of Criticism*, pose an implicit challenge to the new decade's strenuous political demands on poetry. 'Let me start with the supposition that we do not know what poetry is, or what it does or ought to do, or of what use it is', Eliot states: 'we may even discover that we have no very clear idea of what *use* is; at any rate we had better not assume that we know.'[1] Eliot's lectures were obliquely responding to some of the decade's foundational literary-political texts, such as Michael Roberts's emblematic left-wing anthology *New Signatures* (1932) or W. H. Auden's *Poems* (1930) and *The Orators* (1932). Less than a year after the publication of the Harvard lectures, a questionnaire in the British left-wing magazine *New Verse* summed up the decade's key artistic concerns in terms similar to Eliot's: 'Do you intend your poetry to be useful to yourself and others?'[2] Eliot's guarded comments about the 'uses' of poetry were levelled at those members of the literary left who wanted to harness poetry to political causes. His wary distance from the idea of literature's extra-poetic usefulness ('we had better not assume that we know') does not simply deny that literary writing might serve as a vehicle for politics or religion. Rather, his remarks advocate a form of programmatic self-doubt, a recognition of the perplexities engendered by an artistic commitment to religious or political systems of value.

Eliot's professed uncertainty about poetry's political uses is difficult to square with two familiar critical 'myths' about thirties politicized writing.[3]

[1] T. S. Eliot, *The Use of Poetry and the Use of Criticism* [1933] (London: Faber and Faber, 1964), p. 15, emphasis in the original.

[2] 'An Enquiry', *New Verse*, 11 (October 1934), 2–22 (p. 2).

[3] As Bernard Bergonzi has remarked, thirties authors were 'mythologiz[ing] themselves as they lived and wrote'. See Bergonzi, *Reading the Thirties: Texts and Contexts* (Basingstoke: Macmillan, 1978), p. 1. For discussion of these 'myths', see Samuel Hynes, *The Auden Generation: Literature and Politics in England in the 1930s* (London: Bodley Head, 1976), esp. pp. 378–94; Adrian Caesar, *Dividing Lines: Poetry, Class, and Ideology in the 1930s* (Manchester: Manchester University Press, 1991), pp. 24–40; Peter McDonald, 'Believing in the Thirties', in *Rewriting the Thirties: Modernism and After*, ed. by Steven Matthews and Keith Williams (London: Longman, 1997), pp. 71–90 (esp. pp. 71–77).

The first abstract account originated in the decade itself and asserts literature's ability to promote extra-literary agendas.[4] It advocates the search (in Stephen Spender's phrase) for 'a kind of poetry [. . .] which is complementary to action'—for a poetry which defies the bourgeois belief in poetry's aesthetic self-containment.[5] In the eyes of many young left-wing writers, the high modernism of the 1920s came to embody the kind of writing they were reacting against: 'artists to-day turn outwards towards reality', as Spender notes elsewhere, 'because the phase of experimenting in form has proved sterile.'[6] 'These nineteen-twentyish germs must be expelled from my system', Cecil Day Lewis's 'Letter to a Young Revolutionary' chimes in: 'Who are they to tell me that I must not preach?'[7] Artistic-revolutionary optimism of this kind was often joined to the inexorable call to take a stand in the political battle between Left and Right, between communism and the conservative forces of nationalism and fascism. The second conventionalized account of the politicized writing of the 1930s began to be codified towards the end of the decade and concerns the sobering demise of literature's grand political ambitions. The assumption of literature's inadequacy as a vehicle for politics had its early roots in disillusioned poems like Auden's 'September 1, 1939' (1939) and 'In Memory of W. B. Yeats' (1939), as well as in Louis MacNeice's cycle *Autumn Journal* (1938). It stresses the idea that the 1930s started on a high-pitched note of 'ambitious loftedness'—an ideological innocence that was brought low by the experience of war.[8] Both myths conflate a specific understanding of the politics of writing with questions of literary value. While the first version advocates literature's explicit engagement with social issues, the second states the essential incongruity of art and politics. It is Eliot's view which seems to be the odd one out in this constellation, because it distrusts the extremism of both positions: it rejects the decade's overreaching ambitions for literature, but it also refrains from sounding a retreat into the narrowly circumscribed realm of 'pure' writing.

[4] For this first account, see e.g. *The 1930s: A Challenge to Orthodoxy*, ed. by John Lucas (Brighton: Harvester Press, 1978); Andy Croft, *Red-Letter Days: British Fiction in the 1930s* (London: Lawrence and Wishart, 1990); James Fenton, *The Strength of Poetry* (Oxford: Oxford University Press, 2001), esp. pp. 209–27.

[5] Stephen Spender, 'Poetry and Revolution', in *New Country: Prose and Poetry by the Authors of 'New Signatures'*, ed. by Michael Roberts (London: Hogarth Press, 1933), pp. 62–67 (p. 63).

[6] Stephen Spender, *The New Realism: A Discussion* (London: Hogarth Press, 1939), p. 8.

[7] Cecil Day Lewis, 'Letter to a Young Revolutionary', in *New Country*, ed. by Michael Roberts, pp. 25–42 (p. 28).

[8] Valentine Cunningham, *British Writers of the Thirties* (Oxford: Oxford University Press, 1988), p. 468. See also Hynes, *Auden Generation*; and Peter McDonald, *Serious Poetry: Form and Authority from Yeats to Hill* (Oxford: Clarendon Press, 2002), esp. pp. 103–37.

This book argues that the notion of literature's 'uses' in thirties literary discourse is less settled than is commonly granted, and that Eliot's reflections on the term's indeterminacy find an echo in widespread doubts and confusions on the thirties literary left concerning literature's political usefulness. The positions which are discussed in detail in subsequent chapters range from a troubled stance of neutrality (in the case of William Empson) through attempts to conjoin the demands of artistic innovation and political revolution (Surrealism and Mass-Observation) to Edward Upward's apparently unflinching artistic commitment to the communist cause. Scholars have remarked that many thirties left-wing writers were affected by the imperative—most resonantly expressed in the *Left Review* pamphlet *Authors Take Sides on the Spanish War* (1937)—that 'it is impossible any longer to take no side' in the ideological battle between Left and Right, communism and fascism.[9] As I argue, the rhetoric of 'taking sides' was indeed central to the self-definitions of many left-wingers, yet the stalemated critical positions of the 1930s and after have tended to obscure the complex artistic and intellectual adjustments which the seemingly simple actions of 'going over' and 'taking sides' entailed. Thirties writing, even at its most aggressive and polemical, is notable for its deep-seated anxieties regarding literature's political articulacy.

THE APOLITICAL UNCONSCIOUS OF 1930s LITERATURE

It is my central contention that hesitations over the political project of thirties writing are foundational to that writing itself, and that much politicized literature of the decade was produced in direct engagement with these artistic uncertainties. More often than not, the left-wing literature of the 1930s occupies positions outside the radical demands for art as a form of propaganda, on the one hand, and for literature's retreat from the sites of political action, on the other. These anxieties do not compromise the political project of thirties left-wing literature, but they suggest its complexity and in turn complicate the terms on which criticism of the period should be premised. The richness of left-wing aesthetics can remind us of the diverse reciprocal accommodations which take place between the two terms of the phrase 'the politics of writing', and it is the purpose of this book to unravel and chart some of the phrase's inherent ambiguities. I am particularly concerned with what might be called the 'apolitical

[9] *Authors Take Sides on the Spanish War* (London: *Left Review*, 1937), no pagination.

unconscious' of thirties writing—that is, with the fraught attraction to the idea of a supposedly self-contained writing among authors variously associated with the political left. In an influential essay, Theodor Adorno pointed to the dialectical tension which lies at the heart of the concept of poetic integrity. The notion of 'artistic autonomy', Adorno observed, negates its own origins in nineteenth-century bourgeois society by claiming that art can transcend its social determination and emancipate itself from a given universe of discourse and behaviour. It aims to repress history both as a sedimented presence within texts and as the precondition of poetic integrity itself. At the same time, the social prehistory of artistic 'autonomy' remains tacitly inscribed in the concept. 'By virtue of its rejection of the empirical world [. . .] art sanctions the primacy of reality', Adorno remarks, 'Art and artworks into the smallest detail of their autonomy are not only art but something foreign and opposed to it [. . .]. Admixed with art's own concept is the ferment of its own abolition.'[10] Much recent criticism of modernist literature, notably the work carried out under the label of the New Modernist Studies, has challenged the idea of artistic immanence by documenting the social and cultural functions which literary works perform and by elaborating on their location in and interactions with diverse extra-literary contexts. Fredric Jameson's now-classical positing of a 'political unconscious' is an early (and recognizably Marxist) manifestation of this critical impulse, as it responds closely to Adorno's assertion that all aesthetic form is 'sedimented content'.[11]

An analogous process of repression and contamination underpins the works examined here, but in them the terms of Adorno's dialectic are crucially reversed. These texts thematize the historical circumstances of art more self-consciously than the modernist works which are the implicit subject of Adorno's discussion. What is being relegated to the level of their textual 'unconscious' is the first term of the equation: the idea of art's 'autonomy'. 'Art's double character as both autonomous and *fait sociale*', Adorno maintains, 'is incessantly reproduced on the level of its autonomy.'[12] The same tension is also reproduced, I argue, at the level of art's historical consciousness. The idea of poetic integrity, though moved to the background of many politicized texts of the 1930s, continues to exert a

[10] Theodor W. Adorno, 'Art, Society, Aesthetics', in *Aesthetic Theory* [1970], ed. by Gretel Adorno and Rolf Tiedemann, trans. by Robert Hullot-Kentor (London: Continuum, 1997), pp. 1–20 (pp. 2, 5).

[11] Adorno, 'Art, Society, Aesthetics', p. 6. Jameson invokes the process of 'formal sedimentation' to establish a correspondence between the 'form' of a literary text and the social substructure which helps to condition it. See Jameson, *The Political Unconscious: Narrative as a Socially Symbolic Act* [1981] (London: Routledge, 2002), pp. 126–32.

[12] Adorno, 'Art, Society, Aesthetics', p. 6.

spectral presence in them. The critical framework proposed in this study implies an inversion of the dialectic identified by Adorno rather than a genuine synthesis of its two constituent terms. Yet it is precisely because the tension between artistic autonomy and historical self-consciousness fails to be satisfyingly resolved that it resurfaces with such tenacity in the works discussed here.

This internal conflict is mirrored in one of the critical keywords of the 1930s, 'integrity', which comes to designate the formal self-containment of literary discourse (its 'poetic integrity') as well as the notion of literature's accountability to extra-literary obligations (its 'moral integrity'). The reshuffling of these meanings over the course of the decade suggests that writers of the 1930s never quite managed to expunge the 'nineteen-twentyish germs', and the modernist legacy which they encapsulated, from their literary-political agenda. The idea of poetic integrity had featured prominently in Eliot's Preface to the revised edition (1928) of *The Sacred Wood*, one of the central documents of twenties modernism. Eliot noted that the book's first edition from 1920 had focused too narrowly on the 'integrity of poetry', on 'poetry [. . .] as poetry and not another thing'.[13] As I point out in the first chapter, Eliot's discussion of poetic 'integrity' created an influential myth about 'high modernism' that was intended to throw into relief his own more recent interest in literature's religious and political contexts. In Eliot's account, poetic 'integrity' figures as a polemic term, and this hostile charge is carried over, with significant amplification, into the literary and critical discourses of the next decade.

The swift dissemination of the word by the decade's self-proclaimed political poets turns 'integrity' into a shorthand term for an excessively purist view of art. Michael Roberts's use of the concept in his Preface to *New Signatures* (1932), while sympathetic to its modernist connotations, asserted the poet's obligations towards society: if 'poets succeed in their attempt to preserve their integrity without becoming obscure, to speak simply without shoddiness or ambiguity, English poetry may again become a popular, elegant and contemporary art'.[14] Cecil Day Lewis, revising his *A Hope for Poetry* (1934) for a second printing in 1936, added a Postscript which expressed hostility towards an 'element of reaction from the recent preoccupation of poets with social justice', 'a return to the ideals of poetic integrity and artistic individualism: a setting-out-again in the direction of "pure" poetry'.[15] Day Lewis's observation implies an awareness of poetic

[13] T. S. Eliot, *The Sacred Wood* [1920, rev. 1928] (London: Faber and Faber, 1997), p. x.

[14] Michael Roberts, 'Preface', in *New Signatures: Poems by Several Hands*, ed. by Michael Roberts (London: Hogarth Press, 1932), pp. 7–20 (pp. 19–20).

[15] Cecil Day Lewis, *A Hope for Poetry* [1934] (Oxford: Blackwell, 1936), p. 80.

'integrity' as ideologically laden—as bound up with a specifically liberal-bourgeois belief in individualism—and it can serve as a reminder of how closely interwoven the word's aesthetic and moral meanings were. The task for left-wing writers, Spender opined, was to conceptualize 'integrity' in a contrary and anti-modernist sense: they had to view literature as a matter of 'personal'—moral, rather than poetic—'integrity'.[16] It required a strenuous effort to escape the 'safe haven of artistic integrity', and the allure of artistic autonomy constitutes a strong, though often repressed undercurrent in the texts of the decade.[17] A passage from Auden's Introduction to *The Oxford Book of Light Verse* (1938) indicates a further configuration of politicized writing to which this undercurrent gave rise. Anticipating the coming of a classless 'genuine community', Auden concluded that 'in such a society, and in such alone, will it be possible for the poet, without sacrificing any of his subtleties of sensibility or his integrity, to write poetry which is simple, clear, and gay'.[18] In this passage, poetry considered as 'poetry and not another thing' is figured as the forbidden fruit of political writing—a thing aspired to but impossible under the conditions of political struggle. As this small collection of examples suggests, left-wing writing of the 1930s was profoundly divided on some of its central aims, and even the most strongly 'committed' of the writers examined in the following chapters, such as Edward Upward, believed that their work continued to be inextricably bound up with bourgeois and modernist assumptions about literary writing. 'The poetry of the future revolution', as Jean-Paul Sartre commented, looking back in the 1940s to the preceding decade of politically engaged art, 'has remained in the hands of the young well-intentioned bourgeois who draw their inspiration from their psychological contradictions, in the antinomy of their ideal and their class, in the uncertainty of old bourgeois language.'[19] While the possibility of a radical artistic departure and a new literary style remained elusively out of reach, these conflicts also provided a potent impetus and 'inspiration' (in Sartre's phrase) for the young writers' artistic self-investigations.

In the English context I. A. Richards's theories about the formal self-containment of modernist poetry centrally shaped what I have called the decade's 'apolitical unconscious'. Richards had expounded his critical

[16] Stephen Spender, *Poetry Since 1939* (London: Longmans, 1946), p. 38.

[17] Peter McDonald, *Louis MacNeice: The Poet in His Contexts* (Oxford: Clarendon Press, 1991), p. 3.

[18] W. H. Auden, 'Introduction', in *The Oxford Book of Light Verse* [1938] (Oxford: Oxford University Press, 1952), pp. vii–xx (pp. xix–xx).

[19] Jean-Paul Sartre, 'Black Orpheus' [1947], trans. by John MacCombie, in *'What is Literature?' and Other Essays*, ed. by Steven Ungar (Cambridge, MA: Harvard University Press, 1988), pp. 289–330 (p. 295).

doctrines in the 1920s, using Eliot's poetry as his main exhibit, and his ideas played a major role in associating twenties modernism with an advocacy of literature's discrete coherence. Richards's pamphlet *Science and Poetry* (1926) dwelt on the 'integrity' required of 'the poet to-day' and proclaimed 'the complete severance of poetry and *all* beliefs' in *The Waste Land*.[20] His earlier *Principles of Literary Criticism* (1924) had posited a distinct realm of literary 'pseudo-statements'—utterances which are separate from factual propositions about reality and which are not falsifiable because they are frozen in the hypothetical 'as-if' of the artistic imagination. Richards's arguments presented a bifurcated picture of language use which, in the eyes of thirties writers, threatened to open up the possibility of non-referentiality at the heart of (poetic) language, a threat barely hemmed in by Richards's insistence that all utterances serve the purpose of communication. The influence of Richards's theories on the young generation of thirties writers was immense, and it has been noted that *Principles of Literary Criticism* 'contained a programme of critical work for a generation'.[21] The notion of 'pseudo-statements' in particular became a source of artistic anxiety for many thirties writers because it seemed to question literature's ability to engage with reality. Auden, for example, praised Christopher Caudwell's *Illusion and Reality* (1937) as 'the most important book on poetry since the books of Dr I. A. Richards' precisely because of its anti-Ricardian contention that reference enters all language use.[22] The opposition between poetic 'integrity' and literature's ability to attend to its contexts was of course overly schematic, and the view of Richards as a proponent of 'pure' modernist *écriture* stemmed from a biased misreading of his books. As I argue in the first chapter, this misrepresentation of Richards's theories emerged during his debate with Eliot in the mid- and late 1920s. It was Eliot's reductive conception of Richards's position which exerted an important influence on the poetic practice and the aesthetic concerns of thirties writers.[23] Moreover, while the debate

[20] I. A. Richards, *Science and Poetry* (London: Trubner, 1926), pp. 81, 64, emphasis in the original.

[21] Raymond Williams, *Culture and Society, 1780–1950* (London: Chatto and Windus, 1958), p. 244. For the ubiquity of Richards's theories in thirties literature and criticism, see also Cunningham, *Writers of the Thirties*, esp. pp. 58–59.

[22] W. H. Auden, Review of *Illusion and Reality, New Verse*, 25 (May 1937), 20–22 (p. 22).

[23] This distorted account of Richards's views also entered into what Jerome McGann has dubbed 'the aggressively ahistorical procedures' of the New Criticism 'which dominat[ed] hermeneutics since the early 1930s'. See McGann, *The Beauty of Inflections: Literary Investigations in Historical Method and Theory* (Oxford: Clarendon Press, 1985), p. 4. I address some of these continuities in the Coda to this book. The *locus classicus* for the appropriation of Richards and Empson by the New Critics is John Crowe Ransom's chapter 'I. A. Richards: The Psychological Critic. And William Empson, His Pupil', in J. C. Ransom, *The New Criticism* (Norfolk, CT: New Directions, 1941), pp. 3–131.

between Eliot and Richards hinged on the referential properties of poetry, Richards's observations in *Principles of Literary Criticism* had extended the idea of literature's formal autonomy to narrative prose and drama and to other art forms. This slippage between poetry and prose is evident in the self-reflections of many of the authors discussed in this book, and as I illustrate in greater detail in the chapter on Edward Upward, it was linked to concerns that literature more generally would be unable to bear the weight of political causes.

The authors examined in this book studied with or came under the formative influence of Richards at the University of Cambridge between 1924 and 1932. My aim is not, however, to define a homogenous group of any sort. The positions examined in the following chapters cover very different artistic and political temperaments, ranging from William Empson's troubled neutrality and English Surrealism's unrequited dallying with the radical left through Madge's and Jennings's revolutionary aspirations for Mass-Observation to Edward Upward's pugnacious commitment to the communist cause. The focus on these writers illustrates the diverse spectrum of leftist positions that were affected by Richards's theories and by the high-modernist writing from which thirties writers were in complex ways struggling to depart. Richards's influence, though pervasive, was largely negative in providing a foil for the quite different agendas of politicized authors. William Empson's dedication of *Structure of Complex Words* (1951) to Richards can also be applied to the other writers discussed here: many of their ideas about literature were 'arrived at by disagreeing with him'.[24] The most significant corollary of Richards's influence was that it anticipated the disillusionment with literature's political powers which critics have traditionally seen to be setting in towards the end of the decade. The ambiguities of literature's commitment to left-wing politics are thus not limited to 'neutral' authors who sought to resist the decade's orthodox ideological certainties, but possessed a wider discursive presence.[25]

The writers examined here are acutely aware of the difficulties involved in turning literature into a record of ideological content, and sometimes they even seem to value the tension between literature's political mission and its self-referential aspects as a productive stimulus for their writing. According to Stephen Spender, thirties authors 'were extremely non-political with half of themselves and extremely political with the other

[24] William Empson, *The Structure of Complex Words* (London: Chatto and Windus, 1951), p. v.

[25] On the question of political 'neutrality', see especially Valentine Cunningham, 'Neutral?: 1930s Writers and Taking Sides', in *Class, Culture and Social Change: A New View of the 1930s*, ed. by Frank Gloversmith (Brighton: Harvester Press, 1980), pp. 45–69 (p. 49).

half': 'Members of my generation continued to think that poetry should be judged by standards which were not ideological'.[26] Importantly, these concerns did not remain limited to the realm of poetic practice, and it is a central premise of this study that for many thirties authors the levels of literary production and aesthetic reflection were intimately connected. In others words, these writers' self-conscious meditations on the nature of poetic language and on the constraints that arose from writing after and against an older generation of modernists became integral to their literary work. The literary criticism and aesthetic theory of the 1930s reflect the concerns which animate the decade's left-wing literature, but they also in turn helped to shape the modes in which literary writing was conducted. The mutual dependency of both discourses—literary and critical—is not unique to the 1930s but it takes on a particular salience during this decade of politicized art. In order to do justice to this circumstance, I read the literary works of thirties authors alongside their critical essays, programmatic treatises, and self-investigations in letters and diaries. If many of these non-literary writings seem more robust in ideological terms, this is not to say that they are merely ideologically and aesthetically prescriptive in the manner of the Soviet Communist Party's decreed aesthetic of socialist realism. On the contrary, these critical writings offer rich evidence regarding the receptivity of younger thirties writers to the theoretical ideas advanced by Richards—an influence which in its turn became a subject of intense artistic concern.

1930s LITERATURE, LATE MODERNISM, AND THE POLITICS OF WRITING

Few decades have provided a more hotly contested ground for literary historiography than the 1930s. According to a particularly influential account, the literature of the decade was dominated by a small number of literary groups or coteries. The seeming pre-eminence of one of these groups led to the writers of the decade being collectively labelled, by Samuel Hynes and others, the 'Auden generation'. Of course, this tendency has not gone uncontradicted, and some of the most important recent criticism has been committed to revising the view of the decade as one presided over by only a handful of poets. The opening salvo in this revision of the canon was fired by Valentine Cunningham who drew attention to the vast field of cultural production which the myth of the Auden Generation

[26] Stephen Spender, *The Thirties and After: Poetry, Politics, People (1933–75)* (Basingstoke: Macmillan, 1978), pp. 18, 26.

had eclipsed. Cliquishness, according to Cunningham, 'cemented the Old Boys together just as [it] helped keep them in their Permanent Adolescence. The "pylon boys" [. . .] had their own private corner in communizing solidarity.'[27] Feminist critics have subsequently pointed out that this first wave of revisionist criticism—including Cunningham's own study—failed to pay attention to certain other segments of thirties writing, in particular the works by female poets and prose-writers.[28] There has also been a widespread neglect of working-class writing, as scholars have continued to focus on the young generation of authors reviled as public-school and university-educated 'butterflies' in Virginia Woolf's essay 'The Leaning Tower' (1940).[29] This book recognizes that the transmission of Richards's ideas was facilitated by the exclusive (and almost exclusively male) sociability at Oxbridge, and I do not intend to replace one literary-historical parochialism, the notion of an Oxford-educated 'Auden clique' in which a single writer exerted a benign poetic influence on a homogenous group of followers, with another equally restrictive and cliquish myth. Adrian Caesar has warned that 'identification by association is the stuff of mythologies', and it is not my aim to overemphasize the coherence of the group of writers discussed here or to assert total identity of concerns where it did not exist.[30] First, in order to avoid these risks, my discussion will not attempt to map the specific details of Richards's aesthetic theories too neatly onto the works of individual authors; instead I will concentrate on what was often held to be the motivating idea behind Richards's critical position, the notion of poetic autonomy. Second, by stressing the diversity of literary and political attitudes among these writers, I argue that they did not respond to Richards's theories in the same ways. While it is true that the authors considered in the following chapters were educated in a milieu that encouraged them to take note of certain debates about modernism, my argument indicates that ideas about artistic autonomy affected thirties politicized writing more generally.

The mechanisms of inclusion and exclusion which undergird the canonization of certain thirties writers and the non-canonization of countless

[27] Cunningham, *Writers of the Thirties*, p. 148.

[28] Prominent feminist revisions of the thirties canon include Maroula Joannou, *'Ladies Please Don't Smash These Windows': Women's Writing, Feminist Consciousness and Social Change, 1914–1938* (Oxford: Berg, 1995); Jan Montefiore, *Men and Women Writers of the 1930s: The Dangerous Flood of History* (London: Routledge, 1996); *Women Writers of the 1930s: Gender, Politics, and History*, ed. by Maroula Joannou (Edinburgh: Edinburgh University Press, 1999).

[29] Virginia Woolf, 'The Leaning Tower', in *The Moment, and Other Essays* (New York: Harcourt, Brace, 1948), pp. 118–54 (p. 137).

[30] Caesar, *Dividing Lines*, p. 174.

others have produced a relative neglect of literary texts which are located in proximity to political systems of belief, such as communism. This is true in particular of the current tendency within modernist studies to associate the literature of the 1930s with some form of 'late modernism'. These efforts, by critics such as Tyrus Miller, Jed Esty, and Marina MacKay, among others, have done significant critical work by defamiliarizing the 'grand narrative in the study of modernism' in which '"origins", "rise", "emergence", "genealogy", are key terms'.[31] By turning attention away from modernism's foundational texts of the 1910s and 1920s, the concept of a residual or late modernism puts us in a position to 'reconsider what modernism means as a description of distinctive aesthetic modes that were not static but capable of development and transformation'.[32] Yet the growing scholarship on late modernism and the rise of the New Modernist Studies over the past fifteen years have been, in some respects, a mixed blessing. While the New Modernist Studies have produced a richer and more diversified understanding of modernism by moving critical exploration beyond the confines of a notional 'high-modernist' phase in the 1920s, they have also led to the occlusion of certain other parts of the literary-historical map and of the critical questions pertinent to them. In some areas, this new body of scholarship has enforced exclusion mechanisms which are nearly as strict as the ones that used to be associated with the idea of 'high' modernism itself. One kind of writing that is consistently sidelined in recent modernist studies is the large field of thirties politicized writing. As Marina MacKay notes, her important reconfiguration of thirties literature 'draws attention to writers who dissented from the prevailing model of partisanship'.[33] These comments suggest that the aesthetic specificity of late modernist literature begins to emerge against a backdrop of politicized writing that is presented as more or less monolithic—a background hum of artistic orthodoxy and Soviet-influenced dogma.

The reasons for the success of late modernism as a critical category and for the concomitant exclusion of numerous writers from the literary-historical picture of the interwar years are in some cases artistic, but they are also ideological and institutional. It is indicative of this double bind that late modernism and more recently 'intermodernism'—two concepts

[31] Tyrus Miller, *Late Modernism: Politics, Fiction, and the Arts Between the World Wars* (Berkeley: University of California Press, 1999), p. 5. See also Marina MacKay, *Modernism and World War II* (Cambridge: Cambridge University Press, 2007); and Jed Esty, *A Shrinking Island: Modernism and National Culture in England* (Princeton: Princeton University Press, 2003).

[32] MacKay, *Modernism and World War II*, p. 15.

[33] Marina MacKay, '"Doing Business with Totalitaria": British Late Modernism and the Politics of Reputation', *English Literary History*, 73/3 (2006), 729–53 (p. 730).

which were designed as a critique of earlier critical orthodoxies—draw for their academic prestige on that older literary-historical classification, 'modernism'.[34] To be sure, modernist scholars are not alone in feeling profound discomfort about literary texts that are structured around grand political narratives. It is symptomatic of this situation that the recent flourishing of neo-formalist criticism has virtually bypassed thirties literature, with two notable exceptions: Auden's 'September 1, 1939' and his elegy for Yeats with its resonant warning that 'poetry makes nothing happen'. These texts have become touchstones for critics like James Longenbach, Angela Leighton, and Peter McDonald precisely because their air of resignation seems to advocate a wary retreat from political action and into the narrower confines of poetic form.[35] The mechanisms of canonization (and non-canonization) which undergird these critical accounts—new-formalist, modernist, late modernist—seem to be in some crucial respects similar.

The emphasis on the long life of modernism and on modernism's multiple transformations in the 1930s entails, as MacKay observes, 'a very real sense in which the Ivory Tower was, to swap metaphors, a straw man'.[36] Modernism's afterlife under the changed conditions of the 1930s is also central to my study. However, my focus is not on an established first generation of modernists who fell among enemies in the new decade, but on a younger generation of writers whose political impetus was upset by the retrospective vision of a self-contained writing. In order to grasp the specific tensions that characterize the politics of writing during the 1930s, it is necessary to recognize that the works discussed here are representative of a writing against modernism, rather than simply after it. At first glance, my central contention—that we take the idea of poetic autonomy seriously when discussing the politics of writing in the 1930s—appears to run counter to the significant expansion of modernism's geographical, temporal, medial, and aesthetic scope that has taken place in criticism over the past two decades. As the first chapter illustrates in some detail, the version of modernism invoked in this book was itself the outcome of a specific set of aesthetic debates rather than an inherent quality of modernist writing. By returning to a seemingly outdated critical conception of modernism, then, I intend to make a case for the literary-historical significance of this particular understanding of the modernist moment in

[34] On 'intermodernism', see especially *Intermodernism: Literary Culture in Mid-Twentieth-Century Britain*, ed. by Kristin Bluemel (Edinburgh: Edinburgh University Press, 2009).

[35] James Longenbach, *The Resistance to Poetry* (Chicago: University of Chicago Press, 2004), pp. 2–3; Angela Leighton, *On Form: Poetry, Aestheticism, and the Legacy of a Word* (Oxford: Oxford University Press, 2007), p. 22; McDonald, *Serious Poetry*, pp. 111–23.

[36] MacKay, '"Doing Business"', p. 731.

the context of thirties literature. In other words, the notion of the Ivory Tower was important both because it facilitated the creation of another myth—that of the political 1930s—and because it exerted an anxiety of influence that affected a wide spectrum of left-wing writers. As I point out in chapter five, Upward's self-reflexive predictions regarding the non-canonicity of politicized writing have come true. Yet it would be wrong to assume that this non-canonical status is the result of any inherent artistic deficiencies. Instead, the marginalized status of thirties politicized literature is the consequence of certain deeply ingrained assumptions about the long life of modernism that we habitually invoke when we talk about the literature of the interwar years.

It is the aim of this book to illustrate the variety of politicized writing during the 1930s and, in doing so, to reopen some key debates regarding the politics of writing during that decade. As indicated above, I specifically urge a redrafting of the familiar trajectory of thirties writing—from grandiose political expectations to disillusionment—by focusing on a cultural site where anxieties about art's inadequacy as a political weapon were especially intense. But this book also seeks to complicate the revisionist attempt to transcend the literary-historical boundary between the 1920s and the 1930s, and it does so in part by calling for a return to an earlier critical position. It maintains that thirties politicized writing needs to be understood in relation to an Old Left politics which emphasizes the inevitability of social conflict and the extreme urgency of 'taking sides'. The series of historical events which are woven into my account—the Japanese invasions of China in the early and mid-1930s, the outbreak of the Spanish Civil War in 1936, the British abdication crisis and the coronation of George VI, and the collapse of Britain's appeasement policy—elicited a wide and often unpredictable range of literary responses. They are of interest in the context of this study because they helped to polarize political positions within the literary field and because they intensified the need for left-wing writers to come to terms with the artistic tensions and contradictions of the decade.

COMMITTED STYLES

Peter McDonald has observed that left-wing writers of the 1930s were evolving 'a language drained of self-doubt' by paring down the semantic functions of words to those needed for an immediate ideological purpose: 'the kind of literature so ardently desired by many younger writers on the Left in the thirties required "meaning" to be more or less transparent as a term.' Consequently, McDonald submits, these writers sided with the matter-of-factness offered by Richards's category of descriptive, 'scientific' language, while rejecting the idea of 'emotive' pseudo-statements.[37] This book points out that for many thirties writers the exact relation between the two types of language use proposed by Richards, on the one hand, and the nature of politicized literature, on the other, was far from self-evident. The four chapters on Empson, Surrealism, Mass-Observation, and Upward show that the resultant ambiguities are reflected in certain keywords of the decade. These keywords ('honesty', 'revolution', 'fact', 'dream'), far from being semantically transparent, mirror the tensions and indeterminacies between the period's political and artistic commitments, and they function as verbal hinges between two views of literature that are commonly thought of as opposites.[38] The process by which two contrary meanings are placed side by side in a single term is examined in William Empson's *Seven Types of Ambiguity* (1930). Drawing on Sigmund Freud's analysis of primal words, or *Urworte*, Empson observes in his discussion of the seventh type of ambiguity that 'it seems likely, indeed, that words uniting two opposites are seldom or never actually formed in a language to express the conflict between them'.[39] In a similar way, the keywords presented here enable complex processes of semantic mediation between attitudes which are otherwise held to be irreconcilable. They are among the *Urworte* of thirties literary and critical discourse in providing points of convergence for antagonistic concepts of literature's mode of action.

These keywords will serve as thematic guidelines in the main chapters. They do not of course exhaust the list of possible keywords, nor do they in themselves reflect the whole complexity of a specific historical moment. Invoking Raymond Williams's understanding of cultural keywords, I argue that they are 'significant, indicative words in certain forms of thought' as

[37] McDonald, 'Believing in the Thirties', pp. 79, 82–83.

[38] The idea of keywords also had some currency in the decade under discussion. For V. N. Voloshinov's reflections on the 'social multiaccentuality' of individual words, see *Marxism and the Philosophy of Language* [1930], trans. by Ladislav Matejka and I. R. Titunik (Cambridge, MA: Harvard University Press, 1986), p. 23 and *passim*. Nikolai Bukharin's influential essay 'Poetry, Poetics and the Problems of Poetry in the USSR' considered 'the palaeontology of language', arguing that 'within the microcosm of the word is embedded the macrocosm of history'. See *Problems of Soviet Literature: Reports and Speeches at the First Soviet Writers' Conference 1934*, trans. by H.G. Scott (London: Martin Lawrence, 1935), pp. 185–258 (p. 195).

[39] William Empson, *Seven Types of Ambiguity* [1930] (London: Pimlico, 2004), p. 195. For Freud's essay, see 'The Antithetical Meaning of Primal Words' ['Über den Gegensinn der Urworte', 1910], in *The Standard Edition of the Complete Psychological Works of Sigmund Freud*, 24 vols, ed. and trans. by James Strachey and others (London: Hogarth Press, 1953–74), XI (1964), pp. 153–61.

they bind 'together certain ways of seeing culture and society'.[40] They figure centrally both in the literary and in the non-literary works—essays, treatises, reviews, diaries, and letters—to which this book pays attention, yet their role as 'building blocks of cultural understanding' is not as passive as Williams's remarks suggest.[41] Instead of merely reflecting the conflicting impulses of thirties writing, they constitute a vocabulary which authors could use to negotiate these conflicts and which could in turn act as a stimulus for their writing. The dictionary entry for the word 'aesthetic' in Williams's book *Keywords* (1976) offers an example of the displacements which are at work in these terms. 'Aesthetic', Williams comments, 'is a key formation in a group of meanings which at once emphasized and isolated subjective sense-activity as the basis of art and beauty as distinct, for example, from *social* or *cultural* interpretations.'[42] The word's 'social or cultural' meanings, Williams argues, tend to be repressed in everyday usage, but they are accessible to critical analysis. The keywords presented in this book are structurally similar to Williams's description of 'aesthetic', but the two terms of his opposition are reversed as a latent apolitical charge is injected among and into the word's socio-political meanings. The politicized writing of the 1930s was indeed speaking in two 'radically different or radically variable' registers, and we should be prepared to find these ambiguities reflected in the decade's verbal resources.[43]

The first chapter establishes the shared concerns of the writers discussed in subsequent chapters by reconstructing the debate between Richards and Eliot about the role of 'belief' in poetry, and by examining its repercussions in the Cambridge magazine *Experiment* (1928–31). Contributors to *Experiment* included most of the authors discussed in this book, such as William Empson, Hugh Sykes Davies, Humphrey Jennings, and Charles Madge. The Richards-Eliot debate brought to the fore two ideas which subsequently became central to thirties writing: it registered systems of value as a passive presence in poetry, but it also reflected on the possibility of actively propagating these values and beliefs by artistic means. The intensity of the debate between Richards and Eliot is mirrored in the diverse contributions to *Experiment* which pay attention to recent literary and political developments in Soviet Russia and to the question of poetry's

[40] Raymond Williams, *Keywords: A Vocabulary of Culture and Society* [1976] (London: Fontana, 1988), p. 15.

[41] Alan Durant, 'Raymond Williams's *Keywords*: Investigating Meanings "Offered, Felt For, Tested, Confirmed, Asserted, Qualified, Changed"', *Critical Quarterly*, 48/4 (2006), 1–26 (p. 4); see also *Four Ways of Looking at a Keyword*, ed. by Sylvia Adamson and Alan Durant (= *Critical Quarterly*, 49/1 (2007)).

[42] Williams, *Keywords*, p. 32, emphases in the original.

[43] Ibid., p. 17.

extra-literary 'importance'. *Experiment* has commonly been described as a belated attempt at high-modernist *écriture*. By contrast, I point out that the magazine's engagement with Richards's ideas anticipates central critical trends of the 1930s.

The second chapter argues that William Empson's poetry of the 1930s struggles to escape from what Empson called the 'narrowness' of his early verse—from those limitations which, according to Richards, were intrinsic to literature's pseudo-statements. Empson's poems are especially haunted by the fear that the position of political neutrality which he adopted in the 1930s might in its turn effect a blindness to the decade's political conflicts. The chapter pays special attention to Empson's experiences in the Far East. During his stay in Tokyo following the outbreak of hostilities between Japan and China (1932–33), Empson was harshly brought face to face with the propagandistic potential of poetry. His subsequent attempt to develop a position of detachment in the mid-1930s ran into difficulties during his years in China (1937–39), when he was forced into exile after the invasion of Northern China by the Japanese. This experience of real-life escape led Empson to a critical reassessment of poetic 'escapism', a version of which he had advocated in his poetry of the mid-1930s. His reflections about poetry centred on the idea of poetic 'honesty'—a term which Empson held to signify both the adherence to established social and political codes and the poet's independence from those rules.

When Surrealism arrived in England a decade after its inception in France, it came burdened with a complex history of internal strife and of disagreements with the Communist Party. The third chapter focuses in particular on the work of Hugh Sykes Davies and David Gascoyne, and it suggests that English Surrealists responded to the new decade's ideological pressures by echoing André Breton's call to restore Surrealism to its 'pristine purity' of the 1920s. This reorientation was intended to solve the 'regrettable ambiguity' (in Breton's phrase) between the political and artistic dimensions of the Surrealist 'revolution'. The chapter argues that Sykes Davies—a student and later colleague of Richards—associated the idea of Surrealism's stylistic 'purity' with the self-containment of poetic pseudo-statements. The solipsistic tendencies analysed by Sykes Davies complicated English Surrealism's engagement with the pressing political imperatives of the 1930s, but they also prevented it from succumbing to the decade's propagandistic demands on literature. The Mass-Observation movement of the mid-1930s can be seen as a reaction against the stylistic fixity of Surrealism, and chapter four emphasizes the early artistic aspirations which its founders, Humphrey Jennings and Charles Madge, associated with their fledgling enterprise. I argue that the tensions which underlie Mass-Observation's collection of day surveys—between a writing done by the amateur masses and a 'corrective' editing performed by the professional few—can be traced back to the reader reports which Richards solicited from his students in his practical criticism lectures. In analogy to Richards's pedagogical method, Madge and Jennings subjected the raw material of the day surveys to an editorial rewriting that was intended to expunge 'irrelevant associations' from these close readings of English society. The chapter stresses the enduring importance of the role of the bourgeois poet to this process. Madge and Jennings continued to feel attracted to what they labelled over-determined 'poetic facts'—to the writerly complexities of metaphor and allusion—rather than to the messier data generated by the day surveys. The nature of these revisions depended crucially on the different political temperaments of Jennings (who emphasized the movement's emancipatory power) and Madge (who tended towards a doctrinaire version of communism).

Madge maintained a carefully cultivated image as one of the most dogmatic of British left-wing authors, yet his commitment never reached the doctrinaire heights commonly associated with Edward Upward. Upward's literary career is often reduced to the status of a case study illustrating the incompatibility of politics and literature. Chapter five seeks to modify this established view by focusing on the inconclusiveness of Upward's search for a style that would be capable of mirroring his ideological certitude. The chapter examines Upward's unpublished poems and letters, his fantastic Mortmere stories (co-authored with Christopher Isherwood), and his fiction and criticism from the 1930s. I suggest that Upward's works from the 1920s onwards were haunted by Richards's association of literature with a discrete realm of pseudo-statements. His texts envisage two opposed modes of writing, 'fantasy' and 'prophecy', and they negotiate the slippages between the two terms over the notion of 'dreaming'—a word Upward used to refer both to the ideologically saturated 'dreams' of communism and to the immaterial 'daydreams' of poetic fantasy. Upward's texts mark a position on the far left of the literary-political spectrum examined in this book, though it would be wrong to regard Upward merely as an extreme outlier in the literary milieu of the 1930s. Instead, his works indicate the pervasiveness of the search for a literary style that would be capable of conveying the seriousness of political commitment, even when this preoccupation with the right kind of poetic voice could look like a holdover from an earlier, bourgeois era.

1

'Responsible Propagandists'

I. A. Richards, T. S. Eliot, and Cambridge Experiment

Modernist scholars have recently begun to map the place which little magazines occupied in the literary history of the interwar years. Recovering this body of materials has made it possible to write a micro-history of the complex emergence and transformations of modernism as a literary movement; little magazines, as Brian Maidment points out, are significant as 'expositions by which change occurs and is made legible'.[1] This chapter will trace the development of a set of literary-critical arguments in the mid- and late 1920s, and it will examine the role which these arguments played in the incipient critical debates of the 1930s by focusing on the Cambridge magazine *Experiment*. The magazine, which ran to seven issues between 1928 and 1931, included among its contributors many who became prominent literary figures in the 1930s, such as William Empson, the Surrealists Hugh Sykes Davies and Kathleen Raine, as well as Mass-Observers Humphrey Jennings and Charles Madge. While the members of the group went on to pursue diverse careers, their collaborative enterprise *Experiment* testifies to an early shared interest in the issue of 'belief' and in the religious, social, and political contexts of literary discourse.

My discussion begins by revisiting the Richards-Eliot debate over the relationship between poetry and 'belief'. This notorious debate, I argue, helped to inscribe two mutually conflicting critical languages which cohabit incongruously in thirties literary and critical discourse. The controversy between Richards and Eliot registered belief as a passive presence in poetry which complicates the idea of a text-centred critical hermeneutics (I will call this the 'weak' version of the belief-problem), but it also reflected on the possibilities of advertising and propagating belief, whether religious

[1] Brian Maidment, 'Victorian Periodicals and Academic Discourse', quoted in Scott McCracken, 'Cambridge Magazines and Unfinished Business: *Experiment* (1928–31), *The Venture* (1928–30), and *Cambridge Left* (1933–4)', in *The Oxford Critical and Cultural History of Modernist Magazines*, ed. by Peter Brooker and Andrew Thacker (Oxford: Oxford University Press, 2009), pp. 598–622 (p. 600).

or political, by artistic means (I refer to this as the 'strong' version). Both parts of the debate rose to prominence in the 1930s, when they became central to the new literary decade's self-definitions. The Richards-Eliot controversy appeared to end in a deadlock between two irreconcilable positions, one of which (frequently identified with Richards) tended towards a 'textualist' pole, the other (associated with Eliot) towards a 'contextualist' pole. The former position was held to stress the relative independence of poetry and of literary discourse more generally from extraneous systems of belief, while the latter insisted that poetry could not be isolated from its historical contexts. The stalemate between Richards and Eliot was partly the result of an escalating process of mutual misreadings, and the first half of this chapter reconstructs the peculiar dynamic which characterized their critical debate. As I point out, the critical misreading in the 1930s of Richards's theories as a defence of 'pure' writing originated to a significant degree in Eliot's canonical attacks.

The question of literature's contextual ties is very much alive in the pages of *Experiment*, and in many contributions Eliot's investigation of the convergence of poetic language and 'the Grammar of Belief' gains the upper hand over Richards's promulgation of a largely self-enclosed realm of literary pseudo-statements.[2] One reason for these internal tensions is *Experiment*'s fraught adherence to a modernist paradigm of writing which came to be associated, partly through Richards's influence, with an essentially ahistorical outlook. Critics usually pit the writing published in *Experiment* against the more explicitly politicized literature of the 1930s. According to one critic, the contributions to Michael Roberts's iconic anthology of left-wing poetry *New Signatures* (1932), even though it featured poems by former *Experiment* authors William Empson and Richard Eberhart, 'stood counter to almost everything represented by Cambridge "experimental" poetry'.[3] This common view of *Experiment* as a collective espousal of modernist *écriture* obscures just those elements in it which prefigure the 1930s' uneasy take on the languages of poetry and belief, as well as on the relation between literature and political involvement. The present chapter suggests that the outcome of the Richards-Eliot debate facilitated the creation of the myth of the 1930s as a 'political' decade that was distinct from the 'modernist' 1920s.

[2] T. S. Eliot, 'Literature, Science, and Dogma', *The Dial*, 82 (March 1927), 239–42 (p. 240).

[3] Jason Harding, '*Experiment* in Cambridge: "A Manifesto of Young England"', *The Cambridge Quarterly*, 27 (1998), 287–309 (p. 308). For a similar assessment, see Kate Price, 'Finite But Unbounded: *Experiment* Magazine, Cambridge, England, 1928–31', *Jacket Magazine*, 20 (2001) <http://jacketmagazine.com/20/price-expe.html>.

But it also points out that the legacy of modernism, as filtered through Richards's critical doctrines, was more ambivalent and more burdensome than this myth suggests.

'POETRY AS POETRY': THE RICHARDS-ELIOT DEBATE ABOUT BELIEF

The idea of poetry's alleged self-sufficiency, its 'integrity', had been famously recoined from symbolist theories in T. S. Eliot's Preface to the 1928 reissue of *The Sacred Wood*, his important early collection of literary criticism. There, Eliot asserted that the first edition of *The Sacred Wood* from 1920 had claimed that 'when we are considering poetry we must consider it primarily as poetry and not another thing'.[4] The original edition of the book had been more attuned to the question of poetry's extra-literary contexts, to the weak version of the belief-problem, than Eliot was now for strategic purposes willing to concede. The Preface applies the idea of poetry's discrete coherence only in retrospect, lending it the air of a critical myth about modernism. Eliot notes that he recently 'passed on to another problem not touched upon in this book', 'that of the relation of poetry to the spiritual and social life of its time'.[5] The notion of poetic integrity is thus essentially polemic, serving as a foil for certain shifts in Eliot's critical orientation. In addition, the term is rendered unstable by the syntactic environment in which it occurs, as if it were being overshadowed by Eliot's new interest in poetry's 'spiritual and social' background. The tautological structure of Eliot's phrase ('poetry [. . .] as poetry'), rather than emphasizing the idea of poetic integrity, suggests that poetry is internally decentred: its semantic redundancy specifically implies that poetry is open to a range of displacements, 'poetry as ideology', 'poetry as religion', and so on, which threaten to assimilate it to its surrounding contexts. Eliot's cautious wording, 'and not another thing', is designed to seal the sentence off against such ambiguities, yet it paradoxically calls up the alternative thematizations which it seeks to foreclose.

Eliot advertised his break with the self-contained textuality of modernist literature in a number of publications between 1927 and 1930. And his message was heard: writing in the *Cambridge Review* in February 1929, F. R. Leavis remarked that 'Mr Eliot never forgets to see poetry as a texture

[4] T. S. Eliot, *The Sacred Wood* [1920, rev. 1928] (London: Faber and Faber, 1997), p. x.
[5] Ibid.

of words, but he is as much concerned with what lies behind'.[6] The insistence on the importance of poetry's extra-literary dimensions coincided with Eliot's public declaration of his religious and national allegiances in 1927, as manifested in his confirmation in the Church of England and his decision to adopt British citizenship.[7] The significance of a writer's 'social and spiritual life', Eliot now pointed out, was an issue criticism could not afford to ignore. In a well-known long footnote to the second edition (1929) of his essay on Dante, Eliot pushed this argument even further, claiming that 'actually, one probably has more pleasure in the poetry when one shares the beliefs of the poet'.[8] Eliot's phrasing, doubly evasive in the qualifications it places on the claim ('actually', 'probably'), reveals his uneasiness with this new position. And he does seem more at home, and more characteristically assertive, when he declares that

> we must assume that there is literature and literary appreciation; we must assume that the reader can obtain the full 'literary' or (if you will) 'aesthetic' enjoyment without sharing the beliefs of the author. *If* there is 'literature', *if* there is 'poetry', then it must be possible to have full literary or poetic appreciation without sharing the beliefs of the poet. (255 fn., emphases in the original)

This affirmation of poetic integrity reflects the main argument of the 'Dante' essay which Eliot had written a few years earlier. However, as Paul Fry has recently noted, the footnote is generally 'more sceptical about bracketing belief [. . .] than the main text is', and Eliot's invocation of the idea that poetic appreciation is independent of contextual knowledge is indeed all the more jarring for its brevity.[9] The Dante essay, with its conspicuous hiatus between footnote and text, articulates a conflict that resonates well beyond the essay's textual confines, and it specifically points to Eliot's public debate with Richards in the mid- and late 1920s. The attempt to salvage 'poetry as poetry' was a particularly problematic one for Eliot around 1930 because he had come to associate it with the aggressive position of his intellectual opponent.

[6] F. R. Leavis, 'T. S. Eliot: A Reply to the Condescending', *The Cambridge Review*, 8 February 1929, 254–56 (p. 255).

[7] For Eliot's statement of his religious, aesthetic, and political beliefs, see *For Lancelot Andrewes* (London: Faber and Faber, 1928), p. ix.

[8] T. S. Eliot, 'Dante' [1929], in *Selected Essays: 1917–1932* (London: Faber and Faber, 1932), pp. 223–63 (p. 255 fn.).

[9] Paul Fry, 'Hermeneutic Circling: Empson, Rosemund Tuve, and the "Wimsatt Law"', in *Some Versions of Empson*, ed. by Matthew Bevis (Oxford: Oxford University Press, 2007), pp. 201–16 (p. 213). For a discussion of the place of the footnote in the debate between Richards and Eliot, see also John Constable, 'I. A. Richards, T. S. Eliot, and the Poetry of Belief', *Essays in Criticism*, 40 (1990), 222–43 (esp. pp. 231–34).

The author of several books of psychological criticism and cultural diagnosis, Richards exerted a central influence on many writers of the 1930s. His influence was arguably strongest in the pamphlet *Science and Poetry* (1926) with its resonant claim that Eliot's *The Waste Land* 'by effecting a complete severance of poetry and *all* beliefs, and this without any weakening of the poetry, realized what might otherwise have remained largely a speculative possibility'.[10] Richards provided Marxist-minded artists with a way of dispelling the anxiety of influence that came from the poetic *Übervater* Eliot by conveniently dismissing him as a bourgeois author irredeemably out of touch with reality. 'James Joyce, Mrs. Woolf, T. S. Eliot', as the young A. L. Rowse dismissively observed in *Politics and the Younger Generation* (1931), 'are caviare to the bourgeois and academic public'.[11] Eliot's public assertion of his royalist and Anglo-Catholic convictions, as well as his continuing emphasis on poetry's inability to propagate extra-poetic agendas, made him a notoriously difficult figure in the politicized debates of the late 1920s and early 1930s. However, this critical view has tended to obscure the fact that Eliot's attention to 'the relation of poetry to the spiritual and social life of its time' was in many ways closer to the concerns of left-wing authors than Richards's own position.

Principles of Literary Criticism (1924) was Richards's earliest statement of his critical doctrines. It is also in many ways his most moderate, and Richards's argument in this book is difficult to square with his later image as a champion of 'pure' modernist poetry. Early on in his study, Richards is at pains to point out that reading and writing never take place outside the matrix of belief. He ridicules in particular the aestheticist notion of a 'phantom aesthetic state': 'when we look at a picture, or read a poem, or listen to music, we are not doing something quite unlike what we were doing on our way to the Gallery or when we dressed in the morning.'[12] *Principles of Literary Criticism* subsequently elaborates on the idea, central to Richards's conjunction of aesthetic and moral valuation, of art's continuity with life. The third chapter of Richards's book,

[10] I. A. Richards, *Science and Poetry* (London: Trubner, 1926), p. 64, emphasis in the original. For Richards's influence on thirties writers, see Samuel Hynes, *The Auden Generation: Literature and Politics in England in the 1930s* (London: Bodley Head, 1976), pp. 25–29; Valentine Cunningham, *British Writers of the Thirties* (Oxford: Oxford University Press, 1988), pp. 36–70; and Peter McDonald, 'Believing in the Thirties', in *Rewriting the Thirties: Modernism and After*, ed. by Steven Matthews and Keith Williams (London: Longman, 1997), pp. 71–90 (p. 81–85).

[11] A. L. Rowse, *Politics and the Younger Generation* (London: Faber and Faber, 1931), p. 182.

[12] I. A. Richards, *Principles of Literary Criticism* [1924] (London: Routledge, 2001), p. 12.

'The Language of Criticism', critiques narrowly text-centred approaches to literature:

> [In] a full critical statement which states not only that an experience is valuable in certain ways, but also that it is caused by certain features in a contemplated object, the part which describes the value of the experience we shall call the *critical* part. That which describes the object we shall call the *technical* part. (18, emphases in the original)

The literary critic comes into his own, Richards points out, not as a judge of the linguistic and stylistic detail of a poem, but as an *arbiter morum*. His chapter is partly therapeutic in intent, as it aims to cleanse criticism of the 'Mystic Beings' and 'verbal thickets' of aestheticist criticism: 'Design, Form, Rhythm, Expression' (15). Richards instead chooses to address the 'communicative' function of poetry: poets, he observes, are 'social beings and accustomed to communication from infancy' and 'the arts' are accordingly 'the supreme form of the communicative activity' (21). Richards's polemic suggests that the formal features of a text are to be considered primarily as vehicles of a discrete content. The idea that literature ought to be judged by its communicative efficiency thus comes dangerously close to denying that 'the poem itself' (in Richards's recurrent phrase) merits critical attention in its own right.[13]

Despite this insistence that all language serves communication, the Mystic Being of poetic integrity—the 'poem itself' which escapes all attempts to fix its meaning—retains a latent half-life in *Principles*. At a later point in his argument, while commenting on the aestheticist principle of poetry for poetry's sake, Richards is more comfortable declaring what poetry is not rather than affirming what poetry is:

> It is impossible to divide a reader into so many men – an aesthetic man, a moral man, a practical man, a political man, an intellectual man, and so on. [. . .] If he attempts to assume the peculiar attitude of disregarding all but some hypothetically-named aesthetic elements, he joins Henry James's Osmond in his tower, he joins Blake's Kings and Priests in their High Castles and Spires.[14]

Principles does not satisfyingly resolve this fissure between the 'aesthetic' as a feature of poetry occurring in the context of others and poetry as an independently analysable concept. Richards's works of the 1920s frequently

[13] For the phrase 'the poem itself', see Richards, *Practical Criticism: A Study of Literary Judgment* [1929] (London: Transaction Publishers, 2004), pp. 75, 95, 96, and *passim*.

[14] Richards, *Principles*, pp. 71–72.

seem to want it both ways: they are keen to demystify literature by pointing out its manifold ('moral, practical, political, intellectual') contexts, but they also continue to be powerfully attracted to the idea of the 'poem itself'. It is a symptom of this dilemma that *Principles* reintroduces the idea of poetic integrity with a vengeance. 'There are two totally distinct uses of language', Richards claims towards the end of *Principles*: 'a statement may be used for the sake of the *reference* [. . .] this is the *scientific* use of language. But it may also be used for the sake of the effects in emotion and attitude produced by the reference it occasions. This is the *emotive* use of language.' The two uses of language give rise, Richards writes, to factual 'statements', on the one hand, and to 'pseudo-statements', on the other.[15] Richards's theory of 'pseudo-statements' drew a *cordon sanitaire* not just around poetry but around literary discourse more generally by claiming to exempt it from the everyday referential use of language. Richards's theory was initially a theory of art and literature, not just of poetry, and in a later chapter of *Principles* he adduced various literary genres as well as 'the experiences of some music, of some architecture, and of some abstract design' to illustrate his observations regarding art's apolitical nature.[16] This blurring of boundaries between different genres and art forms helps to explain why Richards's theories were capable of affecting poets and prose writers alike.

There had in fact been precedents for Richards's claims about the special status of literary language. The argument of *Principles* implicitly built on earlier discussions of the nature of literary discourse, most notably Hans Vaihinger's *The Philosophy of 'As If'* (translated in 1924 by C. K. Ogden, Richards's colleague and collaborator at Cambridge) and Gottlob Frege's influential distinction between 'sense' and referential 'meaning'.[17] Richards and Ogden's co-authored *The Meaning of Meaning* (1923) had already drawn a distinction between 'scientific' and 'emotive' meaning, thus anticipating the argument of *Principles*.[18] Related positions can also be traced in later studies, such as Roman Jakobson's description of the 'poetic

[15] Ibid., p. 250, emphases in the original.

[16] Ibid., p. 264. Richards's literary examples include *Robinson Crusoe, Don Quixote, King Lear*, and Keats's poetry. Richards notes with a view to narrative prose: 'That is "true" or "internally necessary" which completes or accords with the rest of the experience, which co-operates to arouse our ordered response, whether the response of Beauty or another' (p. 252).

[17] Hans Vaihinger, *The Philosophy of 'As If': System of the Theoretical, Practical and Religious Fictions of Mankind* [1911], trans. by C. K. Ogden (London: Routledge, 1924); Gottlob Frege, 'Über Sinn und Bedeutung', *Zeitschrift für Philosophie und philosophische Kritik*, 100 (1892), 25–50. Frege is discussed in Ogden and Richards's *The Meaning of Meaning: A Study of the Influence of Language upon Thought and of the Science of Symbolism* [1923] (London: Paul Trench, 1927), pp. 273–74.

[18] Ogden/Richards, p. 241.

function' of language or Paul Ricoeur's analysis of metaphor which quotes approvingly from Richards's writings.[19] Eliot, trained as a philosopher at Harvard, was surely aware that the distinction propounded in *Principles* possessed wider philosophical currency, and it is revealing that Richards's restatement of it in *Principles* provoked such hostile comments from him. The main reason for this, I want to suggest, was the intensely polemical edge of Richards's writings and his attempt to turn Eliot into the exponent of a modernist poetry wiped clean of '*all* beliefs'. Eliot's and Richards's statements of shared critical problems can indeed be strikingly different. For example, Richards's formulation that 'the greatest poets, as poets, [. . .] refrain from assertion' finds an echo in Eliot's central demand (in *The Sacred Wood*) to 'consider' poetry 'primarily as poetry'.[20] While Eliot presents the problem as a matter of critical method and hermeneutic perspective, Richards boldly implies that the language of pseudo-statements, the absence of referential 'assertion', is somehow ontologically intrinsic to the medium of poetry. 'A Pseudo-Statement', as Richards elaborated in a letter, 'is something utterly different in function, powers, status, nature, order of being etc., from any scientific, or other verifiable statement, true or false.'[21] Such differences may even suggest that Eliot's invocation of poetic integrity in the 1928 Preface to *The Sacred Wood* and his assertion that he had moved beyond this problem were intended as a covert jibe at Richards.

Left-wing authors in the 1930s were certainly prepared to see Richards as a proponent of modernist aestheticism, and writers like Edward Upward, Christopher Isherwood, and Christopher Caudwell did not tire of criticizing Richards for his theory of 'emotive' language.[22] The idea of poetic integrity, Caudwell observed in a discussion of the belief-debate, epitomized 'the typical bourgeois myth of the free man, the undetermined observer, the man who participates in the social process without being affected by it'.[23] This reductive view of Richards's position was widely

[19] Roman Jakobson, 'Linguistics and Poetics', in *Style in Language*, ed. by Thomas A. Sebeok (Cambridge, MA: MIT Press, 1960), pp. 350–77. Ricoeur notes that 'the strategy of language proper to poetry' consists in 'a sense that intercepts reference and, in the limiting situation, abolishes reality'. See his *The Rule of Metaphor: The Creation of Meaning in Language* [1975], trans. by Robert Czerny (London: Routledge, 2003), p. 262.

[20] Richards, *Principles*, p. 259.

[21] I. A. Richards, Letter to T. S. Eliot, 4 November 1935, in *Selected Letters of I. A. Richards*, ed. by John Constable (Oxford: Oxford University Press, 1990), p. 95.

[22] For Upward and Isherwood, see John Haffenden, *William Empson: Among the Mandarins* (Oxford: Oxford University Press, 2005), pp. 197–98. Caudwell denigrated the 'qualified assent' which 'we give to the statements of poetic art'. See *Illusion and Reality: A Study of the Sources of Poetry* (Basingstoke: Macmillan, 1937), p. 29.

[23] Christopher Caudwell, *Romance and Realism: A Study in English Bourgeois Literature*, ed. by Samuel Hynes (Princeton: Princeton University Press, 1970), p. 129.

shared outside the political left by figures as dissimilar as Kathleen Raine, who thought that Richards conceived of poetry as 'a process beginning and ending in mystery [. . .] the thought was metaphysical',[24] and the New Critic John Crowe Ransom, who attacked Richards's 'esoteric poetic', finding it 'too unrelated to the public sense of a poetic experience'.[25] A comment by Empson, an ambivalent member of the left, indicates the indirect ways by which Richards's critical influence asserted itself: 'I really was much influenced by Richards, but I thought it proper to learn from both sides [i.e. from Richards and Eliot], and would probably have said that I was on the side opposed to him.'[26]

Richards's concept of the 'pseudo-statement' consisted of two distinct yet interrelated parts: on the one hand, it curtailed the extra-poetic dimensions of literature by detaching poetic discourse from its historical contexts; on the other, it seized on poetry's newly gained autonomy to assert its superior, quasi-salvational powers. While Eliot's attack on Richards's critical doctrines concentrated on the assertion that *The Waste Land* had successfully severed itself from '*all* beliefs', his ire had initially been provoked by the second claim. The particular place attributed to poetry in *Principles* afforded Richards the liberty to think of the artist as a special kind of human being, and he variously alleged that ordinary language stands in need of the poet's special verbal powers. 'The rear-guard of society', he asserted, 'cannot be extricated until the vanguard has gone further.'[27] This 'vanguard' included not least the poetic avant-garde whose literary works seemed to hold out the dubiously utopian vision of a life untainted by the viscosity of the world.

An element of apocalyptic expectancy often lurks beneath Richards's scientific terminology. A tone of millenarian hope (quite literally millenarian as Richards predicts poetry's '1,000 years reign'[28]) had already surfaced in the last chapter of *Principles* on 'Poetry and Beliefs' which contained Richards's first sustained speculations about poetry as a substitute for religion:

> Very often the state of mind in which we are left by a poem [. . .] is of a kind which it is natural to describe as a belief. When all provisional acceptances have lapsed, when the single references and their connections which may

[24] Kathleen Raine, *The Land Unknown* (London: Hamish Hamilton, 1975), p. 37.

[25] John Crowe Ransom, 'Criticism as Pure Speculation', in *The Intent of the Critic*, ed. by Donald A. Stauffer (Princeton: Princeton University Press, 1941), pp. 91–124 (p. 95).

[26] William Empson, 'Comment on James Jensen, "The Construction of *Seven Types of Ambiguity*"' [1966], in *Selected Letters of William Empson*, ed. by John Haffenden (Oxford: Oxford University Press, 2006), p. 426.

[27] Richards, *Principles*, p. 54.

[28] Richards, *Science and Poetry*, p. 47.

have led up to the final response are forgotten, we may still have an attitude and an emotion which has to introspection all the characters of a belief.[29]

The passage replaces the extraneous beliefs which enter into poetic language with a speculative 'belief' in the intrinsic worth of poetry. Richards's hopes for poetry as a secular substitute for religion are even greater in an appendix to the second edition (1926) of *Principles*. There, Richards argued that Eliot's poetry was able to 'release the healing waters': 'Some readers find in his poetry not only a clearer, fuller realisation of their plight [. . .] but also through the very energies set free in that realisation a return of the saving passion.'[30] This salvationalist view of poetry enters most prominently into Richards's *Science and Poetry* with its alarmist fear that 'poetry may pass away' following the loss of the 'Magical View' of nature in the wake of modern science, and the book's closing paragraph expresses the hope that poetry will be 'capable of saving us'.[31] Both *Science and Poetry* and the appendix to *Principles* turn to Eliot as the future poet whose works can redeem a world afflicted by a 'dissociation of sensibility'. Richards's belief in poetry as '*a means of ordering, controlling, and consolidating* the whole of experience' (the only italicized passage in *Science and Poetry*) in fact invokes Eliot's comments on the Joycean 'mythical method' which would be capable 'of controlling, of ordering, of giving a shape and a significance to the immense panorama of futility and anarchy which is contemporary history'.[32] Eliot objected to Richards's representation of his poetry, and of *The Waste Land* in particular, as a secular surrogate for religion, and it was Eliot's retaliatory attacks of the late 1920s that helped to paint the picture of Richards as an advocate of pure poetry.

ELIOT, RICHARDS, AND THE 'PERSUASIVE POWER' OF POETRY

Critics have recognized the centrality of Richards's teachings to the literature of the 1930s, but they have tended to see his principal influence in his resonant claim for poetry's salvational powers. This claim, one critic suggests, helped to buttress the new decade's 'hopes for literature

[29] Richards, *Principles*, p. 261.

[30] Ibid., p. 278. The passage seems to allude to the biblical promise of divine 'living water' (John 4:10).

[31] Richards, *Science and Poetry*, p. 82.

[32] Ibid., p. 26; T. S. Eliot, '*Ulysses*, Order, and Myth', *The Dial*, 75 (1923), 480–83 (p. 483).

as a guide to "action"'.[33] Yet despite the well calculated scientific air of Richards's books, their quasi-religious expectations for poetry could seem to belong to the previous century, in particular to the theories of the *fin-de-siècle* Symbolists.[34] The perceived high-artistic elitism of Richards's views ultimately trumps the possibility that Richards established the context 'for the alliance between poetry and political purpose which dominated the 1930s'.[35] Such a view occludes the more significant (and largely negative) influence which Richards's theory of pseudo-statements and his assertion of literature's self-containment exerted on thirties writing. When Eliot launched his attack on Richards's position in a series of reviews in 1927, he was indeed targeting *Science and Poetry* and its call for poetry as an *ersatz* religion, yet his arguments soon homed in on Richards's notion of poetry as a realm of self-contained pseudo-statements. Eliot first criticized the high-pitched rhetoric of poetic redemption in a review of *Science and Poetry* for Wyndham Lewis's monthly *The Enemy*:

> We await, in fact (as Mr. Richards is awaiting the future poet), the great genius who shall triumphantly succeed in believing *something*. For those of us who are higher than the mob, and lower than the man of inspiration, there is always *doubt*; and in doubt we are living parasitically [. . .] on the minds of the men of genius of the past who have believed something.[36]

These lines deflate the alarmism which animates *Science and Poetry*, and the second half of the passage particularly denounces the idea, central to Richards's argument, of a break with tradition and of the initiation of a 'new order' by way of poetry.[37] Eliot replied in his review of *Science and Poetry* that it was foolish to draw a line between 'poetry of all the past and poetry of all the future'.[38] Eliot's rendering of Richards's position in the late 1920s tended to be extreme, and it was designed to make his own scepticism towards poetry as a surrogate for religion seem more plausible. To say that 'poetry "is capable of saving us"', he observed in his review of

[33] McDonald, 'Believing in the Thirties', p. 81.

[34] Compare for example Arthur Symons's observation that Symbolist poetry 'becomes itself a kind of religion, with all the duties and responsibilities of the sacred ritual'. See Symons, *The Symbolist Movement in Literature* (London: Heinemann, 1899), p. 10.

[35] Nick Hubble, 'The Intermodern Assumption of the Future: William Empson, Charles Madge and Mass-Observation', in *Intermodernism: Literary Culture in Mid-Twentieth-Century Britain*, ed. by Kristin Bluemel (Edinburgh: Edinburgh University Press, 2009), pp. 171–88 (p. 181).

[36] T. S. Eliot, 'A Note on Poetry and Belief', *The Enemy*, 1 (January 1927), 15–17 (p. 16), emphases in the original.

[37] Richards, *Science and Poetry*, p. 35.

[38] Eliot, 'Literature, Science, and Dogma', p. 243.

Science and Poetry, 'is like saying that the wall-paper will save us when the walls have crumbled'.[39]

Eliot's tendency to misread (or to exaggerate strategically) Richards's critical views has concealed the fact that his own positions and Richards's were not always as far apart as he would have it. The Richards-Eliot debate actually involved a process of critical osmosis in which Eliot appropriated some of his opponent's critical views even as he vociferously distanced himself from certain others. Richards's *Principles of Literary Criticism* contained a chapter on 'Permanence as a Criterion' which anticipated Eliot's argument, in the 1929 Note to his Dante essay, that the presence of defunct beliefs in literature can disturb the aesthetic enjoyment of a poem. As an example of this commingling of poetry and belief, Richards chose Dante:

> Far more of the great art of the past is actually obsolete than certain critics pretend, who forget what a special apparatus of erudition they themselves bring to their criticism. The *Divina Commedia* is a representative example. It is true that for adequately equipped readers who can imaginatively reproduce the world outlook of Aquinas, and certain attitudes to women and to chastity, which are even more inaccessible, there is no obsolescence.[40]

The 'readability' of Dante only became a *cause célèbre* with Eliot's Note to the second section of his Dante essay. The Note conveyed a keen uneasiness about the limits placed on literary appreciation by belief:

> One probably has more pleasure in the poetry when one shares the beliefs of the poet. On the other hand there is a distinct pleasure in enjoying poetry as poetry when one does *not* share the beliefs [. . .]. It would appear that 'literary' appreciation is an abstraction, and pure poetry a phantom; and that both in creation and enjoyment much always enters which is, from the point of view of 'Art', irrelevant.[41]

The passage plays the conflicting textualist and contextualist claims off against each other, and the casually consensual stance of the first sentence undermines the insistence in the second on the 'distinct pleasure' which is to be derived from 'poetry as poetry'. The closing sentence comes in the guise of a syllogistic conclusion, but it in fact spells out the implications of the first assertion. Poetry, Eliot affirms, is inevitably impure, and it is the task of the critic to explain differences in the appreciation of poems against the backdrop of the writer's and the reader's diverse systems of belief. The

[39] Ibid., p. 243. [40] Richards, *Principles*, p. 208.
[41] Eliot, 'Dante', p. 257 fn., emphasis in the original.

Note to the Dante essay indicates that Eliot was aiming for a middle way between two seemingly antagonistic types of reading which he called 'heresies'. The first 'heresy', which Eliot associated with the critic Montgomery Belgion, contended that poets inadvertently use their poetry to propagate their philosophy of life; by contrast the second critical heresy, misleadingly identified with Richards, sought to purge poetry of all contextual taints. In the 1929 Note, Eliot claims to steer clear of both extremes. However, the intensity of his opposition to Richards's views can be measured by his temporary rapprochement with the first 'heresy'. Invoking Dante again in an essay entitled 'Poetry and Propaganda', Eliot pointed out that Dante and Lucretius are 'what Mr. Belgion would call propagandists, certainly, but they are particularly conscious and responsible ones'.[42] Eliot's advocacy of what he called the 'persuasive power' of poetry is puzzlingly at odds with his refusal, either before or after the publication of this essay, to reduce poetry to a vehicle of religious or political content.[43] The weak version of the belief-problem becomes indistinguishably muddled with the strong one: it is 'impossible to say', Eliot notes, 'how far [poets] write their poetry because of what they believe, and how far they believe a thing merely because they see that they can make poetry out of it'.[44] In 'Poetry and Propaganda', Eliot's opposition to Richards's theory of poetic pseudo-statements carried him to a jarring extreme.

Faced with the emergence of a new set of ideological demands on poetry in the late 1920s and early 1930s, Eliot was better equipped than Richards to acknowledge the contextual claims on poetic integrity. It was Richards's position which began to look problematic, and the results of his own lectures in practical criticism (given in 1925 and 1927, and published as *Practical Criticism: A Study of Literary Judgment* in 1929) demonstrated, if anything, how vast the demands of belief on literature really were. In *Practical Criticism*, Richards extended his attention from the sedimented traces of history within texts to the contextual dimensions of the act of reading, and the volume foregrounded the normative and prescriptive side of Richards's pedagogy. During his lectures, Richards asked students to comment on anonymized poems as a way of assessing their ability to read well and 'correctly'. To his dismay, however, the number of students who got their close readings of the set poems 'right' was embarrassingly small. William Longfellow's 'In the Churchyard at Cambridge' set a sad precedent: 'Only one reader attempted to state the issue between this view [that the poem is didactic] and another view by which it would escape

[42] T. S. Eliot, 'Poetry and Propaganda' [1930], in *Literary Opinion in America*, ed. by Morton Dauwen Zabel (New York: Harper, 1951), pp. 97–107 (p. 103).

[43] Ibid., p. 100. [44] Ibid., p. 103.

these charges', but even this reader 'so overstates his case that he discredits it'.[45] Most of the student readers, Richards lamented, were excessively relying on subjective 'sentiment' (what Richards called 'swoon reading' or 'the "mood" solution of difficulty'), on 'irrelevant associations' ('accidental by-products of a reading which does not realize the poem's meaning'), or on 'stock responses'.[46]

The 'Documentation' section of *Practical Criticism* is crowded with interpretations, catalogued in order of their obtuseness, which get carried away either by a wave of religious feeling (student no. 5.15, writing on a sonnet by Edna St. Vincent Millay, finds in the poem 'a good point for immortality, well worked out and well put. [. . .] I always feel attracted to religious poetry, and anxious to get the best out of it'), or by political affect ('Appeals to me because it sums up my creed as a Socialist, of service not self', notes report 1.194).[47] In the hands of these students, the poems were turning into the vehicles of religious and political propaganda. Richards is exceptionally discerning in sifting the multiplicity of 'misreadings' which litter the students' reports. Yet in sight of the sheer amount of these misreadings, his refusal to accept the reports as a challenge to his theory is little less than baffling. Even his subsequent claim that practical criticism can correct the deeply ingrained habit of misreading fails to convince: the presence of practical-critical vocabulary in the reports paradoxically suggests that the students' immersion in Ricardian critical doctrine was a stumbling block to good reading as much as it was an aid.

Richards observed in a letter to Eliot that *Practical Criticism* contained 'the same view, I think, exactly that I tried to maintain in *Science and Poetry* but I hope clearer and not as easily misunderstood'.[48] In a review of *Practical Criticism* for Eliot's *Criterion*, Montgomery Belgion drew a different and possibly correct conclusion. He found the students' responses 'most instructive' because they allowed him 'not to contradict, but to dismiss' Richards's position—along with Eliot's *The Sacred Wood* on which, he thought, Richards's argument had been modelled.[49] The 'Analysis' section, which makes up the second half of *Practical Criticism*, does in fact read like a stubborn defence of poetic integrity. 'The root question', Richards claimed, 'is whether [the reader's] responses reflect the poem itself, or some private poem prompted by the material set before the reader and by

[45] Richards, *Practical Criticism*, p. 169.

[46] Ibid., pp. 68, 155, 225, 235.

[47] Ibid., pp. 62, 26.

[48] I. A. Richards, Letter to T. S. Eliot, 1 October 1928, in *Selected Letters*, p. 47.

[49] Montgomery Belgion, 'What Is Criticism?', *The Criterion*, 10 (October 1930), 118–39 (pp. 118, 136). Richards retaliated in his 'Notes on the Practice of Interpretation', *The Criterion*, 10 (April 1931), 412–20.

his own reminiscences.'[50] Richards's clinching of this question in chapter seven ('Doctrine in Poetry') of the 'Analysis' section is revealing:

> It would seem evident that poetry which has been built upon firm and definite beliefs about the world, *The Divine Comedy* or *Paradise Lost*, or Donne's *Divine Poems*, or Shelley's *Prometheus Unbound*, or Hardy's *The Dynasts*, must appear differently to readers who do and readers who do not hold similar beliefs. Yet in fact most readers, and nearly all good readers, are very little disturbed by even a direct opposition between their own beliefs and the beliefs of the poet.[51]

The first sentence articulates a position which is remarkably close to Eliot's, while the assertion that 'most readers' are 'little disturbed' by contrary beliefs in poetry is hardly convincing in view of the overwhelming evidence from the students' reports. More than anything else, it was Richards's readiness to overstate his views that put him in direct opposition to Eliot in the later 1920s. Richards was setting too much store by the ahistorical notion of the 'poem itself' which projected the illusion that the close readings of practical criticism could be somehow objectively complete or self-sufficient.

Over the course of the 1930s the role of 'belief' in literature became ever more pressing, both in its weak and its strong formulations. 'One might derive from this slender volume more specific beliefs than from the whole of the Divine Comedy', Allen Tate noted in an early review of Stephen Spender's *Poems* (1933), invoking Eliot's and Richards's discussions of Dante.[52] The public controversy between Eliot and Richards had reached a near-stalemate when *Experiment* started publication in 1928, and the confrontational rhetoric of the debate is reflected in a tendency among *Experiment's* contributors to oppose the supposedly self-contained language of literature and to locate their modernist experimentation around questions of political and religious conviction. While the strong version of the belief-problem—the question of literature's worth as a propaganda tool—still plays a comparatively marginal role in the magazine, its weaker version figures prominently in most of the magazine's numbers.

EXPERIMENT AND THE LANGUAGES OF BELIEF

Experiment was founded in 1928 by an editorial committee comprising five brilliant undergraduates: William Empson, who was pursuing mathematics but changed over to English one year later in order to read for

[50] Richards, *Practical Criticism*, p. 95. [51] Ibid., p. 255.
[52] Allen Tate, 'A New Artist', *New Verse*, 3 (May 1933), 21–23 (p. 22).

a degree under the supervision of Richards; Jacob Bronowski, also majoring in mathematics; William Hare, who had been removed by his father from Oxford for his socialist leanings; future Mass-Observer Humphrey Jennings, studying English under Richards; and later Surrealist factotum Hugh Sykes Davies, reading for a degree in Classics. As John Haffenden points out, several of the contributors to *Experiment* had participated in the lectures, experimental in their own way, that were to form the basis of Richards's *Practical Criticism.*[53] William Empson attended the lectures in 1927 and 1928, as did Humphrey Jennings; Elsie Phare, a frequent contributor to *Experiment*, was also a regular participant; and even Kathleen Raine, generally sceptical of Richards's scientificism, confessed to having attended several of his lectures.[54] 'The climate of *Experiment*', recalled the artist Julian Trevelyan, who had been among the magazine's contributors, 'was determined by Richards's lectures'.[55]

The magazine ran to six numbers between 1928 and 1930 and came to a natural end when its founding members left college, to be revived by Jacob Bronowski for only one last issue as *The New Experiment* (1931). Most prominently, *Experiment* featured work by poets who were to make a name for themselves in the 1930s, such as William Empson, Hugh Sykes Davies, and the American Richard Eberhart. Literary prose, mostly derivative of Woolfian and Joycean modernism, featured to a lesser, and less important, degree. As Jason Harding has correctly observed, the most enduring contributions to the magazine are its critical essays.[56] These essays cover an impressive range of topics; their authors include Jacob Bronowski and Humphrey Jennings, Elsie Phare and the translator and scholar of Russian literature George Reavey, film enthusiast G. F. Noxon, as well as William Empson who supplied excerpts from his critical work-in-progress, *Seven Types of Ambiguity* (1930). The diverse academic backgrounds of the contributors lend the magazine a well-calculated air of experiment both in terms of style and of content: there were opinion pieces on 'Cinema and Censorship', 'Schubert or Schönberg: Melody or Mathematics', 'A Biological Interpretation of Civilisation', and 'Squarcione Today', among other topics. Articles about modernist writers abound: there are pieces on authors as diverse as Paul Valéry and Boris Pasternak, Gertrude Stein, Wyndham Lewis, and D. H. Lawrence; *The New Experiment* even secured

[53] Haffenden, pp. 170–81.

[54] Raine, p. 37. Philippa Bernard has noted that Raine 'attended' the lectures 'frequently'. See Bernard, *No End to Snowdrops: A Biography of Kathleen Raine* (London: Shepheard-Walwyn, 2009), p. 24.

[55] Julian Trevelyan, *Indigo Days* [1957] (Aldershot: Scolar Press, 1996), p. 16.

[56] Harding, '*Experiment* in Cambridge', p. 306.

permission to print excerpts from Joyce's ongoing *Work in Progress*. The editorial statement which opens the last number of *Experiment* is characteristically cautious in putting forward a unified rationale, whether political or literary: 'We have always avoided making protestations of policy, choosing to leave it to the reader to conclude that we really do stand for a single direction of outlook.'[57]

Stylistically at least, there is little doubt as to *Experiment*'s adherence to a brand of avant-garde writing which belonged more properly to the 1920s than to the 1930s. Most noticeably, the poetry published in *Experiment*'s seven numbers is steeped in the spirit of formal experimentation and *vers libre* associated with T. S. Eliot's poetry. References to Eliot abound in the poems of Jacob Bronowski, which evince an Eliotic sense of apocalypse and spiritual renewal ('we have come to the latter season of the year | when kingdoms tremble', 'such that are changeable bleach and age, | April was their begetting'), as well as in the poems of Lionel Birch ('I can not believe | That everyone has gone through the April love-famine'). *Experiment* shares its modernist allegiances with such publications as Eugene Jolas's Paris-based avant-garde journal *transition*, and may have taken its title from that publication.[58] 'Our thoughts at this time were more and more directed towards Paris', Julian Trevelyan recalled, 'of which Cambridge seemed a sordid and distant suburb.'[59] *Experiment* even attracted the attention of Jolas whose magazine had famously proclaimed the modernist 'Revolution of the Word' in 1929.[60] Jolas invited Bronowski to contribute selections from the magazine to the June 1930 issue of *transition*, and the editors of *Experiment* seized on this opportunity to restate their eclectic modernist allegiances, prefacing the selection with a 'Manifesto' that stated the 'need of some new *formal* notation [. . .] a belief in the compact, *local* unit, and in the *impersonal* unit'.[61] Echoing Eliot's call for impersonality and formal terseness in post-war modernist poetry, such statements, along with a cover design influenced by the angular aesthetic of Russian Constructivism, have led critics to align *Experiment* with a modernist outlook and to contrast this stance with the explicitly *engagé* literature of the thirties.[62] *Experiment*, according to these accounts, offers a

57 'Editorial', *The New Experiment*, 7 (Spring 1931), p. 4.

58 The subtitle of *transition* urbanely announced an *International Quarterly for Creative Experiment*.

59 Trevelyan, p. 20.

60 Eugene Jolas and Elliot Paul, 'Proclamation: The Revolution of the Word', *transition*, 16–17 (June 1929), p. 13.

61 'Manifesto', *transition*, 19–20 (June 1930), p. 106, emphases in the original.

62 Harding, '*Experiment* in Cambridge', p. 292; Alan Young, *Dada and After: Extremist Modernism and English Literature* (Manchester: Manchester University Press, 1981), p. 153.

brief respite before the plunge into the 'political' 1930s. When it is read in this way, the magazine becomes a rearguard attempt to carry the Jolasian Revolution of the Word over into the new decade, illustrating how one generation's literary avant-gardism can become a later generation's stylistic backwardness. This view seems to be supported by John Lehmann's recollection that Michael Roberts decided to exclude 'three Cambridge poets, leading lights of *Experiment*' from *New Signatures* 'because he thought them too close to Eliot and to the French surrealists Eluard and Tzara'. 'However estimable their aims might be', Lehmann recalled, 'we were on a different track that he was convinced would in the long run prove more important.'[63] This implies that *Experiment* failed to make the move into the 1930s either stylistically or thematically in spite of Jacob Bronowski's christening of the last number to chime with the fashionable thirties spirit of 'newness'.[64]

Yet the legacy of modernism in the pages of *Experiment* was more ambiguous and more problematic than these assessments indicate. As a result of Richards's association of modernist writing with the semantically self-enclosed realm of pseudo-statements, there was a fear in the magazine of a too thorough absorption in the dehistoricized domain of poetic discourse. Modernist scholars have recently studied the role which little magazines of the 1920s played in the artistic growth and in the geographical spread of modernism. While I am sympathetic towards these attempts, it is difficult to accommodate *Experiment* within this broad understanding of the cultural work performed by little magazines. Instead, the contributions to *Experiment* begin to register their belated modernism as an oppressive presence. In the fifth number of the magazine, for example, Hugh Sykes Davies attacked modernism for its increasing sterility and its 'general tendency towards retreatism'. 'The academic retreat from politics is represented in "The Waste Land" and Pound's "Hugh Selwyn Mauberley"', the article declared: 'For the academic spirit applied to politics—Mr. Eliot's Royalism.'[65] F. R. Leavis, then a young lecturer in the newly founded Cambridge English Faculty, was quick to note *Experiment*'s critical distance from the alleged 'purity' of modernist writing. In an early review of *Experiment*, published in March 1929, he congratulated the magazine's contributors on avoiding the esoteric textual complacencies of what he called 'Sitwellism', referencing the writings of the Sitwell siblings Edith,

[63] John Lehmann, *Autobiography*, 3 vols (London: Longmans, 1955–66), I (1955), p. 174.

[64] For this rhetoric of 'newness', see Cunningham, pp. 112–13.

[65] Hugh Sykes Davies, 'The League of Nations', *Experiment*, 5 (February 1930), 6–10 (p. 6).

Obsert, and Sacheverell.[66] The eschewal of an increasingly self-referential brand of modernism—of 'Sitwellism', in Leavis's convenient shorthand—was the axiomatic problem facing *Experiment*'s contributors.

These tensions are frequently articulated through the terms of the Eliot-Richards debate. Essays devoted exclusively to Eliot's criticism and poetry include William Empson's 'Some Notes on Mr. Eliot' and Elsie Phare's 'An Essay on the Devotional Poetry of T. S. Eliot'. Among the critical essays which invoke Ricardian terminology are Humphrey Jennings's 'A Reconsideration of Herrick' (which cautions against the snares of mis-reading and 'irrelevant associations'), William Hare's 'Beauty: A Problem and an Attitude to Life' (chastising 'intellectual attitudes' in literature) and William Archer's 'Poetry and Beliefs' (which loots Richards's idiom to develop a theory of 'pseudo-environments'). The Richards-Eliot controversy had had its roots in the problem of *religious* belief in poetry, and it is in this incarnation that the debate made its first sustained appearance in *Experiment*. In the summer of 1928, Empson received a letter from Elsie Phare containing a draft of what would become, in the first number of *Experiment*, the essay 'Valéry and Hopkins', an astute close reading of Gerard Manley Hopkins's 'The Windhover'.[67] The correspondence which preceded the publication reveals Empson's admiration of Phare's piece, but Empson's letters also propose his own brilliant interpretation of the poem, a reading which he intended to be 'rather a smack at Richards'.[68] This 'smack' would be aimed, as Empson points out in his first letter to Phare, at an early essay by Richards on Hopkins's poem.[69] Richards's article, published in 1926, had discovered a central ambiguity in 'The Windhover' which turned on the double meaning of the word 'buckle' and which allowed for it to be read both as a praise of ascetic seclusion and as a warning against the exposure of monastic life to religious doubt and inner struggle.[70] The article had claimed to resolve the poem's ambiguities by factoring Hopkins's Christian faith into the critical equation, but it also declared that this presence of Christian belief in 'The Windhover' was a flaw in the poem's design: 'We shall find difficulty in resisting the conclusion that the poet in [Hopkins] was often oppressed and stifled by the priest.'[71] Empson's letters make it clear that he was reluctant to let

[66] F. R. Leavis, 'Cambridge Poetry', *The Cambridge Review*, 1 March 1929, 317–18 (p. 317). Leavis was reviewing *Cambridge Poetry, 1929*, which assembled work by some of the magazine's contributors.

[67] Elsie Phare, 'Valéry and Gerard Hopkins', *Experiment*, 1 (November 1928), 19–23.

[68] William Empson, Letter to Elsie Phare, 14 September 1928, in *Selected Letters*, p. 5.

[69] William Empson, Letter to Elsie Phare, 4 September 1928, in *Selected Letters*, pp. 3–4.

[70] I. A. Richards, 'Gerard Hopkins', *The Dial*, 81 (September 1926), 195–203 (p. 199).

[71] Ibid.

belief interfere with the textual complexities of Hopkins's poem.[72] Elsie Phare's article on 'Valéry and Hopkins', by contrast, stays closer to Richards's blueprint. Settling for less ambiguity than Empson's reading offers, her take on the poem was helped by her intellectual and personal stakes in Eliot's critical tenets. Phare had been confirmed in the Anglican Church in 1928, one year after Eliot, and she had enthusiastically reviewed his *For Lancelot Andrewes* (1928), whose Preface stated his 'classicist', 'royalist', and 'Anglo-Catholic' allegiances, later that year. Eliot's religious convictions, the review noted, invested his criticism and poetry with an 'enviable consistency of outlook'.[73]

The three essays which Phare contributed to *Experiment* constitute the most sympathetic defence of Eliot in the pages of the magazine, and her earliest pieces—on 'The Windhover' and on Hemingway's novels—propagate an artistic 'Classicism' derived from T. E. Hulme and from Eliot himself.[74] By contrast, Phare's third and most substantial contribution to *Experiment*, 'An Essay on the Devotional Poetry of T. S. Eliot' (1930), signals an important modification of the Classicist paradigm. By the late 1920s, Eliot's aesthetic views had become inextricably linked to his religious convictions (and vice versa), and Phare's article grasps the intimate connection between these sets of beliefs. It specifically entails a knowledge that the modernist, or 'Classicist', idea of poetic autarchy is not an independent notion but that it is in its turn premised on a distinct set of extra-literary assumptions. The 'Essay' opens by praising Hulme's theory of poetry because it gives due weight to matters of belief and 'religious attitude', and his Classicism is commended as a remedy against the self-indulgent sentimentality of Georgian poetry.[75] However, Phare regrets the dogmatic unwaveringness of Hulme's assertion of Original Sin: 'Cultivated to the degree in which Hulme recommends it, so that it may become a perpetual "awareness", the recognition of this truth may be positively harmful' (27). She associates the danger of basing poetry on overly rigid ideological premises with 'the phenomenon of spiritual old age'—with the hardening of poetic principles into aesthetic dogma which, she notes, is characteristic of the aging first generation of modernist writers (29). Phare seizes on Eliot's post-conversion poetry to support her case against Hulmean Classicism, and her reading of Eliot's 1927 poem 'Journey of the

72 Less than two years later, Empson used 'The Windhover' to illustrate the seventh type of ambiguity. See *Seven Types of Ambiguity* [1930] (London: Pimlico, 2004), pp. 224–26.

73 Elsie Phare, 'Several White Leopards', *The Granta*, 30 November 1928, p. 197.

74 Phare, 'Valéry and Gerard Hopkins'; and Elsie Phare, 'Ernest Hemingway', *Experiment*, 3 (May 1929), 13–16.

75 Elsie Phare, 'An Essay on the Devotional Poetry of T. S. Eliot', *Experiment*, 6 (October 1930), 27–32.

Magi' is intended to rebut the crushing fatalism of Hulme's posthumous volume *Speculations* (1924). Alluding to a passage from Yeats, Phare notes that Eliot's Magi are

> 'old men of thought' and 'all thought among us is frozen into "something other than human life".' But in the degree to which the old men of thought are Christian, their awareness of the discontinuity between the human and the divine is prevented from becoming the consciousness of an antinomy. Much more Byzantinism and it would begin to quarrel with the dogma of the incarnation; one already feels that Hulme's philosophy moves in that direction. (32)

The article finds fault not only with the aesthetic but also with the Hulmean 'religion' of modernism, with its insistent brooding over Original Sin and human limitation. Phare's essay cuts across the fundamental Hulmean breach between the divine and the human by holding out the promise of divine grace. Eliot's poem can in fact be seen to bear out some of her central claims, as the Magi fail to determine whether they

> were [. . .] led all that way for
> Birth or Death? There was a Birth certainly
> We had evidence and no doubt. I had seen birth and death,
> But had thought they were different; this Birth was
> Hard and bitter agony for us, like Death, our death. (ll.35–39)[76]

The passage contemplates the possibility of metaphysical 'Birth or Death', as well as of their mundane analogues (spelled with lower-case initials). While the first lines express the believer's conviction that there 'was a Birth certainly' in Bethlehem, the third line hesitates over the non-transcendent 'birth and death', and the last verse inconclusively weighs both possibilities ('like Death, our death'). Eliot's poem appears to describe an intense experience of faith which cannot be articulated adequately in the medium of poetry, and it even allows for an element of doubt to linger among the Magi's hyperbolically doubled assertiveness ('We had evidence and no doubt'). The lines which follow this passage are the closing lines of the poem, and they culminate in an anticipation of redemptive grace:

> We returned to our places, these Kingdoms,
> But no longer at ease here, in the old dispensation,
> With an alien people clutching their gods.
> I should be glad of another death. (ll.40–43)

[76] T. S. Eliot, 'Journey of the Magi', in *The Complete Poems and Plays* [1969] (London: Faber and Faber, 2004), pp. 103–104.

The tone of submission and self-sacrifice in the last verse suggests the possibility of a second Birth—the 'return' to a 'Kingdom' that is only imperfectly anticipated in the first line. The poem's last word, 'death', evokes a sense of sheer physical extinction, but it may also suggest the outlook of negative theology as it points to a metaphysical 'Birth' that cannot be expressed by the language of the poem.

Phare's essay on 'Eliot's Devotional Poetry' articulates a profound dissatisfaction with the religion of Hulmean high modernism, but it also proposes a more speculative, Romantic programme for the second generation of modernists:

> It seems possible that to-day the time has come for us to leave off scolding J. J. Rousseau and George Sand: not that they are more in the right than they ever were, but because their wrongness has had all the emphasis it deserves; and apply ourselves if it is not too late, to giving a little self-confidence to our younger contemporaries. (28)

As Phare elaborated in a book on Hopkins's poetry, 'The Windhover' anticipates a more 'catholic Catholicism' than Hulme's theories.[77] Defending Hopkins's religion against the Freudian ambiguities discerned in it by critics like Empson, Phare asserts that he was by no means 'morbidly ashamed of his natural man', and that there is in his poetry no trace of Hulme's 'morbid detestation of human limitations'.[78] But her reading of 'The Windhover' is also intended as a revaluing of Eliot's own faith since 'Hopkins's devotional attitude has much [. . .] in common with that of Eliot'.[79] Phare's *Experiment* 'Essay' likewise reassesses the ideological underpinnings of Eliot's poetry. It does not accept the notion of 'poetry as poetry' as a natural property of poetic discourse, but investigates the (religious) systems of belief which are embedded within it and which lend it substance.

Phare's essays reflect a wider attentiveness in *Experiment* to what I have called the weak version of the belief-problem, and other contributors were quick to grasp the implications of the Richards-Eliot debate beyond Phare's more specific focus on religion. As Eliot had observed in 1927: 'Mr Richards seems to me to be using the word "belief" very hazily, usually with the intimation of *religious* belief, though I do not see why he should limit himself to that.'[80] And Richards's *Science and Poetry* had also discovered that 'at present it is not primarily religious beliefs, in stricter

[77] Elsie Phare, *The Poetry of Gerard Manley Hopkins: A Survey and Commentary* (Cambridge: Cambridge University Press, 1933), p. 138.

[78] Phare, *Hopkins*, pp. 141, 139.

[79] Ibid., pp. 143–44.

[80] Eliot, 'Note on Poetry and Belief', p. 17, emphasis in the original.

and narrower senses of the word which are most likely to be concerned. Emphases alter surprisingly.'[81] Emphases did alter significantly, especially in the early 1930s, and Eliot's and Richards's stretching of 'belief' to include the emerging array of political ideologies helped to stimulate a continuation of their argument in *Experiment*. The debate between Richards and Eliot provided contributors with a language through which they could voice their nascent political interests and reflect on the implications of these interests for their own literary work. Yet while the discussion of modernist writing's ideological underpinnings found its way into the pages of *Experiment* by way of Phare's exploration of literature's religious contexts, subsequent debates about the relationship between politics and literature were conducted almost exclusively by the magazine's male contributors. There had only been a few female contributors when the magazine started publication, and the most prominent among them moved decisively away from radical politics in the early 1930s: while Phare immersed herself in her new-won Anglican faith, Raine adopted a stance of mysticism in her poetry that largely removed her from the concerns of Marxist history. The literary-political concerns which were beginning to crystallize in the pages of *Experiment* were circulated among a predominantly male group of writers.

EXPERIMENT AND POLITICS: THE CASE OF VSEVOLOD IVANOV

The shift of the belief-problem into a more explicitly political matrix was helped by a number of historical developments in the late 1920s. As Scott McCracken has noted in a survey of student activism in mid- and late-1920s Cambridge, 'both politically and aesthetically the period between 1928 and 1934 was a critical one': the 1920s had been a period of labour militancy, leading up to the General Strike in 1926 and the Jarrow hunger marches which passed through Cambridge; the year 1929 saw the Wall Street Crash whose immediate aftershocks continued to be felt well into the next decade.[82] These political developments also changed the climate in which little magazines were operating. Edgell Rickwords's *Calendar of Modern Letters*, for example, failed to translate its *communisant* tendencies into political action during the General Strike, and this failure precipitated

[81] Richards, *Science and Poetry*, p. 80. Richards further noted that 'university societies founded fifteen years ago, for example, to discuss religion, are usually found to be discussing sex today' (*Science and Poetry*, p. 80). The book's 1935 reissue carefully emended that 'they were discussing sex when this was first written in 1926, as they are discussing political ideologies today'. See *Poetries and Sciences* [1935] (London: Routledge, 1970), p. 75.

[82] McCracken, p. 608.

the folding of the magazine as the editors 'decided that they no longer wanted to identify with a [bourgeois] culture that they saw as moribund'.[83] The volatile political atmosphere also affected larger magazines such as Eliot's *Criterion*. Jason Harding has observed that the *Criterion* in its early 'belletristic incarnation'

> did not interest itself overtly in politics. [. . .] In his editorial 'Last Words' [of 1939], Eliot claimed it was only from 1926 that the lineaments of the post-war world became clearly visible. This year, of course, was the year of the General Strike, an event that laid bare bitter and entrenched class divisions in British society. [. . .] From 1926, the *Criterion* saw political commentary as within its province.[84]

The cases of the *Calendar* and the *Criterion* set important precedents for the editorial agenda of *Experiment*. There was in fact a distinct socialist or even communist streak running through the biographies of *Experiment*'s editors: Empson had supported the General Strike of 1926 and remained a socialist throughout the 1930s; Sykes Davies entered the Communist Party a few years into the new decade, as did Bronowski; Jennings was and remained left-wing, even though he did not join the Party. And even if waving the Red Flag was often simply a matter of academic fashion in the late 1920s, intensifying historical pressures were for the first time giving the issue of 'taking sides' real urgency.

Relegated to the last pages of the second issue of *Experiment* (February 1929) is George Reavey's translation of the story 'Mounds' by the Russian writer Vsevolod Ivanov.[85] Ivanov had been brought to the attention of a slightly wider English public by an enthusiastic review of one of his short story collections in the *Times Literary Supplement* in 1928. The review puzzled 'how translators have come to overlook this genial author', and it went on to note that though Ivanov 'is, politically, a Communist, he never once allows one to know it'.[86] There is a grave irony in this comment since it was precisely Ivanov's defiance of communist aesthetics which brought him into conflict with the Soviet Communist Party in the mid-1920s when the

[83] John Lucas, 'Standards of Criticism: The *Calendar of Modern Letters* (1925–7)', in *Modernist Magazines*, ed. by Peter Brooker and Andrew Thacker, pp. 389–404 (pp. 398, 404); see also John Lucas, *The Radical Twenties: Aspects of Writing, Politics and Culture* (Nottingham: Five Leaves, 1997), pp. 217–50.

[84] Jason Harding, *The 'Criterion': Cultural Politics and Periodical Networks in Inter-War Britain* (Oxford: Oxford University Press, 2002), pp. 178–79.

[85] Vsevolod Ivanov, 'Mounds', trans. by George Reavey, *Experiment*, 2 (February 1929), 47–48.

[86] [John Cournos,] Review of Vsevolod Ivanov's *Dikhanie Pustini* [*The Breath of the Desert*], *Times Literary Supplement*, 19 July 1928, p. 536.

tenets of socialist realism were beginning to be formulated.[87] More than any other text in the first two numbers of *Experiment*, Ivanov's story justifies Leavis's congratulatory remark on the magazine's successful eschewal of 'Sitwellism', and Leavis's article was in fact published only one month after the second issue of *Experiment* had come out. Ivanov, born in 1895, is introduced by Reavey as 'a Siberian miner's son':

> On the road at an early age [. . .] he was wrestler, organ grinder, and sailor in turn. It is as a communist and writer that he reaches his apotheosis. After fighting Kolchak and the Czechs in Siberia, he became a 'Serapion Brother,' and transmuted his terrible experiences into a vivid record of the times. (47)

The biographical note marks the story out as an intrusion into the well-tempered modernism of *Experiment*. The reference to the club of Serapion Brothers, a bastion of avant-garde writers in post-revolutionary Russia, is designed to render the contrast less harsh, yet Ivanov's biography in fact illustrates the clash between avant-garde writing and the official Soviet doctrine of Agitprop which outlawed stylistic experiment. Following the publication of his collection *Tainoe Tainykh* (translated as *Mystery of Mysteries*) in 1927, Ivanov's literary 'ornamentalism' had incurred violent polemics from the Russian Association of Proletarian Writers, making him a cultural *persona non grata.*[88]

The plot of 'Mounds' concerns a young Soviet revolutionary whose plans to mount a Shakespeare production at a local theatre are violently disrupted when he is 'informed by the authorities that the presentation of Shakespeare was not essential to the revolutionary stage' (47). Not much later, the narrator is ordered by the same 'authorities' to lead an expedition on a macabre mission:

> I was told that some 8000 corpses had accumulated at the distant station of Tamarska; spring was at hand; and an epidemic was feared. My task accordingly was to dispose of the bodies judiciously. To this end I was given a locomotive, two wagons, a typist, dynamite, and spirit, and, above all, full powers of action. These instructions, finally, were capped by the brief hope that, as a writer, I would no doubt appreciate the experience. (47)

[87] Brandon Taylor has pointed out that 'the period 1926–8' was central to the formulation of political and aesthetic goals by the Soviet CP. See Taylor, 'Socialist Realism: "To Depict Reality in Its Revolutionary Development"', in *Adventures in Realism*, ed. by Matthew Beaumont (Oxford: Blackwell, 2007), pp. 142–57 (esp. pp. 145–50).

[88] For the historical context of Ivanov's early stories, see Valentina G. Brougher's helpful introduction to *Vsevolod Ivanov: Fertility and Other Stories* (Evanston: Northwestern University Press, 1998), pp. xiii–xxxvii. Trotsky had prominently condemned Ivanov and the Serapion Brothers. See Trotsky, *Literature and Revolution* [1925], ed. by William Keach, trans. by Rose Strunsky (Chicago: Haymarket, 2005), pp. 70–73.

The narrator does not inquire into the origin of the corpses ('gaunt and naked bodies of men, women, and children, all frozen, lay stiffly heaped in rows', 47), but the sheer anonymity of the figure points towards the state-organized industrialization and collectivization enforced by Stalin in the mid-1920s which resulted in the starving of several million peasants. The narrator quickly becomes complicit with the calculated use of violence; finding no way to crack open the frozen earth, he forces a peasant at gunpoint to reveal the location of an abandoned quarry: 'At last I shouted, fingering my Revolver – "Do you realise that I have full powers! If you don't tell me within two minutes [. . .] I will shoot, and add you to the 8000 corpses"' (48). After the bodies have been buried, the narrator leaves Tamarska, only to be called back in the spring:

> On the melting of the snow the grave had apparently swelled with the rotting bodies and burst. [. . .] So the unwilling bourgeois were again marched out, and forced to re-cover the grave. The stench was terrible. The very horses refused to approach the spot; yet the bourgeois had to cover it with clay. A lorry, full of bricks, was then driven across. (48)

The reference to the mass of 'bourgeois' workers suggests the anonymous suffering in the early Gulag forced-labour camps, turning the story into a remarkably explicit parable on totalitarian sadism and the dehumanizing effects of a new political order gone morally awry.

It is difficult to account for the task performed by Ivanov's story in the context of a narrow editorial scheme purveying modernist writing to an audience of like-minded academics. The polite cynicism of the telegram, for example, 'capped by the brief hope that, as a writer, I would no doubt appreciate the experience', implies deep-seated doubts regarding the possibility of artistic withdrawal. The retreat into modernist textuality, into the Jolasian Revolution of the Word, is trumped by a historical revolution which is at once more real and more profoundly unsettling in the demands it imposes on writing. Ivanov's story—with its little-concealed criticism of the excesses of the Russian Revolution and of Stalin's early rule—raised *Experiment*'s political stakes, and it acted as an urgent, albeit implicit, call on the magazine's contributors to reassess their left-wing credentials. The critical essays published in the magazine's subsequent numbers suggest the power of the story to upset the detached aestheticist rationale of *Experiment*. These articles do not, in other words, seek to 'protect [. . .] art', as Geoffrey Hartman thought Eliot's *The Sacred Wood* and Richards's practical criticism were designed to do, 'from imperious demands of an ideological nature, emanating from politics'.[89]

[89] Geoffrey Hartman, *Criticism in the Wilderness: The Study of Literature Today* [1980] (New Haven: Yale University Press, 2007), p. 284.

The essay that opens the next number of *Experiment*, face to face with 'Mounds' as it were, constitutes an oblique response to Ivanov's story. Emphasizing literature's social and historical contexts, 'Wyndham Lewis's *Enemy*' (signed 'Five', referring to the magazine's five editors) amounts to an editorial statement of purpose.[90] In the third number of his magazine *The Enemy*, Lewis had launched an indiscriminate attack on the communist politics embraced by members of the French Surrealist group. The Five scramble to the aid of Lewis's victims:

> [Lewis's] polemic is important, because upon it is founded also his political thesis: in his own words – that the artist must 'banish his political sensations altogether or so I believe.' The use of the word 'sensation' is characteristic. [. . .] He cannot analyse the belief and discover it to be [a] manifestation of that unconscious attitude to society which is the ultimate basis of art [. . .]. That theology and politics are implicit in all significant art, because significance is the expression of a positive critical attitude, a *Weltanschauung*, he cannot realise. (3–4)

The passage entails a crucial shift towards what I have called the strong version of the belief-problem. The idea that artists are proponents of a particular '*Weltanschauung*' resembles Eliot's discussion of literature as a type of 'responsible propaganda' rather than his more cautious reflections about the 'uses' of poetry in his 1932 Harvard lectures. Surprisingly, 'Wyndham Lewis's *Enemy*' is an extended critique not only of Lewis's magazine but also of the perceived political escapism of Eugene Jolas's *transition*. The same critical move that is meant to save Surrealist avant-gardism from Lewis's charges paradoxically implicates *transition* in a kind of aestheticist defeatism:

> Of course Mr. Lewis cannot sustain such bubbling independence: but finding himself forced into politics, he makes precisely the same protective manoeuvre as that made by the *transition* group: he invents for himself a set of politics which will effectively isolate him from political reality. (4)

The Five decide to 'smile at the pretty Bohemian communism' of Jolas's magazine 'which deserves all the hard things Mr Lewis has said about it' (4). It is surprising to find this sort of dismissal in a journal commonly identified as a cross-Channel '*hommage à Montparnasse*', and there is indeed little in the essay to support the idea that the Five's opposition to Lewis was 'a gesture of solidarity with the policy of experimentalism adopted by *transition*'.[91]

[90] 'Five', 'Wyndham Lewis's *Enemy*', *Experiment*, 3 (May 1929), 2–5.
[91] Harding, '*Experiment* in Cambridge', p. 292.

TOWARDS THE 1930s: THE 'IMPORTANCE' OF LITERATURE

The attack on Lewis and *transition* taps into a current of critical ideas popularized through the Richards-Eliot debate. Eliot's 'Poetry and Propaganda' essay, for example, suggested that it was becoming increasingly difficult to think of poetry 'primarily as poetry and not another thing'. And Richards's *Science and Poetry*, far from offering a simplistic celebration of the 'severance of poetry from *all* belief', had likewise noted that

> a great deal of poetry can, of course, be written for which total independence of all beliefs is an easy matter. But it is never poetry of the more important kind, because the temptation to introduce beliefs is a sign and measure of the importance of the attitudes involved.[92]

Richards's comment is particularly illuminating, because it is fundamentally at odds with the picture which Eliot had been drawing of his opponent. The issue that is at stake in the quarrel about belief, Richards insists, is the 'importance' of poetry. But what kind of poetry is, after all, 'of the more important kind': the poetry which links explicitly with political and religious systems of belief? Or the 'serious poetry' which affirms, in Peter McDonald's phrase, only the 'authority' of form and 'in which poetry's integrity' is 'independent of [extra-literary] concerns and unaccountable to them'?[93] In subsequent *Experiment* issues, many contributors claimed to relinquish the Hulmean realm of poetic autarchy, searching instead for alternative beliefs which might lend ideological muscle to their writing.

Among the members of the editorial committee, Bronowski showed the greatest zeal when it came to the extra-poetic 'importance' of literature. Bronowski had clearly been impressed by Ivanov's story, and his poems continue to echo the imagery of 'Mounds'. One of his poems is terrified to discover that 'Winter slips from the land | there'll be graves to cover', and the voice of another pleads for burial: 'let me have, that died | three seasons ago, burial'. Scott McCracken, quoting the latter passage, points out its stylistic and thematic indebtedness to *The Waste Land*,[94] yet this view neglects that Bronowski's poems are significant precisely for their admixture of two seemingly incongruous idioms, as they combine modernist echoes from Eliot with the political charge of Ivanov's story. Bronowski's critical contributions are also animated by the question of literature's 'importance'. Five months after the attack on Lewis, Bronowski wrote that

[92] Richards, *Science and Poetry*, pp. 79–80.
[93] McDonald, *Serious Poetry*, p. 108.
[94] McCracken, p. 609.

in poetry the metaphysical '*outlook* is never actually stated; but it is the fundament of the narrative; and upon its complete objectification into narrative, as much as upon the further objectification of the narrative into objects, depends the success of the poem'.[95] This restatement of the weak belief-problem acknowledges that literature is always part of larger ideological formations. But Bronowski's comments also suggest that politics plays a necessary and constructive role in literary texts, as it buttresses the slippery medium of poetic language with a self-consistent *Weltanschauung*.

Richards's critical doctrines, in particular his defence of poetic pseudo-statements, surface again and again as Bronowski's main target. In *Science and Poetry*, following his discussion of *The Waste Land*, Richards had turned to D. H. Lawrence and the poetry of W. B. Yeats as successful examples of the severance of literature from all beliefs. Richards had particularly praised Lawrence whose 'original rejection of a morality not self-supporting but based upon belief makes his work an admirable illustration of my main thesis'.[96] Richards's self-congratulatory posturing is undermined by Bronowski in a contribution ('D. H. Lawrence'), half obituary, half critical assessment, to *The New Experiment*.[97] Bronowski concurs with Richards that it is wrong 'to suppose that Lawrence's statements have a meaning outside the system of meanings [. . .] of the books' (6), but he is suspicious of the attempt to posit a realm of inner-textual, poetic autarchy: 'To struggle for [the] completeness of a name, a symbol, requires the faith to believe the completeness important, to be an end in itself. Lawrence knew that the completeness must be his only end, but he was too sensitive to its limitation to have faith in it' (10). Literature, even if it does not fall back on extraneous systems of belief, requires a special form of 'faith' in the 'completeness' of literary expression—a residual belief resembling what Eliot and Richards had called 'poetry as poetry'. Bronowski recognizes that the ideal of poetic autonomy is not simply given, but that it rests on the ideologically charged assumption that the 'aesthetic' can be tidily differentiated from other (political, religious, social) systems of value. Lawrence, Bronowski points out, lacked this belief in writing for writing's sake: he 'often felt himself to be betraying his symbolism', and it is this 'honesty which thwarted his achievement' (11).

Bronowski's articles were responding to an intensifying debate among *Experiment*'s contributors. Following the clamorous dismissal of Lewis's 'politics', opinions about the role of belief in literature had fractured into

95 Jacob Bronowski and J. M. Reeves, 'Towards a Theory of Poetry', *Experiment*, 4 (November 1929), 20–27 (p. 24), emphasis in the original.

96 Richards, *Science and Poetry*, p. 76–77.

97 Jacob Bronowski, 'D. H. Lawrence', *The New Experiment*, 7 (Spring 1931), 5–13.

two broad groups, and Bronowski sought to fortify his 'contextualist' position against those who opposed the statement issued by the Five. One of Bronowski's antagonists was William Archer, a regular contributor to the magazine. Archer's article 'Poetry and Beliefs' had discussed 'the place of beliefs in poetry', and the essay had made a forceful case, somewhat more in line with the earlier editorial outlook of *Experiment*, against Bronowski's position.[98] Arguing that poetry is 'from the nature of things' esoteric, Archer concluded that extra-literary beliefs are only a minor ingredient in poetry. 'For the essence of the poetic experience we must look elsewhere', the article comments: 'What determines whether a poem is good as a poem is the relations between its statements and not the statements themselves. [. . .] Beliefs therefore are irrelevant for "poetic" purposes' (31). Archer's prioritizing of the discursive, or 'relational', effects of literary language echoes Richards's argument in favour of pseudo-statements, and it attributes only secondary importance to the referential meaning of individual utterances. Moreover, his tautological definition of the quality of 'a poem [. . .] as a poem' harks back quite explicitly to Eliot's (and Richards's) appraisal of 'poetry [. . .] as poetry and not another thing'. Bronowski reasserted his own position in a 'Postscript' to Archer's article which insisted that literature, and literary criticism, 'can be distinguished from private experience'.[99] However, his reply to Archer's textualist broadside is strangely dampened, and it reflects a general waning of interest in the extra-poetic importance of literature after the publication of *Experiment* material in Jolas's *transition*.

The disputes and disagreements in *Experiment* are indicative of the countless adjustments and struggles which characterized modernist little magazines, yet in the special case of *Experiment* they also mirror broader critical and literary trends which marked the transition from the 1920s to the 1930s. These internal divisions are most evident in the 'Manifesto', penned jointly by the editors of *Experiment*, which prefaces the selection in *transition*. The text is torn between two kinds of belief. It professes

> [a] sense that literature is in need of some new *formal* notation: an attempt to show how such a notation can be built out of *academic* notations, where academic means perhaps no more than non-moral, and is after all best explained in our poetry: a belief in the compact, local unit: and in the impersonal unit: a belief finally, and a disbelief – for it is about this mainly that we are at odds – in *literature* as a singular and different experience [. . .]. You see how haphazard it all is.[100]

[98] William Archer, 'Poetry and Beliefs', *Experiment*, 5 (February 1930), 29–34 (p. 29).
[99] Jacob Bronowski, 'Postscript', *Experiment*, 5 (February 1930), 34.
[100] 'Manifesto', p. 106, emphases in the original.

Martin Puchner has recently recalled the centrality of manifestoes to the development of the modernist avant-gardes, pointing out that manifestoes 'are ideal instances of performative speech'. Like its precursors in the arena of radical politics, the avant-garde manifesto 'projects itself forward, anticipating what will have happened; it is the space of unauthorized theatricality and performative *poesis*'.[101] In the case of *Experiment*'s 'Manifesto', this sense of anticipation is undermined by an anticlimactic sense of hesitation and internal conflict—of 'a belief finally, and a disbelief'. The hybrid 'Manifesto', instead of propounding a statement of shared aims, only succeeds in announcing a profound sense of uncertainty and deferral. The piece is in fact trumped in rhetorical effectiveness by Jacob Bronowski's lengthy disquisition 'Experiment' which immediately followed it in *transition*. Bronowski's programmatic article provided glosses on some of the key passages of the 'Manifesto'. Most notably, it commented on the call for a 'new *formal* notation' in the 'Manifesto':

> we must find a *notation* to replace the old moral notation, in terms of which we can write. In a sense that is a formal problem; not in the sense in which *formal* means 'depending upon a happy arrangement of words', but in the sense in which it means 'to be solved in terms of the literary medium'. And the medium of literature is the sum total of all its relevant contents: outlook, narrative, 'objects', and then the words symbolising objects. These are of one unity; and the writer's problem is to convert his adjustment to the world into literature in terms of this unity. [. . .] When we have found it, it will perhaps lead us into a new belief.[102]

Bronowski's text claims to put the modernist rhetoric of 'formal' experimentation back on its feet by breaking Ricardian pseudo-statements and the ideal of poetic integrity down to their basic constituents: poetry and prose consist of referential 'words symbolising objects' and their key function is to articulate the author's 'adjustment to the world'. Even though the essay makes no mention of communism, the implications of Bronowski's eagerly awaited 'new belief' were immediately apparent to *Experiment*'s other contributors. As George Reavey, one of the magazine's less committed leftist contributors, commented in a letter to Julian Trevelyan in 1931, it had been a 'terrible faux pas that Bruno [Jacob Bronowski] made at the end by announcing himself the editor of the

[101] Martin Puchner, *Poetry of the Revolution: Marx, Manifestos, and the Avant-Gardes* (Princeton: Princeton University Press, 2006), pp. 5, 31–32.

[102] Jacob Bronowski, 'Experiment', *transition*, 19–20 (June 1930), 107–12 (p. 111), emphases in the original.

European Caravan'.[103] The division among *Experiment*'s contributors was running along political lines, as much as along aesthetic ones. 'I do not know whether any of us are going to write well', Bronowski concludes, 'I only know that several of us are going to think well: and that some of us may even persuade literature to think well. And I know of noone [sic] else who will' (112). The 'we' here is dogmatically exclusive, addressing the ones ready to join the political left, rather than those engaging in modernist experimentation.

Bronowski's essay points towards modes of ideological critique associated with the 1930s, yet its radical propositions made little impact on the last two numbers of *Experiment*. The reassertion of 'the compact, local unit' in the programmatic 'Manifesto' left little room for considerations of the extra-literary 'importance' of literature. Later discussions of the politically charged poetry of post-revolutionary Russia have no critical and intertextual afterlife comparable to that of 'Mounds'. Reavey's polite discussion of Aleksandr Blok, Sergey Essenin, Vladimir Mayakosky, and Boris Pasternak in the penultimate number of *Experiment* indulges a distinctly Jolasian interest in the Revolution of the Word, but it also opposes attempts to import political 'statements' into the 'pseudo-statements' of literature:

> Mayakovsky, positive, political, aware of the movement, revolutionised the word in order to emphasise the statement; and so his later poetry becomes didactic, poster-poetry. Here begins the divergence between the *politic* and the *poetic*, between Mayakovsky and Pasternak; for it is Pasternak who reconciles futurism with the poetic tradition, and first uses the revolutionised word to revivify the lyric.[104]

The publication of *Experiment* material in *transition* meant that the magazine once more came to be identified, by the majority of its contributors and readers, with 'the *poetic*' rather than 'the *politic*'. Reavey's article, for example, celebrates Pasternak's poetry as a 'parthenon of impersonality after the agonies and perorations of Essenin and Mayakovsky' (17). The essay mentions Mayakovsky's suicide in April 1930 in order to illustrate communism's brutal repression of avant-garde art, but crucially there is

[103] JTA, Correspondence with George Reavey, Box 24, Uncat. and undated letter from Julian Trevelyan to George Reavey [1931]. 'Wyndham Lewis's *Enemy*' had already called for a 'clearing up of beliefs' and a 'building up of a uniform and contemporary artistic attitude' (p. 5).

[104] George Reavey, 'First Essay Towards Pasternak', *Experiment*, 6 (1930), 14–17 (p. 15), emphases in the original.

no reference to Pasternak's rapprochement with socialist realism in the mid-1920s. In a related vein, the flyer which announced the opening of the *Experiment* Gallery in 1931 (a joint exhibition of Cambridge talent and Continental artists) promised that 'a comprehensive selection of the art of the U.S.S.R. is in preparation', but hastened to add that the only artists to be included were those 'who are in sympathy with the modern movement'.[105]

The issue that carried Reavey's critical essay also contained a translation of a passage from the prose collection *C'est le cabaret* (1919) by the French left-wing author Alexandre Arnoux. The excerpt opens with a rousing revolutionary scene, and the original subtitle of Arnoux's work, *Recueil de nouvelles de guerre* (omitted in the *Experiment* translation), points to the book's roots in the violent upheavals of recent European history. The force of the passage derives from a central ambiguity: it can be read either as the celebration of a revolutionary *élan vital*, or as a warning against the dehumanizing forces implicit in revolutionary collectivism. It is hard to escape the sense of brooding expectation and apocalypse that lingers over the scene:

> Now it is that the Inn starts into life. The self-centred dreams of lonely individuals give place to the brawls of man against man [. . .]. In this crucible, this hot and narrow parlour, where humanity effervesces and ferments, the individual has melted away; voices are coarsened, faces emboldened by quarrelling; each one has surrendered a little of himself to the rest; and into me some of each has penetrated. Across the mist of steam, faces are unrecognisable, expressions indistinguishable. The Inn has now its own tone; and, concocting the different sounds within one mortar, annihilating personal accents under the pounding of its rhythm, it speaks in the universal voice of song.[106]

A voice which emerges from this mass sings 'in sad, in mocking tones, like a Parisian workman', and is 'drunk with the high hopes of revolution, with those violent dreams which lead men through blood from hope to hope'. The song, which echoes the Internationale, indicts patriotism and envisions a worldwide union of 'workmen': 'Les peuples unis | Seront tous amis' (8). The other critical and literary contributions in this number of *Experiment* are curiously deaf to the historical overtones of Arnoux's story. As in Reavey's essay on post-revolutionary Russian poetry, critical interest seems reduced to the level of style, to the way in which the rush of

[105] JTA, Correspondence with John Davenport, Box 4, Uncat. flyer for *Experiment* Gallery.

[106] Alexandre Arnoux, 'From "Le Cabaret"', trans. by Ralph Parker, *Experiment*, 6 (1930), 7–12 (p. 7).

paratactic clauses succeeds in rendering a novelistic mass scene. This stylistic concern owes more to *transition*'s avant-garde fascination with the buzzing city scenes of Alfred Döblin's *Berlin Alexanderplatz* (1929) than to Ivanov's artistic examination of the depersonalization effected by collectivist ideologies.[107] The revived concern with poetic style and with the level of pseudo-statements draws attention to the fact that *Experiment*, even at its most political, only succeeded in talking about historical and political pressures obliquely by adopting mediating voices like those of Eliot or Ivanov.

Experiment's position on the cusp of the new decade is valuable in making 'legible' (to use Brian Maidmant's phrase) a transformational process which blurs the conventional literary-historical boundary between the modernist 1920s and the political 1930s. I have focused on the impact of the Richards-Eliot debate about belief to suggest that *Experiment*'s proleptic momentum—its anticipation of some of the central concerns of the 1930s—also entailed an anxious look back to a particular strand of modernist aesthetics. While this chapter has looked backward, the following chapters will focus more explicitly on writing of the 1930s. Contrary to what recent appraisals of *Experiment* may lead us to believe, the magazine was not treated as an alien and anachronistic object by members of the thirties left. Helen Davis and Harry Kemp, writing on 'The Rise and Fall of Bourgeois Poetry' in a 1934 number of *Cambridge Left*, quoted approvingly from *Experiment*'s critical essays, and in Scott McCracken's view such points of contact 'confirm the importance' of certain shared 'debates' between the two magazines.[108] *Experiment*'s timely avoidance of what F. R. Leavis called 'Sitwellism' also found an echo, half a decade later, in Geoffrey Grigson's condemnation of modernist *écriture*: 'The worst rubbish', Grigson noted in a 1935 review for *New Verse*, 'comes from that old Jane, Edith Sitwell and her plump brother Osbert.'[109] Such affinities between *Experiment* and certain emblematic thirties journals may serve as a reminder that this little magazine was something more, and something other, than a belated modernist venture. *Experiment* illustrates a literary-historical process in which debates from the 1920s were helping to shape the political and artistic investments of thirties literary discourse and to anticipate some of its internal conflicts. It needs to be noted, however, that *Experiment* offers relatively little explicit discussion of the strong version

[107] Extracts from Döblin's novel were published in *transition*, 29–30 (1930), 250–57.

[108] Helen Davis and H. V. Kemp, 'The Rise and Fall of Bourgeois Poetry', *Cambridge Left*, 1 (Summer 1934), 68–77 (pp. 70–71); McCracken, p. 620.

[109] Geoffrey Grigson, Review of *The Year's Poetry 1935*, *New Verse*, 18 (December 1935), 21–22 (p. 22).

of the belief-problem. It is only with the shift into the aggressive registers of propaganda-literature over the course of the following decade that this version comes to the fore. However, the pervasiveness of the weak version of the belief-debate helps to set the stage for these more pointed and more pressing questions.

The history of *Experiment* thus captures a moment at which two key registers of poetic language were beginning to drift apart. This 'divergence' (in Reavey's phrase) 'between the *politic* and the *poetic*' resulted in a tendency to think of the latent tensions between these two poles as though they amounted to an irreconcilable contradiction. When *Experiment* ceased publication in 1931 it could be said to have evolved a form of artistic 'Sitwellism' that was booting out religious and political forms of belief—a set of 'politics' (as the Five had it) which effectively 'isolated' it 'from political reality'. The chapters which follow explore how the anxieties about art's separation from its historical milieu are articulated in a cross-section of thirties literature. As the next chapter points out, Empson's early engagement with Richards's theory of pseudo-statements reflects the debates conducted in *Experiment*, but it also moves beyond them by searching for a type of critical impartiality and political neutrality that would be capable of registering the decade's political pressures.

2

An Honest Decade

William Empson and the Uses of Poetry

It has become a critical commonplace to observe that William Empson succeeded in maintaining a form of 'mental equilibrium' in the face of the ideological conflicts of the 1930s.[1] The present chapter will revisit and reassess these claims. It argues that while 'the possibility of independence' was indeed a central aspiration of his criticism and his poetry, Empson also felt a profound uneasiness with this position as he feared that it might isolate him from the political turmoil of the decade.[2] Empson's poetic style went through an important transformation in the 1930s as he attempted to abandon the style of his early verse. His early work, written in the late 1920s while he was studying with Richards in Cambridge, is dense with intertextual allusions which evoke the self-referentiality of poetic pseudo-statements. However, Empson's crucial experiences in the Far East—in Tokyo in 1931 and 1932, and then in China, in 1937 and 1938—and the publication of some of his poems in Michael Roberts's emblematic left-wing anthology, *New Signatures* (1932), led him to feel the 'narrowness' of this type of writing.[3] Empson's struggle for a position of political neutrality in the 1930s remained uneasy for similar reasons. As he realized, the search for a standpoint outside the decade's conflicts could too easily look like a form of political defeatism that would throw poetry back into a different kind of artistic 'narrowness'.

While Empson's literary output resonates more widely with the position of left-leaning writers who were wary of taking sides, his own anxieties are mirrored in his attempts to come to terms with the notion of artistic 'honesty'. Roberts's Preface to *New Signatures* had presented intellectual

[1] Jason Harding, 'The Gifts of China', in *Some Versions of Empson*, ed. by Matthew Bevis (Oxford: Oxford University Press, 2007), pp. 84–103 (p. 89).

[2] Paul Fry, 'Hermeneutic Circling: Empson, Rosemund Tuve, and the "Wimsatt Law"', in *Some Versions of Empson*, ed. by Matthew Bevis, pp. 201–16 (p. 207).

[3] William Empson, Letter to Robert Herring, 14 July 1938, in *Selected Letters of William Empson*, ed. by John Haffenden (Oxford: Oxford University Press, 2006), p. 111.

'honesty' as the paramount virtue of communist writers who were seeking to expose the social prejudices of capitalist society. Empson was quick to grasp the word's significance in the politicized literary and critical discourses of the decade, and over the course of the 1930s he made extensive notes on the term and lectured on it while teaching in Japan. A growing dissatisfaction with the 'narrowness' of his own poetry, I argue, led Empson to look for a type of poetic 'honesty' that would enable a stance of detachment without implying a retreat from the sites of political action.

INSINCERITY AND THE 'FAMILY' TRADITIONS OF POETRY

Empson's early poems can be seen to engage with the critical doctrines of Richards, who was his tutor at Magdalene College in the mid-1920s. They are particularly troubled by the concept of 'sincerity' which Richards had elevated to a criterion of 'good' poetry in his lectures. As Richards explained in *Practical Criticism* (1929),

> [s]incere emotions, we say, are genuine or authentic. [. . .] It will be worth while hunting a little longer for a satisfactory sense of 'sincerity'. Whatever it is, it is the quality we most insistently require in poetry. It is also the quality we most need as critics.[4]

The chapter from which this passage is taken, 'Doctrine in Poetry', concludes by providing a list of universal 'attitudes' relevant to the human situation and, by implication, to 'sincere' poetry. These 'feelings whose sincerity is beyond our questioning' include 'Man's loneliness (the isolation of the human situation)', 'the facts of birth and death', and 'the inconceivable immensity of the Universe'.[5] Richards saw emotional 'sincerity' as a continuation of his thinking about 'emotive' pseudo-statements in *Principles of Literary Criticism*. In important ways, however, the concept of 'sincerity' was at odds with the theory of poetic pseudo-statements: while the latter stressed the special status of poetic language, Richards's remarks on 'sincerity' foregrounded poetry's 'communicative efficiency', talking about poems as if they were simply vehicles for human interaction.[6] Prior to its 'official' statement in *Practical Criticism*, Richards had

[4] I. A. Richards, *Practical Criticism: A Study of Literary Judgment* [1929] (London: Transaction Publishers, 2004), pp. 264–65.

[5] Ibid., p. 273.

[6] Ibid., p. 51.

himself been more sceptical of the idea of 'sincerity'. In *Principles* he had warned that the 'sincere tone' of a poem can deceive us about the actual value of the feelings involved: 'we can *feel* very sincere', even as 'bogus forms of virtue waylay us – confident inner assurances and invasive rootless convictions'.[7]

The intensity with which thirties writers discussed the notion of artistic 'sincerity' emanated in part from Richards's writings, where it was linked to a belief in poetry's salvational powers. W. H. Auden and Louis MacNeice, for example, in their poem 'Last Will and Testament', singled out as Richards's central legacy his 'study' of 'the facts of birth and death | In their inexplicable oddity'.[8] Edward Upward and Christopher Isherwood had also come under Richards's influence, having attended his lectures in the mid-1920s. As Upward recalled later, he felt a Ricardian dissatisfaction with some of Auden's precocious early poems because they flaunted 'an exhibitionistic intellectualism that reminded me somewhat of a kind of undergraduate talk that Isherwood and I had disapproved of as "insincere" when we had encountered it at Cambridge'.[9] Richards's emphasis on poetic sincerity anticipated the development, over the course of the 1930s, of a critical idiom that privileged poetry's content over its formal intricacies. 'We must make sure that [the work of the revolutionary poet] is technically good', Cecil Day Lewis noted in 1935, 'that it is not imitative, sentimental, insincere, or banal. The poet *is* his poem.'[10] Christopher Caudwell added that art, before it was able to engage with revolutionary politics, must provide a record of the crumbling of bourgeois culture. The 'unendurable tension' of class differences, he observed in *Illusion and Reality* (1937), 'is shown in the chaotic and intoxicated confusion of all *sincere* modern bourgeois art, decomposing and whirling about in a flux of perplexed agony'.[11] Michael Roberts was more cautious: his Preface to *New Country* helped to define some of the decade's central artistic concerns, but it also warned that 'we must not think that our own "sincerity" makes our work more "important" than that of any other generation'.[12] The frequent

[7] I. A. Richards, *Principles of Literary Criticism* [1924] (London: Routledge, 2001), p. 266, emphasis in the original.

[8] W. H. Auden and Louis MacNeice, *Letters from Iceland* (London: Faber and Faber, 1937), p. 242.

[9] Edward Upward, *Remembering the Earlier Auden* (London: Enitharmon, 1998), p. 5.

[10] Cecil Day Lewis, 'Revolutionaries and Poetry' [1935], in *Revolution in Writing* (New York: Haskell, 1972), pp. 32–44 (p. 38).

[11] Christopher Caudwell, *Illusion and Reality: A Study of the Sources of Poetry* (Basingstoke: Macmillan, 1937), p. 317, emphasis in the original.

[12] Michael Roberts, 'Preface', in *New Country: Prose and Poetry by the Authors of 'New Signatures'*, ed. by Michael Roberts (London: Hogarth Press, 1933), pp. 9–21 (p. 17).

invocation of 'sincerity' in left-wing tracts of the decade paradoxically suggests that it might become an end in itself—a desired rhetorical effect which, as Richards had warned, could bracket questions of ethical value, while opening the field of literature up to (political and personal) 'rootless convictions'.

Empson's writings from the late 1920s and early 1930s are also steeped in a rhetoric of sincerity, but they subject it to searching criticism. In his view, the aesthetic criterion of sincerity entailed a reductive view of poetry. The mode of communication enabled by pseudo-statements, he claimed, was too oblique to warrant the analogy with everyday communication on which Richards's argument rested. A note in one of the diaries which Empson kept during his first term at Cambridge turns Richards's rhetoric on its head by insisting on poetry's 'insincerity': 'One must, on paper, feel an emotion strongly and without conflict see the absurdity of it at the same time. [. . .] A person who is wholly in earnest, and only of one mind in a matter is either not sufficiently wide awake or too stupid to think at all.'[13] Literature, this suggests, turns the truths of everyday life into fictions which resist classification into the logical categories of 'true' and 'false'. Empson's attitude towards sincerity comes close to Eliot's doubtfulness with regard to poetry's extra-literary uses. In his 1932 Harvard Lectures, Eliot singled out for ridicule the Ricardian 'recipe of sincerity': 'We can say', he explained, 'that in poetry there is communication from writer to reader, but should not proceed from this to think of the poetry as being primarily the vehicle of communication.'[14] Empson's poems from the 1920s question the idea of poetry's communicative efficiency, and their riddling allusiveness serves to foreground the constructedness of poetic discourse. 'As for Mr Richards's particular recipe for being "sincere"', Empson noted in another essay from 1930, 'I am very willing to believe that it does not work for everyone.'[15] The attempt to show that the concept of 'sincerity' might 'not work' for poetry figures as a central impulse of Empson's early verse. His poems point out how poetic conventions inflect the accent of the individual writer, even as he inhabits them and uses them as a conduit for his own voice. The insincerity of poetic

[13] Quoted in John Haffenden, *William Empson: Among the Mandarins* (Oxford: Oxford University Press, 2005), pp. 101–3.

[14] T. S. Eliot, *The Use of Poetry and the Use of Criticism* [1933] (London: Faber and Faber, 1964), pp. 131, 115.

[15] William Empson, 'I. A. Richards and Practical Criticism' [1930], in *Argufying: Essays on Literature and Culture*, ed. by John Haffenden (Iowa City: Iowa University Press, 1987), pp. 193–202 (p. 195).

language, on this view, is essentially a function of its place in and familiarity with literary tradition.

'Literature, especially poetry, and lyric poetry most of all, is a kind of family joke, with little or no value outside its own language-group', George Orwell wrote in 1941.[16] Empson's poems have many voices and speak in many tongues; they adopt both scientific and literary registers, and modulate widely between undergraduate slang and the poetic grand style. Yet for all their casual multilingualism they are also, and importantly, 'family jokes': their 'argufying' belongs firmly, as Deborah Bowman has recently commented, in the 'aural continuity of a "langue maternelle" which provides a common home'.[17] The allusiveness of Empson's poems constantly reminds us that words cannot be wiped clean of the poetic genealogy with which they have been involved. 'It is extremely probable', Richards had predicted in *Principles*, 'that poets will become not less but more allusive, that their work will depend more and more not only upon other poetry but upon all manner of special fields of familiarity.'[18] Because poetry builds on a 'narrow' knowledge of 'family' traditions, Empson expanded in a later essay, it is profoundly undemocratic:

> You hear it said that in a real democracy the writer can tap the life of the whole country, whereas in a class-conscious country he is tied to his clique and the stuff is bound to be narrower in range. I doubt whether this applies much to verse, which has narrowed its range anyway because people feel you need special reasons for choosing the verse form at all.[19]

The footnotes that accompanied Empson's first volume of verse, *Poems*, in 1935 were designed to battle the 'unfortunate suggestion of writing for a clique' that beleaguered 'a good deal of recent poetry'—in particular the poems of the Auden group.[20] Yet at the same time most of the poetry in Empson's own debut volume had been written for just such a small audience of science-minded Cambridge contemporaries with much the same interests and training.

[16] George Orwell, 'The Lion and the Unicorn: Socialism and the English Genius' [1941], in *The Complete Works of George Orwell*, 20 vols (London: Seckler and Warburg, 1986–98), XII: *A Patriot After All, 1940–1941*, ed. by Peter Davison (1998), pp. 391–434 (p. 399).

[17] Deborah Bowman, 'Argufying and the Generation Gap', in *Some Versions of Empson*, ed. by Matthew Bevis, pp. 21–41 (p. 38).

[18] Richards, *Principles*, p. 204.

[19] William Empson, 'A London Letter' [1937], in *Argufying*, pp. 414–17 (p. 416).

[20] William Empson, *Poems* (London: Chatto and Windus, 1935), p. 39.

One of Empson's earliest pieces, 'Song of the amateur psychologist' (1926), resumes the discussion of poetic insincerity begun in the 1925 diary:

> Let us descend now
> But carefully, they are high steps
> And steep, for walking.
> [. . .]
> ah, I can quite imagine you saying it, with an air of apocalyptic
> and desperate capability, sincerity, security almost –
>
> 'The low roof goes
> down, the stairs
> arriving proudly
> at no final pinpoint
> go straight down
> only, down always.'[21] (ll.51–3, 67–74)

The first line invokes the beginning of Eliot's 'The Love Song of J. Alfred Prufrock', while the dubious authority of the majestic plural implicates the poem's mute addressee in the amateur psychologist's quasi-mythological, Orphean descent into the depths of the psyche. The prose lines, spoken by the amateur psychologist himself, lay the ground for the epiphany that follows, with its topsy-turvy enjambments. There is even in those closing lines a deeply ironic echo of Christian damnation, of the bottomless pit, that comes out of *Paradise Lost* (the reiterations of 'down' at the endings and beginnings of lines are favourites of Milton's: Satan 'from his loftie stand on that high Tree | Down alights', and the angels falling 'headlong themselves they threw | Down from the verge of Heav'n').[22] Empson's poem has also learnt a lesson from Robert Browning's dramatic monologues, as the closing lines are put into the mouth of the silent addressee by the psychologist-guide ('ah, I can quite imagine you saying it') in a way that annuls their stated claim to 'sincerity'. As a result, the central movement of the poem's closing lines is one of calculated insincerity, of ventriloquist manipulation. The text's proliferation of mythological and literary allusions serves to highlight its own poeticity in a way that challenges the Ricardian ideal of 'communicative efficiency'.

If, as John Haffenden has observed, Empson wanted his poetry to be 'the vehicle of powerful emotion', there is also a crucial element of rhetorical and

[21] All quotations from Empson's poems refer to *Complete Poems*, ed. by John Haffenden (London: Penguin, 2000).

[22] John Milton, *Paradise Lost*, ed. by Alastair Fowler (London: Longman, 1998), 3.395–96 and 6.864–66.

intertextual self-awareness in his early poems—an impulse that subordinates Ricardian sincerity to the largely self-referential forces of poetic tradition and influence.[23] What Empson's early poetry seems to be sincere about is 'despair', both over the tragic aloofness of the beloved (for example in the poems 'The Ants', 'Vilanelle', 'Letter I' to 'Letter IV') and over the unattainability of transcendent bliss in this world ('This Last Pain', 'Doctrinal Point'):

> You can't beat English lawns. Our final hope
> Is flat despair. Each morning therefore ere
> I greet the office, through the weekday air,
> Holding the Holy Roller at the slope
> (The English fetish, not the Texas Pope)
> Hither and thither on my toes with care
> I roll ours flatter and flatter. (ll.1-8)

The poem, 'Rolling the Lawn' (published in *The Cambridge Review* in 1928), subjects despair to the repetitive routine of garden-keeping, making 'flat' the starting point of an extended pun, but it also metaphorically connects the flattening of the lawn to the mental processes that repress despair by pushing it away into the depths of the unconscious. The text's particular way of cultivating despair is revealed in a footnote in the 1935 *Poems*. The footnote brings into focus the poem's poetic 'langue maternelle' by directing the reader's attention to Belial's speech to the fallen angels in book two of *Paradise Lost*:

> [. . .] Thus repulsed, our final hope
> Is flat despair: we must exasperate
> The almighty victor to spend all his rage,
> And that must end us, that must be our cure.

The reference to Belial introduces a metaphysical despair into Empson's lines, but the footnote also performs an additional task. As in many other of Empson's early poems, the allusiveness of 'Rolling the Lawn' sublimates Empson's subjective experience of anxiety by displacing it into a poetic realm that Richards had described as fundamentally self-contained.

Empson elaborated on the process of poetic abstraction that is at work in 'Rolling the Lawn' in an essay from 1937. This time it is not Milton but A. E. Housman who stands in as precursor and model:

> It is true I think that all Despair Poetry needs a good deal of 'distance' (of the poet from the theme); you can only call despair a profound general truth when you are looking beyond all the practical particulars, which might well

[23] John Haffenden, 'Introduction', in *Complete Poems*, pp. xi–lxv (pp. xxxii–xxxiii).

> have been hopeful if the man had been stronger. [. . .] Housman himself gives this reason why this one of his stock themes can carry a large implication, in a poem that imitates Andrew Marvell. [. . .] 'All things may end, for all began':
>
> But this unlucky love should last
> When answered passions thin to air;
> Eternal fate so deep has cast
> Its sure foundation of despair.
>
> And indeed the foundations of this narrow and haunting poetry seem to me very solid.[24]

'Rolling the Lawn', with its allusion to Milton, adopts a strategy of intertextual distancing that is very similar to Housman's evocation of Marvell.[25] But the reference to Housman also points to a specific genealogy of poetic forbears—a mother tongue which connects the 'Despair Poetry' of Marvell and Housman with Empson's own writings.[26] The 'Empsonian vision', Roger Sale has remarked, 'conquers history heroically' by invoking 'moments that create a community'.[27] This evocation of poetic tradition, of a small family of literary precursors, complicates Richards's 'technique or ritual for heightening sincerity' and his recourse to a group of experiences which are held to be universal.[28] Whenever Empson's early poems try to go beyond subjective experience, they continue to be self-consciously and 'narrowly' (as the passage on Housman suggests) poetic. If these poems are, as Christopher Ricks notes, about types of 'pregnancies', about the anxiety of begetting, they are also (in the words of Eliot's 'Gerontion') about 'the word within a word', about the way in which words are shaped by their own poetic lineage.[29] A poem from 1926, 'Centos', satirizes this habit of poetic allusiveness by adding seventeen footnotes to a poem which consists of only twelve lines. Empson began to feel the solipsistic tendencies of his kind of writing in the late 1920s, and as late as 1938 he complained that he was still struggling to escape from the 'narrowness

[24] William Empson, 'Foundations of Despair' [1937], in *Argufying*, pp. 418–20 (pp. 419–20).

[25] Empson is probably thinking of Marvell's 'Definition of Love'.

[26] The line of poetic forbears proposed by F. R. Leavis—Donne-Eliot-Empson—has all but eclipsed Housman's influence on Empson. See Leavis, *New Bearings in English Poetry: A Study of the Contemporary Situation* (London: Chatto and Windus, 1932), pp. 198–201.

[27] Roger Sale, *Modern Heroism: Essays on D. H. Lawrence, William Empson, and J. R. R. Tolkien* (Berkeley: University of California Press, 1973), pp. 133, 141.

[28] Richards, *Practical Criticism*, pp. 272–73.

[29] See Christopher Ricks, 'Empson's Poetry', in *William Empson: The Man and His Work*, ed. by Roma Gill (London: Routledge, 1974), pp. 145–207. See also Susan Wolfson, 'Empson's Pregnancies', in *Some Versions of Empson*, ed. by Matthew Bevis, pp. 264–88.

of my early verse'.[30] In particular, it was the combined effects of Empson's teaching experience in Japan in 1931 and 1932 and the inclusion of some of his poems in Michael Roberts's anthology *New Signatures* which lent renewed urgency to the problem of the proper mode of action of poetry. The idea of art as a harbinger of the coming social revolution, while widespread among members of the far left, was profoundly at odds with Empson's special attention to poetry's insincerity. Faced with the ideological pressures of the new decade and haunted by a feeling of isolation during his stays in the Far East, Empson was, as Paul Fry has observed, in many ways a Miltonic outcast from the lost paradise of Cambridge.[31] His position as an outsider in Japan and China meant that he felt cut off not just from political developments in Europe but also from the shared ground of its 'familiar' poetic traditions.

ARTISTIC 'HONESTY' AND THE MANIPULATIVE POWERS OF POETRY

Most of the pieces in Empson's first collection had been written and published in the late 1920s while he was still at Cambridge. However, the volume was compiled for publication only in 1935, at a time when Empson's notion of poetry's mode of action was taking a new direction. Haffenden's dating of Empson's poems and letters reveals a gap between the bulk of *Poems* and the three last pieces in the volume which also points to an important biographical divide. These three poems—'Doctrinal Point', 'Letter V', and 'Bacchus'—were written after Empson had begun to teach English at Tokyo University in August 1931, shortly before the Japanese invasion of Chinese Manchuria on 7 November 1931. Sending a copy of 'Letter V' to Sylvia Townsend Warner early in 1932, Empson wrote from Tokyo: 'I shan't write [more] verse till I leave this country and am sending you a thing I wrote in my first month here, before the clogging effect had got to work.'[32] Empson's letters return again and again to the 'clogging effect' that kept him from writing for almost two and a half years: 'I am stopping trying to do literary work: it seems too hollow for some reason', he wrote to Richards in February 1933.[33] Another letter to Townsend Warner finds it 'very pleasant but not very invigorating, to have you write

[30] Empson, Letter to Robert Herring, 14 July 1938, in *Selected Letters*, p. 111.

[31] Paul Fry, *William Empson: Prophet Against Sacrifice* (London: Routledge, 1991), p. 118.

[32] Quoted in *Complete Poems*, p. 283.

[33] William Empson, Letter to I. A. Richards, 13–18 February [1933], in *Selected Letters*, p. 55.

so generously about my verses: they were mostly done at Cambridge, and aren't like what I want to do now'.[34] Empson's comments on 'Despair Poetry' in the 1937 essay on Housman contain a reference to the experience that was causing his writer's block. 'The foundations of [Housman's] narrow poetry seem to me very solid', Empson closed his essay, 'but it is the only poetry I have yet seen having a pernicious effect on the young.'[35] A letter to John Hayward, Empson's older contemporary at Cambridge, from March 1932 relates the relevant episode from Empson's time as an English professor in Tokyo:

> We were reading Housman in one class, which I thought would suit them (suicide is the national sport, of course), but it was embarrassing to read a series of dull essays saying that Housman must be a good poet because he really did make them want to kill themselves, especially to go and die in Shanghai – I wish we could know them . . . the lads that will die in their glory – and so on (one of that class was sent to Shanghai and killed, and various others mobilized). I wonder if it would have made the old gentleman feel ashamed of himself?[36]

John Haffenden has remarked of Empson's letter to Hayward that 'although he reported [the incident] as a joke, he felt genuinely shocked by the students' response'.[37] The episode even found its way into the opening pages of *The Structure of Complex Words* (1951), published almost twenty years later.[38] Empson was hardly prepared to see how radically reading—even of the 'narrow' type of poetry—could be altered by cultural situation and tradition. Housman's poetry had seemed full of grim irony to post-Great War British students, but it was a lesson in honour for this generation of Japanese. In their hands, Housman's poems turned into nationalist propaganda, and the 'narrowness' of Housman's poetry was replaced by a different type of inner constraint—what Auden's epigraph to *Look, Stranger!* (1936) called the 'narrow strictness' of propagandistic writing.[39] Poetic didacticism was of course one of the central aspirations of thirties left-wing writing and teaching one of its key tropes, yet few writers were brought face to face with literature's manipulative potential as early and as harshly as Empson.

Empson was haunted by the thought that he might be guilty for the death of his student, and this feeling was exacerbated by his deeply

34 William Empson, Letter to Sylvia Townsend Warner, 4 June 1932, ibid., p. 44.

35 Empson, 'Foundations of Despair', p. 420.

36 William Empson, Letter to John Hayward [March 1932(?)], in *Selected Letters*, p. 40.

37 Haffenden, *William Empson: Among the Mandarins*, p. 299 and p. 626 fn.

38 Empson, *The Structure of Complex Words* (London: Chatto and Windus, 1951), pp. 12–13.

39 W. H. Auden, *Look, Stranger!* (London: Faber and Faber, 1936), p. 7.

ingrained loathing of all sacrifice. It was with a note of relief that he recalled in a 1936 BBC radio talk: 'I am thankful to say that he left early in the term, so that I cannot have pumped too much poison into him, otherwise I might feel partly responsible for his death.'[40] The radio talk attributes the reasons for his students' 'ideal of death' not to nationalist sentiment, but to the low status of individuality in Buddhism, the religion to which most of his pupils belonged. In an earlier essay, 'Death and its Desires', which Empson appears to have drafted in response to his teaching experiences of 1931 and 1932, he noted that in Buddhism the 'rationalising escape from the fear of death is carried so far that there is much less sense of tragedy and of the fascination of a sacrificial death than in Christianity'.[41] Empson's growing fascination with Buddhism gains the upper hand in 'Death and its Desires' as well as in the radio talk, and both pieces deflect Empson's stinging feeling of guilt by glossing over the nationalist longing for self-sacrifice which drove his students.

Empson's fraught awareness of the persuasive powers of poetry was reinforced by the publication of several of his early poems in Michael Roberts's anthology *New Signatures*. Roberts's Preface to the volume claimed that 'the artist cannot expect to write well unless he is abreast of his times, honest with himself'.[42] Honesty, Roberts insists, is the prime virtue of the revolutionary poet who recognizes the prejudices of his own class: the honest poet is 'in some ways, a leader' who offers 'an imaginative solution of [the] problems' (10) of his society. Roberts stresses the similarities between Empson's poems and the poetry of Auden, Spender, and Day Lewis, who were all represented in the volume:

> Even Mr Empson, whose poetry may still be difficult, is definitely trying to say something to an audience. His poetry repays study, for its obscurity is due solely to a necessary compression, not to any use of accidental association. [. . .] In Mr Empson's poetry there is no scope for vagueness of interpretation [. . .]. (12)

This statement misses the tone of Empson's poems almost completely. Roberts may have been aware that Empson was trying to move beyond the stylistic constraints of his early verse, yet the attempt to align his work with propaganda-poetry is in jarring conflict with the lessons Empson had learned in Japan, especially with his opposition to any rhetoric that claimed social healing powers for poetry.

40 Haffenden, *William Empson: Among the Mandarins*, p. 626 fn.

41 William Empson, 'Death and its Desires' [1933], in *Argufying*, pp. 534–56 (p. 536).

42 Michael Roberts, 'Preface', in *New Signatures: Poems by Several Hands*, ed. by Michael Roberts (London: Hogarth Press, 1932), pp. 7–20 (p. 8).

Quentin Skinner has proposed that we 'recover the nature of the normative vocabulary available' to us by compiling a 'cultural lexicon' of the words we use for 'description and appraisal'.[43] The idea of poetic 'honesty' is central to the myth of the 1930s, and if one were to compile a 'cultural lexicon' for the literary history of the 1930s, the term would certainly have to be included in it. Like its alias 'sincerity', the word is 'normative' in Skinner's sense in the way it shapes the aesthetic and moral investments of thirties literary discourse. The communist critic Alick West, for example, invoked Marxist honesty against neo-Romantic expressiveness, declaring that 'since romanticism, bourgeois thought has been dishonest'.[44] 'We are only allowed two virtues', Cecil Day Lewis's 'Letter to a Young Revolutionary' (1933) agreed: 'courage and "intellectual honesty".'[45] Such demands for writerly honesty dovetailed seamlessly with calls for a new and anti-bourgeois *Tendenzpoesie*, for an ideologically saturated New Realism which would replace the perceived modernist preoccupation with poetic form. Francis Scarfe, looking back to the decade in his perceptive study *Auden and After* (1942), detected a 'characteristic honesty' in Day Lewis's 'Transitional Poem' which he held to be indicative of the wider intellectual climate of thirties writing.[46] Auden's notorious dismissal of the 1930s as 'a low dishonest decade' in the poem 'September 1, 1939' offers a precise inversion of this rhetoric, as does the retrospective indictment of his own poetry of the decade for being 'infected with an incurable dishonesty'.[47]

During his stay in Tokyo in the early 1930s, Empson felt out of touch with the recent literary and political developments in England, and in a letter to Roberts from November 1932 he demanded clarification, not least about the political identity of the Auden group of which *New Signatures* had made him, as it were, an honorary member. Empson was particularly worried by the ubiquitous call on artists to take sides in the decade's emerging ideological battles. 'Dear Roberts', his letter begins,

> You are very clear what this war is, what side you are on, and that you have allies; I feel rather out of all this. What is 'The Oxford Movement' I keep hearing about? Is it Hitler or Auden's Boy Scout attitude? What political

[43] Quentin Skinner, 'The Idea of a Cultural Lexicon', *Essays in Criticism*, 29 (1979), 205–24 (p. 222).

[44] Alick West, 'Marx and Romanticism', in *Crisis and Criticism* [1937] *and Selected Literary Essays* (London: Lawrence and Wishart, 1975), pp. 68–72 (p. 68).

[45] Cecil Day Lewis, 'Letter to a Young Revolutionary', in *New Country*, ed. by Michael Roberts, pp. 25–42 (p. 25).

[46] Francis Scarfe, *Auden and After: The Liberation of Poetry, 1930–1941* (London: Routledge, 1942), p. 2.

[47] Quoted in Edward Mendelson, *Early Auden* (London: Faber and Faber, 1981), p. 201.

views are you fighting for, if any? I am taking in the New English Weekly; is there anything in that? I am in need of letters.[48]

Critics have puzzled why Empson stopped publishing poetry in 1940, but they have not given due weight to the 'clogging' events of 1931 and 1932 and their power to upset the aesthetic rationale of Empson's earlier poems. The question that has remained unanswered is, as John Fuller noted some forty years ago, 'not why [Empson] more or less stopped in 1940, but why he wrote fewer poems after 1930 and how the poems of the 'thirties are different from poems of the 'twenties'.[49] In order to understand Empson's troubles with the position of the independent observer, it is necessary to take into account the hopes and the keen disappointments connected with his stays in Japan and China, countries which Empson, at different points in the 1930s, thought of as places of emotional and intellectual refuge. In less than two years, Empson's attempt to escape the narrow style of his Cambridge poetry seemed to have catapulted him to one extreme of the political spectrum, and into the company of the decade's young left-wing poets. 'Honest' poetry of the kind presented by Roberts, he pointed out in *The Structure of Complex Words*, was 'too masterful, too accustomed to make assertions out of its little ironies'.[50] This awareness of the propagandistic potential of poetry and of the decade's collectivist ideologies, both communist and nationalist, continues to reverberate in many of Empson's poems, and it complicates his attempts at maintaining a position of detachment in the face of the political antagonisms of the decade.

Empson quickly caught on to the fraught concept of poetic 'honesty', and the letters he wrote between 1931 and 1933 document his attempt to come to grips with the term. His first extended analysis of 'honesty' took the form of an article which he intended to write for a dictionary of verbal analysis edited by Richards.[51] 'I feel very greedy to have something to do with your dictionary', he announces in a letter to his former tutor from September 1933, 'and send with this some notes on the uses of *honest.*'[52] And again to Richards a few months later: 'I shall send you my nagging

[48] William Empson, Letter to Michael Roberts, 12 November 1932, in *Selected Letters*, p. 51.

[49] John Fuller, 'An Edifice of Meaning', *Encounter*, 45/5 (November 1974), 75–79 (p. 78).

[50] Empson, *Structure of Complex Words*, p. 216.

[51] For Richards's outline of his uncompleted enterprise, see 'Preface to a Dictionary', *Psyche*, 13 (1933), 10–24. See also William Empson, 'Dictionaries', in *Structure for Complex Words*, pp. 391–413.

[52] William Empson, Letter to I. A. Richards, 5 September 1933, in *Selected Letters*, p. 68, emphasis in the original.

little honest.'[53] Empson lectured on the term in Japan in the winter of 1932, but he did not finish the dictionary entry on 'honest'.[54] However, the preparatory 'notes' which he enclosed in the letter to Richards have survived in manuscript.[55] The three typescript pages offer a revealing, if oblique, comment on Empson's own situation as a poet in the 1930s. The multiple meanings of 'honest', Empson explains, cluster around two major semantic poles. According to the first of these, 'value for the individual' is 'assumed to be normally but not necessarily achieved by keeping to the social rules'. Honesty of this kind denotes a conformity with established social codes that is 'derived from "honour", e.g. in the romantic or chivalric sense that may demand crimes'. This sense of the term, summarized under the heading of 'social conduct', had been dramatically brought home to Empson by his Japanese students' ardent desire to assert national honour through personal sacrifice—a desire which the anthropologist Ruth Benedict identified a decade later with the Japanese cultural concept of 'giri'.[56] By contrast, the second main sense of honesty 'implies some other moral idea as within "true" honesty', 'hence "independent, in action or judgment"'. 'Individual' honesty, Empson elaborates, involves '*not deceiving oneself about one's own desires or emotions,* though perhaps about external facts or legal obligations. The "honest fellow" idea. A paradox about selfishness is inherent in it; he is generous because his feelings have "honest warmth".'[57]

Empson's notes recognize the respective claims of individuality and of life in a collective. As the decade progressed, however, he feared that a split might occur between these two meanings, uprooting the 'independent' man's sense of community while making the collectivist projects of the decade, both nationalist and communist, blind to the dignity of the individual. Empson restated the two key meanings of 'honest' in his 1940 article 'Honest Man'. 'Honest', the essay details, denotes either a 'feeling of moral approval' in accordance with social rules or the idea that 'the honest man [. . .] is the independent man, the Noble Savage'.[58] Empson identified more and more strongly with the second meaning of 'honesty', as an 'independent' habit of thought capable of acknowledging the validity of contradictory beliefs. The concept thus came to serve as a link that

[53] William Empson, Letter to I. A. Richards, [1934], ibid., p. 78.

[54] Haffenden, *William Empson: Among the Mandarins*, p. 294.

[55] RA, William Empson, Uncat. notes appended to letter to I. A. Richards, 5 September 1933.

[56] Ruth Benedict, *The Chrysanthemum and the Sword: Patterns of Japanese Culture* [1946] (New York: Mariner, 2005), esp. pp. 133–46.

[57] Emphasis in the original.

[58] William Empson, 'Honest Man', *Southern Review*, 5 (1940), 711–30 (p. 719).

connected Empson's diverse interests in the 1930s, from verbal analysis through cultural criticism to his attempt at maintaining a form of political neutrality in the face of the decade's ideological conflicts.

With the rise of these ideological formations over the course of the 1930s, 'honesty-as-conformity' and 'honesty-as-independence' came to be discussed by many as though they were mutually exclusive. Empson was one of the possible neutrals who did not contribute to Nancy Cunard and Brian Howard's iconic *Left Review* questionnaire *Authors Take Sides on the Spanish War*.[59] On the left, this decision not to choose sides tended to be identified with the morally skewed stance of bourgeois liberalism: 'bourgeois "impartiality"', John Cornford inveighed in 1933, was 'a deliberate self-protection from the conclusion to which an objective study of the world to-day will lead'. There was 'no middle position between revolution and reaction', Cornford elaborated: 'Not to take sides is to support the *status quo*.'[60] Empson's artistic and political independence left his poetry open to the impugning suspicion of more committed left-wingers because it could look like a lack of political muscle, but also because the refusal to take sides was itself considered an ideologically charged gesture.

There have been incisive readings of Empson's deconstruction of the figures of the 'independent man' and the 'Noble Savage' in *Some Versions of Pastoral* (1935), but critics have paradoxically failed to account for the ways in which Empson's own stance of independence reacted to and was shaped by the literary-political contexts of the 1930s. As Paul Alpers has observed, Empson's reflections about pastoral also afforded him a model for the role of the poet. According to Empson, the artist's independence was in previous centuries held in check by the sense of community conveyed through poetic tradition: the validity of literary conventions such as pastoral allowed 'for the stable presentation of conflicts and contradictions and for putting the complexities of life into the "simple" effects of art'.[61] It was only more recently that the poet emerged as a 'lone figure' whose style 'can no longer do the work of reconciling or even warding off the contradictions of life'. Alpers finds an amplified version of this 'peculiarly modern plight' in Empson's poetry and criticism of the 1930s: 'one wonders how the poet and critic [. . .] can find his way back from his raft upon the main to a solid sense of society.'[62] Empson's observations—concerning

[59] See Valentine Cunningham, 'Neutral?: 1930s Writers and Taking Sides', in *Class, Culture and Social Change: A New View of the 1930s*, ed. by Frank Gloversmith (Brighton: Harvester Press, 1980), pp. 45–69 (p. 49).

[60] John Cornford, 'Left?', *Cambridge Left*, 2 (Winter 1933–34), 25–29 (p. 26).

[61] Paul Alpers, 'Empson on Pastoral', *New Literary History*, 10/1 (1978), 101–23 (p. 112).

[62] Ibid., p. 108.

the 'lone figure' of the poet and his or her inability to reconcile historical 'conflicts and contradictions'—are exemplarily borne out by his own experiences in Japan and China. Empson's sense of isolation, his inability to comprehend fully the cultural dimensions of the conflicts he was witnessing at first-hand, intensified the difficulties he experienced in maintaining a stance of 'honesty-as-independence'. It led, as Paul Fry has noted, to his abrupt 'linguistic and ethical conversion away from unitary [pastoral] symbols'.[63] Empson's poems from the mid- and late-1930s are animated by a search for human community outside the 'narrow' family traditions of poetry—a search that ultimately led him to take sides with the Chinese during the Second Sino-Japanese War. Empson's engagement with the ideological turmoil of the 1930s can thus be used to interrogate two literary-critical myths: it rejects the left-wing rhetoric of 'taking sides' as alarmist, but it also poses a challenge to those critics who claim that Empson succeeded in escaping the decade's political demands by adopting the position of an impartial spectator.

'Empson's interest in both poetry and criticism', Geoffrey Hill has observed, 'is fixated on the perennial problems of conduct and belief.'[64] Departing from this common universalizing strand of Empson criticism, we should recognize that Empson was also crucially concerned with the 'problems of conduct and belief' that arose in the specific literary context of the 1930s. Empson's effort to leave behind the narrowness of his early poems mirrors the impulse that underlies much left-wing writing of the decade—to broaden poetry's experiential base and to open literary discourse towards the diversity of social life. His poetry seeks to develop a form of impartiality and detachment which maintains a precarious distance from the political and aesthetic pressures of the decade without claiming to isolate itself from them.

'A GAZE OVER THE DROP': DETACHMENT IN EMPSON'S MID-1930s POETRY

Two years prior to the 'clogging' events of 1932, Empson had himself written a poem, 'Note on Local Flora', which dealt obliquely with the topic of revolutionary sacrifice. The poem had originally appeared in the February

[63] Fry, *Prophet Against Sacrifice*, p. 115. Fry continues that 'I am painfully aware [. . .] that I have not explained *why* Empson changed his mind about the efficacy of pastoral symbols': 'the key to the puzzle is in the hands of the critical biographer [. . .]. Empson himself keeps pointing to lessons learned from living in the East' (pp. 117–18, emphasis in the original).

[64] Geoffrey Hill, 'The Dream of Reason', *Essays in Criticism*, 14 (1964), 91–101 (p. 92).

1930 issue of *Experiment*, and was reprinted in *New Signatures*. More than any other poem by Empson, 'Note on Local Flora' seems to warrant his inclusion in Roberts's volume:

> There is a tree native in Turkestan,
> Or further east towards the Tree of Heaven,
> Whose hard cold cones, not being wards to time,
> Will leave their mother only for good cause;
> Will ripen only in a forest fire;
> Wait, to be fathered as was Bacchus once,
> Through men's long lives, that image of time's end.
> I knew the Phoenix was a vegetable.
> So Semele desired her deity
> As this in Kew thirsts for the Red Dawn.

The poem longs for sacrifice, but it is also repelled by it. As Ricks has pointed out, the reference to Semele, killed by her lover Zeus, 'reminds the poem of the pangs of birth and of the terribly unforeseen; [. . .] and the Red Dawn is something from which only this extraordinary tree (not native here, remember, though "local flora") can have no impulse whatsoever to flinch'.[65] But the poem can also be understood to contain a more conservatively political message, and to express what many communist texts of the time, taking their cue from Lenin's *What Is To Be Done?* (1902) and *The State and Revolution* (1918), were saying: that only a few leaders would be prepared for surrender to the revolutionary cause.[66] Importantly, Empson's text offers an oblique reprise of a poem by Auden, 'It was Easter as I walked in the public gardens', which had been written a few months earlier and which was published in his volume *Poems* (1930). Like 'Note on Local Flora', Auden's poem hinged on the idea of sacrifice. Its central lines, 'So I remember all of those whose death | Is necessary condition of the season's setting forth', combine echoes from Eliot's poetry with a belief in historical necessity that also informs Auden's later, more doctrinaire line about the 'necessary murder' in the Spanish Civil War poem 'Spain'.[67] Empson's poem suggests a similar connection between the idea of sacrifice and the political ideologies of its day, but it ironizes the expectation of revolutionary apocalypse by locating the 'Tree of Heaven' firmly within the geography of the botanical gardens at Kew. Despite its tonal nuances,

[65] Ricks, p. 201.

[66] See for instance Michael Roberts's introduction to *New Country*: 'it is for us to prepare the way for an English Lenin' ('Preface', p. 14).

[67] W. H. Auden, *The English Auden*, ed. by Edward Mendelson (London: Faber and Faber, 1977), p. 37.

the place of 'Note on Local Flora' towards the end of *Poems* also marks it out as a stylistic departure from the other pieces in the volume. Empson declared in later years that there was 'always this curious curl of the tongue in [Auden's] voice, which I think many people later disliked very much. But it seemed wonderful then. [. . .] And Auden somehow made it sound perfectly sincere.'[68] Empson himself, by contrast, had 'never learned the technique' of 'all those geared-up propaganda boys' and 'so was never considered a political poet'.[69] It is likely that 'Note on Local Flora' signals the attempt to claim Auden's 'curl of the tongue' for Empson's own 'political' poetry.[70] Throughout the 1930s, Empson felt the temptation to try his hand at the kind of 'sincere' poetry which Auden was writing and which seemed effortlessly to escape the 'narrowness' of Ricardian pseudo-statements. On this reading, 'Note on Local Flora' offers itself to be read as Empson's odd period piece, though one complexly attuned to the fashionable Marxism of its time.

In Empson's debut collection, 'Note on Local Flora' is followed by another flora poem of sorts, 'Doctrinal Point'. 'Doctrinal Point' was one of the first poems Empson wrote after the events of 1931 and 1932, and it reflects his desire for disengagement from the realm of ideological conflict. The text's juxtaposition in *Poems* to 'Note on Local Flora' suggests a significant shift in Empson's artistic concerns:

> The god approached dissolves into the air.
>
> Magnolias, for instance, when in bud,
> Are right in doing anything they can think of;
> Free by predestination in the blood,
> Saved by their own sap, shed for themselves,
> Their texture can impose their architecture;
> Their sapient matter is always already informed.
>
> Whether they burgeon, massed wax flames, or flare
> Plump spaced-out saints, in their gross prime, at prayer,
> Or leave the sooted branches bare
> To sag at tip from a sole blossom there
> They know no act that will not make them fair. (ll.1–12)

[68] William Empson, 'Early Auden' [1963], in *Argufying*, pp. 375–77 (p. 375).

[69] William Empson, Letter to Christopher Ricks, 19 January 1975, in *Selected Letters*, p. 597.

[70] Empson noted that his second volume of poems, *The Gathering Storm* (1940), was 'all about politics'. See 'Empson in Conversation with Christopher Ricks', in *Complete Poems*, pp. 115–25 (p. 118). Critics, following the lead of John Wain, have not given Empson's observation the attention it deserves: 'Empson's remark to Ricks is of course the kind of thing that one says in conservation when seeking to establish areas of very broad agreement.' See Wain, *Professing Poetry* (Basingstoke: Macmillan, 1977), p. 310.

These opening lines lack the prophetic passion of 'Note on Local Flora', and 'Doctrinal Point' can be seen to mimic the earlier poem's sense of imminent apocalypse: the conflagration associated with the Tree of Heaven is no longer brought on from outside, but is figured as a natural part of the plant's organism. The poem clearly reflects Empson's growing interest in the contemplative stance which he associated with Buddhism.[71] Buddhism lent particular support to Empson's insight that it was necessary to balance contradictory states of being and to attach oneself to neither. This eschewal of the need to choose between conflicting values is mirrored in the opening stanza's vision of a reconciliation between the feeling of personal autonomy ('doing anything they can think of') and a life based on social and material factors ('Their sapient matter is always already formed').

'Doctrinal Point' draws on a traditional genre of Japanese and Chinese poetry, the reflection on an individual plant. Arthur Waley's book of translations *A Hundred and Seventy Chinese Poems*, from which Empson had quoted in *Seven Types of Ambiguity* (1930), featured various specimens of this type.[72] The 'plant poem', Waley explained, was one 'of the habitual *clichés* of Chinese verse', and 'Doctrinal Point' draws on the conventions of this literary genre as a way of tapping into the meditative energies of Buddhism.[73] The poem conveys an air of awed envy at the plant's poise, even as its tone remains remarkably matter of fact:

> If you describe things with the right tensors
> All law becomes the fact that they can be described with them;
> This is the Assumption of the description.
> The duality of choice becomes the singularity of existence;
> The effort of virtue the unconsciousness of foreknowledge. (ll.15–19)

'Doctrinal Point' envisions a state of mystical union in which the poem's verbal 'texture' becomes indistinguishable from the 'architecture' of the magnolia: the plant's ability to contain contradictions within its organism becomes a metaphor for poetry itself. The poem's meditative vision of this 'Assumption' gestures towards a primal act of naming which weds language to the object world in an indivisible 'singularity of existence'.

[71] See Haffenden, *William Empson: Among the Mandarins*, pp. 310–319. *Some Versions of Pastoral*, which Empson was composing around the same time, linked the related vision of Andrew Marvell's 'Thoughts in a Garden' to Buddhism. See *Some Versions of Pastoral* [1935] (London: Penguin, 1995), pp. 108, 116.

[72] For Empson's reference to Waley's translation, see *Seven Types of Ambiguity* [1930] (London: Pimlico, 2004), pp. 13–14. The lines quoted by Empson are in *A Hundred and Seventy Chinese Poems*, ed. and trans. by Arthur Waley (London: Constable, 1918), p. 79.

[73] Ibid., p. 39.

'Doctrinal Point' creates a continuity with Chinese literary traditions that allows Empson to present a key element of his thinking about pastoral—the idea that art consists of 'putting the complex into the simple'.[74] While the opening lines of 'Doctrinal Point' offer Empson's most optimistic assessment of this kind of detached and contemplative 'description', the poem's closing lines record a deep-seated anxiety:

> They have no gap to spare that they should share
> The rare calyx we stare at in despair.
> They have no other that they should compare.
> Their arch of promise the wide Heaviside layer
> They rise above a vault into the air. (ll.22–26)

The poem recognizes that the magnolia's aloofness is a rare accomplishment, and 'despair' at the tree's majestic self-sufficiency spreads contagiously by way of assonance into the rhymes and into the lines themselves ('spare', 'share', 'compare', 'their', and so on). The ending of 'Doctrinal Point' is indicative of a wider ambivalence in Empson's poems of the mid- and late 1930s: these texts frequently feature the speaker as a contemplating onlooker and outsider, but they are also uneasily aware that such detachment might finally be beyond human reach. 'Note on Local Flora' and 'Doctrinal Point' both recur to the stylized genre of the plant poem as a way of imagining radically different solutions to life's contradictions. The metaphorical conceit of the plant performs the trick of presenting this reconciliation as a natural process which requires no effort, but it also threatens to displace the possibility of such a solution into the distant realm of poetic artifice.

Empson's critical writings from the mid-1930s—ranging from his articles on Buddhism to *Some Versions of Pastoral*—participate in the search for a position outside the decade's ideological frontlines. However, these texts often gloss over the difficulties and perplexities which are so perceptively recorded in his poetry. Their more optimistic view of poetic honesty is prefigured in an article from 1930 which defends Richards against an attack by the Oxford scholar John Sparrow. Empson's brilliant defence projects onto *Principles of Literary Criticism* much that isn't Richards's. Most importantly, Empson points out that Richards has neglected the role of poetry as a medium for thought: was it 'impossible to feel and think at the same time? Obviously [this] is the whole crux of that difficult and easily vulgarized notion of sincerity.'[75] On Empson's view, poetic language extends the resources of

[74] Empson, *Some Versions*, p. 25.
[75] Empson, 'Richards and Practical Criticism' pp. 195–96.

sense-making characteristic of language use more generally. Poetry opens up a space of retreat in which a reflexive attitude towards reality may become possible, creating 'a forum where one could make up one's own mind'.[76]

A comment in *Some Versions of Pastoral* about *La Condition humaine* (1933), André Malraux's novel about the failed 1927 communist uprising in Shanghai, resonates most closely with Empson's own experiences in Japan. Empson argues that the book's adoption of the point of view of a European outsider—the fact that it is redeemingly 'out of touch with the proletariat'—guarantees its 'freedom from propaganda'.[77] *Some Versions of Pastoral*, written at a key moment in Empson's poetic and intellectual development, signals a parallel attempt to make art immune to the temptations of collectivist ideologies and to assert (in the words of Paul Fry) 'the apparent paradox that individuality, not collectivity, is what is common to all human experience'.[78] The chapter on John Gay, for example, observes that in *The Beggar's Opera* 'honesty' implies the 'pathetic right to selfishness, the ideal of Independence'.[79] *Some Versions of Pastoral* explained the idea of honesty-as-independence about which Empson had been worrying since 1932 to a wider audience, and the book was intended as a programmatic 'argument against the communist aesthetic'.[80] 'The artist never is at one with any public', states the closing chapter on Lewis Carroll's *Alice* books: it is only 'the sincerity of the child that criticizes the folly of convention'.[81] The artist, Empson elaborated later, 'must say ruthlessly what he himself likes or wants, and only by this selfishness can he help his fellows'.[82] The comments about Alice continue the discussion of the 'paradox of selfishness' begun in the notes to Richards by presenting the 'sincerity of the child' as a blueprint for the detachment of the artist. Empson's immersion in the philosophical and theological systems of Buddhism and Taoism, it seems, afforded him a brief respite from the decade's historical and political constraints. The success with which *Some Versions of Pastoral* hides the self-doubts characteristic of Empson's poetry is reflected in contemporary reviews of the book. Empson 'is in the lucky position of being removed from immediate political struggles', an anonymous contributor wrote in *New Verse*, 'and yet sufficiently self-confident intellectually not to feel this to be a source of inferiority'.[83] Empson's poems from the mid-1930s make use of some of the metaphors established in *Some Versions of*

[76] Adam Piette, 'Empson, Piaget, and Child Logic in Wartime', in *Some Versions of Empson*, ed. by Matthew Bevis, pp. 42–59 (p. 45).
[77] Empson, *Some Versions*, p. 16.
[78] Fry, *Prophet Against Sacrifice*, p. 110.
[79] Empson, *Some Versions*, p. 184.
[80] Ibid., p. 16.
[81] Ibid., p. 222.
[82] William Empson, 'The Ancient Mariner' [1964], in *Argufying*, pp. 297–319 (p. 317).
[83] Anonymous, Review of *Some Versions of Pastoral*, *New Verse*, 18 (December 1935), 17–18 (p. 18).

Pastoral such as the Alice-like child, but in them the idea of 'honesty-as-independence' becomes problematic. As I have suggested above, there is a developmental movement inscribed into *Some Versions of Pastoral* which traces the loss of a sense of community in the seventeenth century and the emergence of individualism over the course of the eighteenth and nineteenth centuries. Empson's poems reflect the fear that poetry's 'narrowness' might finally be insurmountable and that an excess of artistic independence might itself become strenuous or even paralysing.

The gathering political storms of the mid-1930s made a position of political and artistic detachment all the more urgent and all the more difficult to realize. The following lines from 'Your Teeth are Ivory Towers' deploy a new metaphor alongside the familiar image of the child, though one that assumes a disturbingly passive view of the poet:

> [. . .] The safety valve alone
>
> Knows the worst truth about the engine; only the child
> Has not yet been misled. You say you hate
> Your valve or child? You may be wise or mild.
>
> The claim is that no final judge can state
> The truth between you; there is no such man.
> This leads to anarchy; we must deliberate. (ll.15–21)

The lack of a common ground—the 'claim' that 'no judge can state | The truth between you'—is mirrored in the syntactic disruption which runs through these lines: sentences are wrapped around line-breaks and individual verses are split to yield semantically self-contained half-lines. At the same time, these half-lines are tied together by the rhythm and rhyme pattern of the poem, as if to suggest that poetry can defuse such internal divisions. This attempt to attain a stance of formal poise is also mirrored at the level of the poem's imagery: the speaker's detachment carries him well beyond the domain of human interaction and conflict, and leads him to adopt the strangely passive aloofness of the 'safety valve'. 'Your Teeth are Ivory Towers' is one of Empson's most troubled and troubling poems because it suggests that intellectual independence can only be maintained by assuming a position which borders on emotional apathy. Empson's 'work is cool in tone, wry, controlled and unimpressed', Al Alvarez commented in an influential essay, 'it has no truck with the large political gestures and that fixed stare on the immediately contemporary which was the most characteristic poetic posture before the Second World War'.[84] Alvarez's

[84] Al Alvarez, *The Shaping Spirit: Studies in Modern English and American Poets* (London: Chatto and Windus, 1958), p. 74.

observation reflects a wide consensus, as literary critics have tended to follow the gist of Empson's programmatic footnotes in *The Gathering Storm* (1940). The 'relation of the artist to his society may include acting as a safety valve or keeping the fresh eye, etc. of the child', states the footnote to 'Your Teeth are Ivory Towers', 'and therefore can't be blamed out of hand for escapism or infantilism'.[85] Scholars have underestimated Empson's wariness of the apathy to which cool detachment and 'mental equilibrium' might lead. Like the earlier 'Doctrinal Point', 'Your Teeth are Ivory Towers' registers the instability of the founding metaphors of its own lyric voice.

Empson's poems often seem to talk about the domain of human conflicts in abstract and universalizing terms. 'Doctrinal Point' illustrates this process whereby the experience of concrete external pressures is sublimated into the language of individual psychology. In other poems, revolutions and wars are presented as if they were the outcome of a lack of nerve, of a failure to bear the divisions and contradictions which characterize human life more generally: 'But as to risings, I can tell you why. | It is on contradiction that they grow', announces 'Aubade' from the mid-1930s. Scholars who have stressed this tendency, most notably Christopher Ricks, assume that these poems can be detached from their historical moment.[86] The establishment of this critical orthodoxy was significantly helped through the early appropriation of Empson by the New Critics who turned the abstract idea of poetry's inherent 'tensions' into a token of literary value.[87] This aestheticizing and 'universalizing' view of Empson's poetry has cast a long shadow on subsequent scholarship, and it has obscured the fact that the ambiguities of Empson's thirties poetry are rooted in the political turmoil of the decade and in the problem of occupying a position of neutrality. As

[85] William Empson, *The Gathering Storm* (London: Faber and Faber, 1940), pp. 62–63.

[86] Ricks's seminal essay 'Empson's Poetry' suggested that 'in Empson's poems, as in the life of any sensitive person, the fear of a commitment to love is entwined with the fear of that most daunting and exhilarating of all human commitments, the begetting of life' (p. 153). In a letter, Ricks admitted that his 'essay seems to slight the political poems, or the politicalness of the poems' (Letter to William Empson from Christopher Ricks, 26 January 1975, in *Selected Letters*, p. 601). John Fuller has similarly noted that 'the only true vision' of Empson's poetry lies in 'discovering what man's position in the world really is' (p. 76). This line of argument has been continued in a different key by Nick Hubble who detects in Empson's criticism a 'trend towards a universal audience' 'encompassing members of all social classes'. See Hubble, 'Intermodern Pastoral: William Empson and George Orwell', in *New Versions of Pastoral: Post-Romantic, Modern, and Contemporary Responses to the Tradition*, ed. by David James and Philip Tew (Madison: Fairleigh Dickinson University Press, 2009), pp. 125–35 (p. 126).

[87] Allen Tate's central New Critical essay 'Tension in Poetry' argued that 'the varieties of ambiguity and contradiction possible beneath the logical surface are endless, as Mr. Empson has demonstrated'. See 'Tension in Poetry' [1938], in *Reason in Madness: Critical Essays* (New York: Putnam, 1941), pp. 62–81 (p. 68).

a result, critics often find themselves in the paradoxical situation of praising Empson's critical writings for establishing certain key procedures of contextualist criticism, while leaving the political and social specificity of his own poetry largely unexamined. By contrast, I suggest that Empson's poems interrogate the possibility of such an 'escape' from their historical environment; they question their own strategies of abstraction, and they also resist the Ricardian view of poetry as a repository of 'universal' experiences.[88] Empson's search for a standpoint that could encompass and contain the strident ideological pressures of the 1930s remained ambivalent because it could too easily resemble a defeatist retreat from social and political action.

To be 'honest', Empson's essay 'Honest Man' notes summarily, means being 'a great observer'.[89] At its best, the detached voice of Empson's poems generates astute insights into the mass allure of political and religious ideologies. 'Ignorance of Death', for instance, drafted in 1936 and printed in *The Gathering Storm*, finds in the ideologies of its day a blend of cynical pragmatism ('The Communists however disapprove of death | Except when practical') and of revolutionary messianism:

> Heaven me, when a man is ready to die about something
> Other than himself, and is in fact ready because of that,
> Not because of himself, that is something clear about himself. (ll.16–18)

The last line is double-edged, registering an overpowering sense of collective and individual purpose, but also recognizing the dangers of ideological delusion and deception. Empson's strenuous affirmation of artistic and political detachment is scrutinized in two other poems, 'Reflection from Rochester' and 'Courage means Running'. 'Courage means Running', written in or around 1936, associates honesty-as-independence with a salutary feeling of fear:

> Fearful 'had the root of the matter', bringing
> Him things to fear, and he read well that ran;
> Muchafraid went over the river singing
>
> Though none knew what she sang. Usual for a man
> Of Bunyan's courage to respect fear. (ll.1–5)

Empson's political attitudes are referenced obliquely through an allusion to John Bunyan's *The Pilgrim's Progress*, from which the figures of Fearful and Muchafraid are taken. Empson elsewhere linked Fearful to one of the

88 Richards, *Practical Criticism*, pp. 272–73.
89 Empson, 'Honest Man', pp. 721–22

central allegorical characters in *The Pilgrim's Progress*, Honest. 'Honest', he noted, 'though brave had much to do with Fearing [sic], a man, [Bunyan] says, that had the root of the matter in him, and has been acquainted with Self-Will.'[90]

'Courage means Running' presents 'honesty' and 'fearing' as key elements of its own aesthetic rationale: 'No purpose, view, | Or song but's weak if without the ballast of fear', the poem warns (ll.9–10). Empson came to see 'fear' and 'running' as fundamental principles of anti-war politics, and 'Courage means Running' can be read as a defence of Britain's precarious strategy of political appeasement:

> As to be hurt is petty, and to be hard
> Stupidity; as the economists raise
> Bafflement to a boast we all take as guard.
>
> As the wise patience of England is a gaze
> Over the drop, and 'high' policy means clinging;
> There is not much else that we dare praise. (ll.25–30)

Rather than offering a conclusion of the poem's argumentative complexities, these closing lines simply assert that there is nothing more to say, that moving forward from this point would be foolish. Empson's poem sides with Britain's neutrality, and the inclusive 'we' of the last line signals an abstraction of fearfulness, of abstention, into a principle of international politics. But 'Courage means Running' also ponders the central dilemma of 'Your Teeth are Ivory Towers', that detachment may only be escapism in disguise:

> To escape emotion (a common hope) and attain
> Cold truth is essentially to get
>
> Out by a rival emotion fear. We gain
> Truth, to put it sanely, by gift of pleasure
> And courage, but, since pleasure knits with pain,
>
> Both presume fear. To take fear as the measure
> May be a measure of self-respect. (ll.14–20)

The poem discards the idea of a serenely detached 'cold truth'—what 'Your Teeth are Ivory Towers' proclaimed to be 'the worst truth about the engine'. Detachment remains dialectically tied to the world by way of a negative awareness which the poem calls 'fear' and 'pain'. These affects serve as reminders that the diverse forms of artistic and political detachment can

90 Ibid., p. 721; and *Structure of Complex Words*, p. 195.

only be comprehended in relation to their opposites: 'independence' looks back to a state of dependency, and 'impartiality' implies a knowledge of what it means to be partial and to take sides. In analogous fashion, Empson's painful experiences of 1931 and 1932 exert a spectral presence in his later poems by providing the central impetus which drives their struggle for detachment. Empson's 'respect for fear', Hugh Haughton has correctly observed, 'is one of the major sources of his poetry.'[91] But Empson's affirmation of fear also renounces the more robustly ideological convictions of other thirties writers: 'to write in plain, vigorous language', George Orwell noted in 1946, looking back to the previous decade, 'one has to think fearlessly, and if one thinks fearlessly one cannot be politically orthodox.'[92] Fearlessness of this kind, Empson warns, can itself become dogmatic because it lacks knowledge of its own 'rival emotion'.

The insistence on 'fear' in 'Courage means Running' suggests that the intensifying ideological battles of the 1930s brought Empson face to face with the limitations of artistic independence. Crucially, the bird's-eye point of view adopted in Empson's poems from the mid-1930s is troped not as a coolly surveying glance but as a vertiginous look into the abyss: the earthquake-shaken 'house on a cliff' in 'Aubade' belongs in this category, as does the dizzying 'gaze | Over the drop' in 'Courage means Running'. Empson recognized that neutrality came at a cost, and in later years he was distressed by the idea that 'Courage means Running' could be read as a defence of the Munich Agreement.[93] When Empson picked the poems that were to be published in his second collection of verse, *The Gathering Storm*, he decided not to include 'Courage means Running', presumably because he found that the poem's optimistic view of independence—both as the moral choice of an individual and as Britain's master narrative for national isolation—had been rendered obsolete by the outbreak of war in Europe.

'THIS PASSIVE STYLE': EMPSON IN CHINA, 1937–1938

Empson may also have chosen not to include 'Courage means Running' in *The Gathering Storm* because the geographical centre of attention of his

[91] Hugh Haughton, 'Alice and Ulysses's Bough: Nonsense in Empson', in *Some Versions of Empson*, ed. by Matthew Bevis, pp. 158–81 (p. 163).

[92] George Orwell, 'The Prevention of Literature' [1946], in *The Complete Works of George Orwell*, 20 vols (London: Seckler and Warburg, 1986–98), XVII: *I Belong to the Left, 1945*, ed. by Peter Davison (1998), pp. 369–81 (p. 376).

[93] Empson, 'Corrigenda' to *Collected Poems* (1955), quoted in *Complete Poems*, p. 340.

poetry had shifted once more to the Far East, and he did not feel qualified to comment on recent political developments in Europe. Empson had come to identify his fraught stance of political and artistic detachment with a specific locale, China, where he spent several years as a university teacher in the mid- and late 1930s. 'Time I went to China', Empson scribbled in the margins of a 1933 letter to Richards as he began to feel the 'clogging effect' of his experiences in Japan.[94] And to China he went: first, for a brief visit in the spring of 1933, to indulge his growing fascination with Buddhist sculpture, and then again between 1937 and 1939 to teach English literature at National Peking University. It is unlikely that, following the experiences in Tokyo, Empson was expecting to occupy the role of the European outsider when he arrived in China in the autumn of 1937. Empson's endurance was once again subjected to a harrowing test when, shortly after his arrival, the Japanese army invaded Northern China and he was forced into exile with his university. The shared experience of exodus intensified Empson's inclination to identify with the Chinese, putting his political neutrality under strain. Under conditions of war, certain kinds of neutrality were less desirable than others: 'That pacifist book [*Ends and Means*, 1938] by [Aldous] Huxley seems rather stupid here', Empson wrote to Edith Sitwell when, after a mere two months' respite in the Chinese province of Hunan in the spring of 1938, the universities had to move again to escape from the Japanese invaders.[95] In 1932 and 1933, Empson had struggled to escape from the 'narrowness' of his early poems. Now, five years later, his central anxiety was that the stance of critical detachment which he had designed in his poetry might in its turn lead to a narrowed conception of poetic activity, separating it from its social and historical milieus.

Empson's poem 'Autumn on Nan-Yüeh', written during the Northern universities' sojourn in Hunan between November 1937 and February 1938, is thick with self-doubt. 'Autumn on Nan-Yüeh' stands apart from Empson's other poems regarding both its length and its form (eighteen stanzas, consisting of twelve or fourteen iambic lines each). The explicitly autobiographical focus of the poem signifies a shift away from the poetry Empson wrote in the mid-1930s towards an investigation of the social and historical preconditions on which his detachment needed to be premised. The poem's allusions to lines and phrases from other writers, rather than looking back to the careful intertextual references of Empson's first volume of poems, evoke the improvised teaching conditions

[94] Empson, Letter to I. A. Richards, 13–18 February [1933], p. 55.
[95] William Empson, Letter to Edith Sitwell, 28 April 1938, in *Selected Letters*, p. 105.

at Nan-Yueh which forced Empson to reproduce the class readings from memory. The poem notes: '"The soul remembering" is just | What we professors have to do' (ll.39–40). Both in terms of its autobiographical theme and of its underlying aesthetic concerns, 'Autumn on Nan-Yüeh' is a poem of escape:

> I have flown here, part of the way,
> Being air-minded where I must
> (The Victorian train supplies a bed;
> Without it, where I could, I bussed),
> But here for quite a time I stay
> Acquiring moss and so forth – rust,
> And it is true I flew, I fled,
> I ran about on hope, on trust[.] (ll.13–20)

'I flew, I fled': detachment can look like escape in this poem, and Empson's invocation of Percy Bysshe Shelley's skylark in the first stanza ('Scorners eternal of the ground', l.7) expresses a yearning for poetic aloofness that is subsequently denounced as too absolute. 'Escape verse has grown mortal sin', 'Your Teeth are Ivory Towers' had remarked with an eye to the political poets of the decade, and it is Empson's own poetic stance of 'Escape', of abstention from the political broil, which the poem scrutinizes:

> Indeed I finally agree
> You do in practice have to say
> This crude talk about Escape
> Cannot be theorized away. (ll.117–20)

'In practice' here means the ethical practice of individuals who make decisions in order to determine who they are, but the phrase also evokes the act of writing, of poetic practice. 'The artist', Empson's footnote to 'Your Teeth are Ivory Towers' asserted, 'can't be blamed out of hand for escapism or infantilism.' 'Autumn on Nan-Yüeh' maintains a wry distance from the oratorical poetry of the decade, but it does 'finally agree' that its stance of detachment might amount to a harmful type of escapism. The main fear recorded in the poem, then, is not of a return of its historical and political unconscious but of the potentially debilitating effects of Empson's own poetic stance of detachment.

Empson's attempts to work and write during the universities' extended period of exile were disappointing. The Yeatsian epigraph to the poem: 'There is no deformity | But saves us from a dream', announces that the hauntingly grotesque 'dreams' of real life were serving as a check to the possible aloofness of poetic visions and dreams:

The holy mountain where I live
   Has got some bearing on the Yeats.
Sacred to Buddha, and a god
   Itself, it straddles the two fates;
And has deformities to give
   You dreams by all its paths and gates.
They may be dreamless. It is odd
   To hear them yell out jokes and hates
And pass the pilgrims through a sieve,
   Brought here in baskets or in crates. (ll.27–36)

Empson's esteem for the Buddhist ideal of mental equilibrium, of the unmoved contemplation of irreconcilable opposites, finds an echo in the image of the 'holy mountain' which 'straddles the two fates'. But the stanza also suggests the difficulties of attaining such a detached position. During the pilgrimage season in autumn, thousands of pilgrims, many of whom were crippled or disabled ('brought here in baskets or in crates'), undertook the twenty kilometre ascent to the summit of Nan-Yueh, a mountain sacred to Taoism. In the draft of an essay on China, Empson noted that the pilgrims offered no pleasant sight: 'The main way up [. . .] has the most grisly collection of beggars. My own brand of charity would not dream of extending itself to anything so far removed from humanity.'[96] Empson's capacity to adapt to new environments was certainly great, but it did not prevent the kind of culture shock (and class shock) which is blaring through his disgust here. In a typescript version of the poem, he crossed out the last line of the stanza, emending it to 'So lively, carried there in crates'.[97] The correction suggests the deep attachment which he felt towards China, but it also hints at his temporary willingness to gloss over the sense of estrangement and disillusionment which he encountered during his sojourn. As Empson observed in a letter to Julian Trevelyan in 1936 before leaving for the Far East, he tended to idealize China: 'It would be fun really to write a long self-analytical letter about why I fall in love with nearly all Chinese.'[98] The poem's vacillations mirror the painful tensions between Empson's own yearning for detachment and his increasing involvement in the Sino-Japanese conflict. His experience of this conflict—the writing of 'Autumn on Nan-Yüeh' coincided with the Nanking Massacre in December 1937, a key event of the war—differed crucially from his experiences in Tokyo, and Empson identified much more

[96] William Empson, Draft of 'Letter to China', quoted in *Complete Poems*, p. 385.

[97] RA, William Empson, Uncat. typescript of 'Autumn on Nan-Yüeh' with handwritten corrections. Empson discarded the correction when the poem was printed in *The Gathering Storm*.

[98] JTA, Correspondence with William Empson, Box 25, Uncat. letter from William Empson to Julian Trevelyan, 10 September 1936.

closely with China in 1938 than he had with Japan in 1932. Despite the hardships which he had to endure during the universities' escape into the Chinese provinces of Hunan and Yunnan, the country remained a place of refuge for him, a place removed (culturally, ideologically, historically) from the aggressive nationalisms of Europe and Japan.

Yet in spite of his sympathy with Chinese culture, the speaker feels out of place, and even the sight of the holy mountain of Nan-Yueh offers little comfort. Empson was not, as many critics have asserted, 'at home anywhere in the world'.[99] As the poem remembers England, Nan-Yueh—the place as well as its people—seems elusively out of reach:

> 'Thank God I left' (this is my smatter)
>   'That pernicious hubble-bubble
> If only to hear baboons chatter
>   And coolies beat their wives.' A brother
> I feel and it is me I flatter. (ll.61–6)

It is not 'shameful to aver | A vague desire to be about | Where the important things occur', the poem reassures itself (ll.212–14). Even so, while Empson's students were rallying to join Chiang Kai-shek's nationalist war against Japan, the absence of obligations, what Empson called in a letter 'the laziness of the place', occasionally becomes oppressive:[100]

> Politics are what verse should
>   Not fly from, or it goes all wrong.
> I feel the force of that alright,
>   And had I speeches they were song.
> [. . .]
> The heat-mists that my vision hood
>   Shudder precisely with the throng.
> England I think an eagle flight
>   May come too late, may take too long.
> What would I teach it? Where it could
>   The place has answered like a gong. (ll.143–56)

Critics have tended to assert that China taught Empson about the importance of detachment and impartiality.[101] Yet 'Autumn on Nan-Yüeh' is

[99] Alpers, p. 103.

[100] JTA, Correspondence with William Empson, Box 25, Uncat. letter from William Empson to Julian Trevelyan, 1 November 1938.

[101] This view has been complicated only recently by John Haffenden's biography of Empson which points to the important rifts within the Chinese population—between nationalists and communists, as well as between the metropolitan elites and what they held to be 'the illiterate masses'. See *William Empson: Among the Mandarins*, p. 511.

profoundly unsure what lessons were to be learned from his experiences and what he might be able to 'teach' England. His letters offer a comprehensive record of this bafflement: 'I have begun you a letter once or twice, and stopped because it seemed stupid to send you a letter without an article about China', begins a disappointed epistle to Robert Herring, editor of *Life and Letters Today*, from July 1938. Empson admitted to feeling 'ignorance' when he composed the letter to Herring, but he was not inclined to belittle the force of historical events:

> The poem I sent you from Nanyueh ['Autumn on Nan-Yüeh', which Herring had turned down] I remember now as the kind of bad-tempered letter that makes people you are fond of quarrel with you. My attempts at getting out of the narrowness of my early verse are painfully half-baked. The fact is my opinions about politics are half-baked; it seems to shine through. [. . .] You want a more coherent politics than mine.[102]

The letter takes account of the decade's increasing political strains, and it may even be flirting with the idea of a closer involvement in the politics of the 1930s. But it also announces an important departure: Empson notes that he feels 'less able to write' for Herring's magazine which had become a forum for the poetry of Auden, Spender, and MacNeice.

Hugh Haughton has recently observed that 'Autumn on Nan-Yüeh' 'has a witty, Audenesque air'.[103] The poem intimates the attraction of Auden's 'sincere' 'curl of the tongue', but it also remains sceptical of the oratorical poetry of Auden's 'boys': 'I do not really like | The verses about "Up the Boys", | The revolutionary romp' (ll.105–7). In the following stanza, the image of the 'soaring' observer visualizes what *Some Versions of Pastoral* called the 'sincerity of the child', but it also mimics the commandingly panoramic vision of the Audenesque eagle:

> Verse has been lectured to a treat
>   Against Escape and being blah.
> It struck me trying not to fly
>   Let them escape a bit too far.
> It is an aeronautic feat
>   Called soaring, makes you quite a star
> (The Queen and Alice did) to try
>   And keep yourself just where you are. (ll.79–86)

Some Versions of Pastoral pointed out that 'the sane man can take no other view of the world, even for controlling it, than the child does'.[104] Adam

[102] Empson, Letter to Robert Herring, 14 July 1938, in *Selected Letters*, pp. 110–11.
[103] Haughton, p. 177. [104] Empson, *Some Versions*, p. 221.

Piette has noted of this 'sanely detached' withdrawal that 'the child's-eye view of the world is a view that resists being misled by the propaganda of war, however locally necessary'.[105] 'Autumn on Nan-Yüeh', by contrast, is more aware of the rhetorical gap between the perspective of the child and the adult poet's ventriloquist imitation of this point of view than Empson's critics have conceded. The poem recognizes that the adoption of this perspective is not as ideologically innocent as the image of the child suggests, and that it might specifically serve to hide a blindness to the exigencies of a particular historical situation. It interrogates the role of the 'neutral observer', of the aloof 'neutral, unjudging bird', which Auden and Isherwood (following other China-travellers of the period) fashioned for themselves in their travelogue *Journey to a War* (1939).[106] The exodus to Hunan and Yunnan intensified Empson's emotional involvement with China's political fate, and unlike 'Doctrinal Point' 'Autumn on Nan-Yüeh' acknowledges that making decisions and choosing between conflicting opposites is fundamental to human life. In the later poem, attempts at artistic detachment and 'Escape' become complexly intertwined with the real-life experience of 'escape'. Under the circumstances of the Second Sino-Japanese War, escape—the decision to join the further exodus of the universities—became Empson's way of taking sides.

In 'Autumn on Nan-Yüeh', 'Escape' is not associated with poetic authority or intellectual detachment, but with the perplexities of a lyric voice 'on the run'. The poem's pervasive use of gerunds ('being blah', 'trying not to fly', 'soaring') works to a similar effect: the idea of a frozen (yet internally unstable and dynamic) present disrupts the concept of time as a sequential progress from past to future, substituting an open-ended and non-directional movement for the notion of history as a chain of causes and effects. Progressive verb forms are central to the design of Empson's poetry in the 1930s because of their ability to express a sense of indeterminacy and inbetweenness. 'Life', Empson wrote in a much-quoted footnote to 'Bacchus', 'involves maintaining oneself between contradictions that can't be solved by analysis.'[107] The footnote has served as a key exhibit for critics who celebrate the 'mental equilibrium' of Empson's poems, but the sentence also encapsulates the inner tensions and the provisionality of the attempt to find a position from which to speak.[108]

The experience of war and rumours of Japanese atrocities made it ever more difficult to maintain the position of the European outsider that

[105] Piette, pp. 47, 46.

[106] W. H. Auden and Christopher Isherwood, *Journey to a War* [1939] (London: Faber and Faber, 1973), pp. 18, 97.

[107] Empson, *Gathering Storm*, p. 56.

[108] See e.g. Wain, p. 296; and Ricks, p. 149.

Empson had celebrated in Malraux's *La Condition humaine*. And even the notion of 'soaring' brings to mind images of battle: 'So far I seem to have forgot | About the men who really soar', the speaker remembers the Japanese planes bombing Northern China: 'We think about them quite a bit; | Elsewhere there's reason to think more' (ll.131–34). Towards the end, the poem invents a voice which is recognizably Empson's, but which also indicts the detachment of his poems from the mid-1930s such as 'Your Teeth are Ivory Towers' and 'Courage means Running':

> 'This passive style might pass perhaps
>   Squatting in England with the beer.
> But if that's all you think of, what
>   In God's name are you doing here?
> If economics sent the Japs
>   They have the rudder that will steer;
> Pretence of sympathy is not
>   So rare it pays you for a tear.['] (ll.195–202)

'Autumn on Nan-Yüeh' reflects the political and aesthetic adjustments that were pressed on Empson during the political and military developments of 1937 and 1938. In the end, the poem fails to 'soar' as the universities are once again forced to fly from the Japanese invaders. 'I said I wouldn't fly again | For quite a bit', the last stanza begins,

>   I did not know.
> Even in breathing tempest-tossed,
>   Scattering to winnow and to sow,
> With convolutions for a brain,
>   Man moves, and we have got to go.
> Claiming no heavy personal cost
>   I feel the poem would be slow
> Furtively finished on the plain.
>   We have had the autumn here. But oh
> That lovely balcony is lost
>   Just as the mountains take the snow.
> The soldiers will come here and train.
>   The streams will chatter as they flow. (ll.221–34)

The poem's transition from Empson's particular experience of 'flight' to the level of pastoral abstraction remains unconvincing. The stanza gives the impression of having been scribbled down hastily on departure, putting an abrupt end to the poem's abstract contemplation of 'the large thing that is there'. The poem acknowledges the necessity to fly, but it decides to linger behind, recording the sparse emotional attachments formed during Empson's stay at Nan-Yueh ('that lovely balcony', 'the mountains').

Despite the poem's attempts to make 'Escape' look like a matter of course, like a gain even, the subdued grief of the closing lines keenly registers the loss involved in departing. The last stanza echoes Matthew Arnold's 'Switzerland' poems as a way of articulating Empson's own sense of exile. The final lines of 'Autumn on Nan-Yüeh' seem to be modelled on the ending of 'Absence', the closing piece of Arnold's cycle: 'I struggle towards the light – but oh, | While yet the night is chill | Upon time's barren, stormy flow, | Stay with me, Marguerite, still.'[109] Anticipating the exodus of the Northern universities, the coda of 'Autumn on Nan-Yüeh' presents a view of the world as it will be like when the speaker is no longer there to see it, while the unintelligible 'chatter' of the water—its 'barren, stormy flow', in Arnold's phrase—offers a disconcerting image of an empty and chaotic future. The speaker has relinquished the position of the solitary observer and joined the exodus of the Chinese universities. Empson's lines point to the gap between the stance of 'disinterestedness' which Arnold professed in his criticism and the keen sensation of isolation articulated in the 'Switzerland' poems, but they also recall the importance which Empson attributed to 'fear' and 'pain'. In 'Autumn on Nan-Yüeh', as in Arnold's 'Absence', the pain of departing calls up its complementary emotion, the desire to belong.

'The heart of standing is you cannot fly', the refrain of Empson's poem 'Aubade' observed in 1937. In 'Autumn on Nan-Yüeh' the need to belong, to take sides, gains an upper hand over the apprehension that (again in the words of 'Aubade') 'It seemed the best thing to be up and go'. 'Autumn on Nan-Yüeh' presents artistic detachment not as the cool indifference of the 'safety valve' or as the moral recklessness of the child who is blissfully unaware of societal constraints. Innocence is not as easy to recapture as the image of the child suggests, and the poem's fraught independence is (in Adorno's phrase) 'a naïveté of a second order'. 'Autumn on Nan-Yüeh' experiences a radical 'uncertainty over what purpose it serves', it is 'uncertain whether art is still possible' when it becomes more and more difficult to maintain oneself between contradictions.[110]

'My war started in 1937', Empson confessed in a letter to Ricks in 1975.[111] Empson's reference in 'Aubade' to a 'quake' followed by a 'long pause and then the bigger shake' creates a link between the military convulsions of the Second Sino-Japanese war and the anticipated cataclysm of the Second World War, but it also draws a connection between Empson's

[109] Matthew Arnold, *The Poems of Matthew Arnold, 1849–1867*, ed. by A. T. Quiller-Couch (Oxford: Oxford University Press, 1926), p. 121.

[110] Theodor W. Adorno, 'Art, Society, Aesthetics', in *Aesthetic Theory* [1970], ed. by Gretel Adorno and Rolf Tiedemann, trans. by Robert Hullot-Kentor (London: Continuum, 1997), pp. 1–20 (p. 2).

[111] Empson, Letter to Christopher Ricks, 19 January 1975, p. 598.

experiences in Japan and the terrors of 1937 and 1938. His position as a foreigner in China and Japan, rather than cushioning the impact of historical events, contributed to Empson's awareness of the antagonisms of the decade. His experiences in the Far East alerted him to the dangers of turning poetry into a vehicle of politics, but they also affirmed his conviction that poetry must be able to engage with the particularity of its historical moment. He felt that the detachment aspired to in his poetry of the mid-1930s was no longer possible—not because he doubted the inherent value of trying to understand both sides in a conflict, but because he was afraid that such detachment might in turn effect a narrowing of his moral vision.

The late 1930s saw a surge in publications about China—such as Edgar Snow's popular *Red Star Over China* (1937), Carl Crow's *I Speak for the Chinese* (1937), Anna Louise Strong's *China Fights for Freedom* (1939), and Israel Epstein's *The People's War* (1939)—which celebrated the rise of the Chinese nation after centuries of aggression from Russia, Japan, and the Western colonial powers. Empson also tended to idealize China, and it is necessary to stress the disillusionment which the events of 1937 and 1938 inflicted on him. The growth of nationalist sentiment in China surprised and troubled Empson. Of the 1500 students who had followed the universities to Nan-Yueh, 500 left within a month to join the resistance against Japan, and many more were to follow over the next one and a half months.[112] 'Autumn on Nan-Yüeh' had still hoped that in China 'Not nationalism nor yet race | Poisons the mind, poisons the air', but the nationalist fervour of his students unsettled Empson's earlier and largely celebratory view of Buddhism. Only a few months after writing the poem he felt forced to recant: 'it is tragic to see the Chinese being forced to cultivate Jingo nationalism; that's a bad thing, but the mental effects on a proud group held as slaves are worse.'[113] John Haffenden has observed that Empson's views of Chinese culture were centrally informed by his interest in Buddhism, Taoism, and Confucianism, and that his poetry inclines towards the contemplative posture associated with the first two rather than towards the duty-oriented dogmas of the latter.[114] Richards had noted in his 1932 study *Mencius on the Mind* that Confucianism was 'openly suasive in character, makes only such distinctions as are useful in supporting social aims, and takes note of facts only so far as their recognition is compatible with an approved social system'.[115] Empson identified

112 Haffenden, *William Empson: Among the Mandarins*, p. 460.
113 Empson, Letter to Edith Sitwell, 28 April 1938, p. 105.
114 Haffenden, *William Empson: Among the Mandarins*, pp. 498–500.
115 I. A. Richards, *Mencius on the Mind* [1932], ed. by John Constable (London: Routledge, 2001), p. 62.

Confucian teaching specifically with Japan, underestimating its place in Chinese culture. One of Empson's co-travellers in the autumn of 1937, Victor Purcell, wrote a memoir of their exodus through Southern China, *The Chinese Evergreen* (1938), which reflects Empson's ideas about China and Japan, but which also cautions against 'the common summing up that one hears so often —"China will always be the same. Whatever happens, she will never change".'[116] Purcell chastizes the 'ignorant glee' which Empson later detected in his own attitude towards China.[117] This 'ignorance' made it possible for Westerners to turn the corrupt Chiang Kai-shek into a hero, and it runs strongly in the Orientalizing pages of other travelogues of the decade, such as Auden and Isherwood's *Journey to a War*.

When it comes to the lessons Empson learned in China, critics have tended to share his optimism, while ignoring his profound sense of disillusionment. 'His own years in China taught him about the necessity of maintaining one's balance when faced with conflicting socio-cultural values', Jason Harding has recently noted.[118] However, the gifts of China were more ambiguous than these remarks suggest. Empson's poetry recognizes that the position of honesty-as-independence always runs the risk of being drawn back into its dialectical opposite; it understands the importance of detachment, but it also acknowledges that such independence cannot take the place of action. Empson's awareness of this dilemma finds an echo in Lionel Trilling's opening remarks to his 1939 study of Matthew Arnold. Trilling's 'Introductory Note' purports to speak about Arnold, but the type of political commitment which it sketches in fact contains an oblique comment on Trilling's and Empson's own decade:

> He looked with coolness upon action, it is true, but not because he had any quarrel with action itself, only because he knew that action is not always itself – that it goes beyond itself, becomes a means of faith, a way of escaping thought and what seem to be the humiliations of necessary doubt. Now, in a day when intellectual men are often called upon to question their intellect and to believe that thought is inferior to action and opposed to it, that blind partisanship is fidelity to an idea, [he] has still a word to say – not against the taking of sides but against the belief that taking a side settles things or requires the suspension of reason.[119]

[116] Victor Purcell, *Chinese Evergreen* (London: Joseph, 1938), p. 266. For an account of the 'disintegration of the Chinese holistic world outlook', see Lydia Liu, *Translingual Practice: Literature, National Culture, and Translated Modernity—China, 1900–1937* (Stanford: Stanford University Press, 1995), pp. 239–56 (p. 240).

[117] Empson, *Complete Poems*, p. 373.

[118] Harding, p. 103.

[119] Lionel Trilling, *Matthew Arnold* (London: Allen and Unwin, 1939), pp. xii–xiii.

Empson had much in common with this type of left-leaning liberalism, and Trilling's comments provide a necessary corrective to the widespread view that Empson's 'wry, controlled and unimpressed' stance of impartiality is fundamentally at odds with, or even excludes, the possibility of commitment.[120] 'Autumn on Nan-Yüeh' illustrates the process by which 'action' 'goes beyond itself' by showing how the decision to take sides removes the speaker from the geographical space of the poem, but it also resists the idea of 'blind partisanship' by registering the disorientation that results from 'escaping thought'. Empson wrote so discerningly about these problems because he came to feel the need to take sides himself. His poetry illustrates a key paradox of the thirties myth of 'taking sides', of literature as a means to action: that even those writers who were not part of it, who opted out of it, who were on its margins, were defined by it. During his time in China, Empson realized that 'nationalism' was 'really the great force' in contemporary politics and that 'even the Chinese' had 'caught it like a bug'.[121] When the decade came to a premature if not unanticipated close in September 1939, Empson took his stand on the side of the no longer neutral England by doing propaganda work for the BBC, and the same year saw the publication of his second, and last, collection of poetry, *The Gathering Storm*. The coincidence of these two events, while largely symbolic, points to the twin impulses that run through Empson's poems of the mid- and late 1930s: the urge to escape from the political and military broil and the desire to take his stand on one side of the ideological divide.

[120] Writing of Empson's propaganda work for the BBC during World War II, John Haffenden has continued this apologetic line of Empson-criticism: 'Propaganda is the art of anticipating a response and thus of devising a form of persuasion which will secure acceptance and conviction; literary criticism is its close kin. [. . .] In truth, making propaganda stretches the imagination'. See *William Empson: Against the Christians* (Oxford: Oxford University Press, 2006), pp. 17, 22.

[121] Empson, Letter to Robert Herring, 14 July 1938, in *Selected Letters*, p. 111.

3

Between Communism and 'Purity' of Style

The Revolutions of English Surrealism

Over the course of the 1930s, the Surrealist movement on both sides of the Channel had to defend itself against charges that it was fundamentally apolitical, individualist, and bourgeois. By an ironic twist, one of the most energetic avant-garde movements of the 1920s, and the one that had been most outspokenly communist, found itself lodged in the political rearguard. In critical accounts of the 1930s, English Surrealism tends to get pushed out of the picture by the busy literary contexts which surround it: by the towering paternal influence of the French Surrealists, on the one hand, and by the poetry of the more clamantly political writers of the decade, on the other. As a result, the history of English Surrealism's literary-political defences—and the questions about poetry's 'usefulness' which it explicitly and implicitly raises—is an under-evaluated, though central part of the literary history of the 1930s. This chapter stresses the strong political undercurrent of English Surrealism and it points to the diversity of the movement's radical impulses; it argues that the movement did not initially subsume its political aspirations under its artistic aims but that its political ambitions were increasingly complicated through the fraught relationship between French Surrealism and the Communist Party.

English Surrealist literature is rife with calls for a 'revolution' and for an intervention in 'history', but the meanings of these terms are arguably less fixed than in some of the more robustly politicized texts of the decade. Hugh Sykes Davies, a member of the English Surrealist group and one of the organizers of the International Surrealist Exhibition in London in 1936, noted in the mid-1930s that there were two ways to become a 'sympathizer' with Surrealism. First, there was 'the way of simple souls', 'of practising artists who see or read surrealist work, and respond to it strongly [. . .]. This type of person is generally without great capacity for theoretical work [. . .] in these conditions, the theory is of a poor quality'. More common, however, was the road of theoretical reflection. 'It is perfectly possible', Sykes Davies wrote, 'in these days [. . .] for a creative artist to find himself confronted by certain theoretical problems at a very early stage in his development.'[1] English Surrealism inherited from its French counterpart a strong inclination for theoretical discussion and self-reflection, and these debates in turn helped to shape the aspect of Surrealist writing in England. The central problem which haunted English Surrealism and which inflected its 'revolutionary' aspirations was its belatedness as an avant-garde movement. I suggest in particular that the movement's political ambitions were limited from within by the constraints of an established poetic style and by the attempt to restore Surrealism to its artistic 'purity' (in Breton's phrase) of the 1920s. My analysis focuses on two authors, David Gascoyne and Hugh Sykes Davies, whose writings illustrate both the strong political impetus of English Surrealism and its simultaneous concern with some form of stylistic purity. It is indicative of the conflicted positions of English Surrealism that the authors who most strongly inveighed against the search for artistic purity are also those whose work is most liable to such charges. For example, Sykes Davies's essays from the 1930s indicate that the relative fixity of Surrealism's stylistic parameters in the 1930s lent new urgency to I. A. Richards's claim that literature was limited to the self-contained realm of poetic pseudo-statements. An awareness of these internal constraints is implicit in the movement's key literary and critical documents, but it tends to be consciously thematized only towards the end of the decade when the threat of war became imminent. The artistic trajectory of English Surrealism in the 1930s cannot be separated from the history of French Surrealism. A key place in this chapter will therefore be occupied by a sequence of events, the so-called Aragon affair of 1932, which was central to French Surrealism's fraught relationship to communism and which contained the seeds for the English movement's ambivalence towards politicized writing.

THE POLITICAL IMPULSE OF ENGLISH SURREALISM

David Gascoyne was the first spokesperson of Surrealism in England who could claim some familiarity with the French movement, and his *A Short Survey of Surrealism* (1935) is often viewed as the founding document

[1] Hugh Sykes Davies, 'Sympathies with Surrealism', *New Verse*, 20 (April–May 1936), 15–21 (p. 16).

of English Surrealism. However, it is in Gascoyne's unpublished notebooks and occasional essays from 1935 and 1936, rather than in the more widely known *Short Survey*, that he can be seen to develop a political programme for the English incarnation of the Surrealist movement. The essay 'Poetry and Reality' from 1936, for example, belongs to the period of Gascoyne's growing involvement with communism, and it takes issue with the attempt to identify poetry with the rhetorical registers of propaganda. Just because 'certain poems are not about strikes, factories, the armaments camp', it would be wrong to assume that their authors are 'unwilling or unable really to face the concrete facts of the world in which they live'. '[R]ather than constituting a refuge or retreat from reality', Gascoyne points out, 'such poems are written in opposition to, or in defiance of the existing conception of the real.'[2] These comments sketch the blueprint for a politicized writing that is lodged outside the narrow confines of communist propaganda art. On Gascoyne's account, Surrealism's course to revolutionary action is an indirect one: it indicts the bourgeois ideology of 'the real', but it does not actively propagate an alternative to the dominant socio-economic conditions of life. Poetry, as Gascoyne put it in a letter to his friend George Barker, was 'to be propaganda for being aware'.[3] Other members of the English Surrealist group agreed with Gascoyne's opposition to more overtly propagandistic types of political writing. In an essay on the nature of 'revolutionary art', Herbert Read, the most prolific member of the English Surrealist group when it came to the movement's self-definitions, had similarly exempted Surrealism from the 'injunction to paint pictures of red flags, hammers and sickles, factories and machines, or revolutionary subjects in general'.[4] Critics have tended to take such remarks about Surrealism's indirect course of action out of context and to subordinate the politics of the movement to its artistic principles.[5] Yet this view, which opposes the poetics of Surrealism to its politics, neglects the rich spectrum of artistic and political positions occupied by English Surrealism, as well as the ways in which Surrealists attempted to reconcile their various commitments.

[2] David Gascoyne, 'Poetry and Reality' [1936], in *Selected Prose 1934–96*, ed. by Roger Scott (London: Enitharmon 1998), pp. 74–77 (p. 74).

[3] David Gascoyne, *Journal 1936–1937* (London: Enitharmon, 1980), p. 67.

[4] Herbert Read, 'What is Revolutionary Art?', in *5 on Revolutionary Art* (London: Wishart, 1935), pp. 11–22 (p. 12).

[5] See, for example, Peter Nicholls, *Modernisms: A Literary Guide* (Basingstoke: Macmillan, 1994), p. 286; Adrian Caesar, *Dividing Lines: Poetry, Class and Ideology in the 1930s* (Manchester: Manchester University Press, 1991), pp. 173–202. For an early instantiation of this critical trend, see Derek Stanford's chapter on Gascoyne in *The Freedom of Poetry: Studies in Contemporary Verse* (London: The Falcon Press, 1947), pp. 40–73.

Gascoyne sought to dispel any doubts regarding his Marxist credentials with his 'First English Surrealist Manifesto'. Published in the French magazine *Cahiers d'art* in 1935, Gascoyne's text stressed Surrealism's 'absolute reliance' on the dialectical materialism of Marx, Lenin, and Engels.[6] Similarly the impetus that starts the journals which David Gascoyne kept between 1936 and 1939 is not literary, but political. 'I joined the C. P. yesterday', notes the entry for 22 September 1936, and the pages which follow capture the atmosphere of political unrest that marked the mid- and late 1930s. The journal testifies to the seriousness of Gascoyne's commitment to communism, and one of the entries records the 'singing [of] fragments of the Internationale and the Red Flag, and shouting "Red United Fighting Front!"' at a demonstration against Oswald Mosley.[7] Gascoyne was also prepared to defend his newly-won convictions against gainsayers such as the Belgian Surrealist E. L. T. Mesens who had angered him by 'seiz[ing] upon me as an occasion to be very long-winded and didactic about my having joined the C. P., the Moscow Trial, the 4th International, etc.'.[8] Not all English Surrealists were eager to join the Communist Party, but Marxist sentiment was running as strongly among the Surrealist group as anywhere on the English intellectual left: Hugh Sykes Davies was a friend of the Cambridge spies Guy Burgess and Anthony Blunt, and he joined the Communist Party in the 1930s (as did Charles Madge and Roger Roughton); Roland Penrose, by contrast, was firmly left-wing but remained outside the party, like Humphrey Jennings and Julian Trevelyan. By general consent Gascoyne was considered England's Surrealist *Wunderkind*, and he was quick to make friends among the young left-wingers who had contributed to the Cambridge magazine *Experiment*. Having met several of the contributors at David Archer's radical bookshop in Parton Street, London, Gascoyne became close friends with Trevelyan and George Reavey after relocating to Paris in 1933 at the precocious age of 17; and only a few years later he would translate Benjamin Péret's poems with Jennings.[9]

Gascoyne's essay 'Poetry and Reality' indicates that he was eager to transmit the strong political charge of French Surrealism to England. The piece insists that the Marxist affiliations of Surrealism predated those of the Auden group, 'the so-called "left-wing" English Poets': 'The curious

[6] David Gascoyne, 'Premier manifeste anglais du surréalisme (fragment)', *Cahiers d'art* 10 (1935), p. 106.

[7] Gascoyne, *Journal 1936–1937*, p. 30. [8] Ibid., p. 38.

[9] For Gascoyne's close personal ties to the former *Experiment* circle, see Robert Fraser, *Night Thoughts: The Surreal Life of the Poet David Gascoyne* (Oxford: Oxford University Press, 2012), pp. 56–62.

thing is that the surrealist poets, far from being politically disinterested, were among the first European writers of bourgeois origin to turn to Communism and to adopt, integrally, the philosophy of dialectical materialism'.[10] Gascoyne recalls the 1925 Marxist conversion *en masse* of the Paris group—of André Breton, Louis Aragon, Michel Leiris, and others—which had been followed by Breton's programmatic review of Leon Trotsky's biography of Lenin.[11] Another text by Breton, 'Legitimate Defence', had aligned Surrealism firmly with the politics of the Communist Party. Surrealists, Breton argued, had no stake in Symbolist *poésie pure*: they had 'always declared and still maintain that the emancipation of style, which is to a certain degree possible in bourgeois society, cannot consist in a laboratory operation bearing abstractly on words'.[12] But Breton also pointed out that literature could not easily be turned into propaganda—an idea which finds an echo in Gascoyne's remarks about Surrealism's indirect path to revolutionary action. Roger Roughton, editor of the short-lived Surrealist periodical *Contemporary Poetry and Prose* and one of the most outspokenly communist members of the group, agreed that

> Surrealist work, while not calling directly for revolutionary intervention, can be classed as revolutionary in so far as it can break down irrational bourgeois-taught prejudices, thus preparing the mental ground for positive revolutionary thought and action.[13]

On this view, the 'revolutionary intervention' of Surrealism performs a determinate task preceding the political revolution proper. Its function is to expunge bourgeois prejudice and to prepare the ground for the constructive work of communism. Surrealism is presented as a serious form of political engagement, and one which is potentially more 'radical' because it subverts deeply ingrained ways of seeing reality. In a related vein, Gascoyne's *Short Survey* insisted on the compatibility of Surrealism's artistic and political revolutions: 'I think that the Surrealists should be regarded as desirable "fellow-travellers". [. . .] They can in their way do just as much good for the Revolution, ultimately, as the propaganda writers are doing in theirs.'[14]

[10] Gascoyne, 'Poetry and Reality', p. 74.

[11] André Breton, Review of Leon Trotsky's *Lenin*, *La Révolution surréaliste*, 5 (1925), 29.

[12] Breton, 'Légitime défense', *La Révolution surréaliste*, 8 (1926), 30–36 (p. 33), my translation.

[13] Roger Roughton, 'Surrealism and Communism', *Contemporary Poetry and Prose*, 4–5 (August–September 1936), 74–75 (p. 74).

[14] David Gascoyne, *A Short Survey of Surrealism* [1935] (London: Enitharmon, 2000), p. 87.

The reflections on Surrealism's political dimensions in Gascoyne's published works are also mirrored in the poems which he chose to translate or excerpt in his notebooks from 1935 and 1936. These works—notably by Paul Eluard and Arthur Rimbaud—contrast with the more familiar kinds of Surrealist poetry published around the same time in left-wing periodicals. For example, while *New Verse* was publishing Norman Cameron's rendering of Arthur Rimbaud's comparatively well-known long poem from 1871, 'Le Bateau ivre', Gascoyne was translating Eluard's unsettling 'La personnalité toujours nouvelle' (1934), a poem apparently more up-to-date with the revolutionary drift of the times:

> Knives to weep and never weep again
> Knives to attack the flowered paper of dawn
> Knives to demolish the foundations of life [. . .]
> Knives like a glass of poison in the breath
> Like the bare arms of a dazzling morning
> To watch over the agony of floods
> In order to know the end of the absurd.

Surprisingly for a text by one of the members of Breton's inner circle, Eluard's poem imagines what it would be like for poets to push beyond the merely ludic aggressions of Surrealism. The last line in particular appears to anticipate a shift from the unpredictable and idiosyncratic spur of Surrealist writing towards a sense of ideological purpose. On the same page of his notebook, Gascoyne jotted down a stanza from Rimbaud's 'Qu'est-ce que pour nous, mon coeur', written in 1871, not long after the Paris Commune:

> Tout à la guerre, à la vengeance, à la terreur.
> Mon esprit! Tournons dans la morsure: Ah passez,
> Républiques de ce monde! Des empereurs,
> Des régiments, des colons, des peuples: assez![15]
>
> [All to war, to vengeance and to terror,
> My spirit! Let us turn about in the Biting Jaws: Ah! vanish,
> Republics of this world! Of emperors,
> Regiments, colonists, peoples, enough!][16]

The excerpts from Eluard and Rimbaud are of interest because they serve as reminders of the range of political temperaments which Surrealism

[15] DGP, Notebook, 1936, ADD 56040.

[16] Arthur Rimbaud, *Complete Works, Selected Letters: A Bilingual Edition*, ed. and trans. by Wallace Fowlie (Chicago: The University of Chicago Press, 2005), p. 215.

inhabited, but their shared tone—effectively a kind of poetic call-to-arms—is also at odds with the more conventional Surrealist poems which Gascoyne was translating for the English press in the mid-1930s.

The more orthodox communist strand of Surrealism found articulation in the monthly magazine *Contemporary Poetry and Prose*, edited by Roger Roughton, which ran for about a year in 1936 and 1937. According to Geoffrey Grigson, Roughton and Gascoyne belonged to the 'newest cherub[s], pink from the egg, plodding after tough Eluard and Breton'.[17] Grigson's nasty remark recognizes that Surrealism was an almost exclusively male affair, and it pits the Truly Strong Men of the French movement against the homosocial bonds that were lending support to the fledgling English group. Grigson specifically implies that the heterosexual 'tough[ness]' of Breton and Eluard, whose poetic celebrations of women and their bodies frequently bordered on machismo, outmuscles the apparently more dubious (sexual and artistic) activities of Roughton and Gascoyne who had shared lodgings in Southwark for some months in the early 1930s.[18] But the nucleus of the English Surrealist movement was by no means as homogenous in its literary preoccupations as Grigson claimed. While Gascoyne decided to travel to Paris in the summer of 1935 to conduct research for his seminal *Short Survey*, Roughton (now a Communist Party member) visited the USSR and in January 1936 began to work as a reviewer for the communist *Daily Worker*. Around this time, he also came under the political influence of A. L. Lloyd, a dogmatic communist and a vociferous opponent of Surrealism. When Gascoyne met Roughton again in September 1936, he detected 'a certain smugness which irritate[s] me in Communists of my acquaintance, particularly Roger Roughton'.[19] The case of English Surrealism's 'newest cherubs' illustrates how quickly political radicalization could take place in the 1930s, but it also shows up the tensions which existed between the twinned political and artistic impulses of Surrealist writing. One of Roughton's own poems to be published in *Contemporary Poetry and Prose* was 'Animal Crackers in Your Croup':

> I have told you that there is a laugh in every corner
> And a pocket-book stuffed with rolls of skins
> To pay off the bills of the costive
> To buy a new pipe for the dog
> To send a committee or bury a stone

[17] Geoffrey Grigson, 'A Letter from England', *Poetry*, 49/2 (November 1936), 101–3 (p. 101).

[18] On the rumoured sexual relationship between Roughton and Gascoyne, see Fraser, *Night Thoughts*, pp. 72–73.

[19] Gascoyne, *Journal 1936–1937*, p. 23.

I have told you all this
But do you know that
Tomorrow the psalmist will lunch on his crystal
Tomorrow REVOLT will be written in human hair
Tomorrow the hangman's rope will tie itself in a bow
[. . .]
Tomorrow Karl Marx will descend in a fire-balloon
Tomorrow the word that you lost will ask you home
[. . .]
Yes listen
Tomorrow the clocks will chime like voices
Tomorrow a train will set out for the sky[20]

The poem starts by portraying the banal tediousness of social life under capitalism, and the absurdity of the first few images seems intended to caricature the hollowness and risibility ('a laugh in every corner') of the bourgeoisie. However, the poem also begins to imagine a different social and economic order as it replaces the capitalist system, in which objects are reduced to faceless exchangeable goods, with the vision of a sphere in which humans no longer exist in an alienated relationship to the world of objects that surrounds them ('the world that you lost will ask you home', 'the clocks will chime like voices'). The rut of bourgeois life depicted in the opening lines is contrasted in particular with the prophetic and revolutionary fervour that characterizes the rest of the poem. One of French Surrealism's early aspirations had been the realization of a revelatory—quite literally sur-real—vision capable of suspending the oppressive routines of everyday life. Roughton's poem participates in this tradition, as the reciprocal movements of the descending 'fire-balloon' and the train 'set[ting] out for the sky' hint at an apocalyptic scenario in which the world is turned on its head. But the poem also breaks with the tone of many other Surrealist poems by drawing attention to the subject-position of the speaker as the source of its peculiar prophetic authority: the disjunctive style aimed at by Surrealism and the exhortations characteristic of propaganda-poetry sit uneasily side by side in Roughton's poem, as the metonymic slide of the first lines is quickly reined in by a mode of direct address ('I have told you [. . .] I have told you all this') that insists on the rightful artistic and ideological primacy of orthodox communist dogma.

The tensions which run through 'Animal Crackers'—between the undirected poetic impulse of Surrealism and the more tightly policed

[20] Roger Roughton, 'Animal Crackers in Your Croup', *Contemporary Poetry and Prose*, 2 (June 1936), p. 36.

rhetorical patterns of *communisant* literature—are made explicit in some of the pieces of literary and political commentary which Roughton contributed to *Contemporary Poetry and Prose*. In 1936, for example, Roughton's revolutionary bile had been stirred by an open letter from Ezra Pound which attacked 'The Coward Surrealists'. Pound, a fascist since the early 1930s, claimed that Surrealism lacked a political rationale and that its escape from the representational conventions of realism amounted to an escape from reality as such: 'The mere flight from and evasion of defined words and historic fact is NOT *sur-* but SUB-realism, it is no more revolutionary than the dim ditherings of the aesthetes in 1888 which supplied the oatmeal of the "nineties".'[21] Roughton's retort ('Eyewash, Do You?') in the same number of *Contemporary Poetry and Prose* defended Surrealism, but it also revealed the beginning of a rift that was running through the ranks of the English group. 'Surrealism', Roughton declared,

> is intrinsically a revolutionary element of limited but certain importance, [even though] an overdose of Freudianism may lead, and has led, some surrealists to an individualistic, anarchic trotskyism. Thus I, though a member of the English surrealist group, cannot speak for all the surrealists [. . .]. But I can speak for those surrealists who do not use revolutionary phraseology for counter-revolutionary ends.[22]

Roughton's division of Surrealists into communists and 'individualist, anarchic' pseudo-revolutionaries relies on a heavily politicized meaning of the term 'revolution'. Roughton's mentor A. L. Lloyd had adopted a similarly dogmatic stance in his review of Herbert Read's volume *Surrealism*: 'Surrealism', he noted in *Left Review*, 'is a particularly subtle form of fake revolution.'[23] By drawing a neat line around the political meaning of the term, Roughton and Lloyd were cancelling out the ambiguities which resided between the concepts of artistic and political 'revolution' and which became central to the re-shuffling of Surrealism's political identities over the course of the decade.

Gascoyne's poem 'No Solution' from 1934 is instructive in its differences from Roughton's slightly later 'Animal Crackers in Your Croup'. The first stanza of the poem reads:

[21] Ezra Pound, 'The Coward Surrealists', *Contemporary Poetry and Prose*, 7 (November 1936), p. 136.

[22] Roger Roughton, 'Eyewash, Do You? A Reply to Mr. Pound', *Contemporary Poetry and Prose*, 7 (November 1936), 137–38 (p. 137).

[23] A. L. Lloyd, 'Surrealism & Revolutions', *Left Review*, 2/16 (January 1937), 895–98 (p. 897).

Above and below
The roll of days spread out like a cloth
Days engraved on everyone's forehead
Yesterday folding Tomorrow opening
Today like a horse without a rider
Today a drop of water falling into a lake
Today a white light above and below[24]

The repetition of 'Today' at the beginning of each of the final lines contrasts with the insistence on the historical momentousness of the future in 'Animal Crackers'. Gascoyne's poem upends Roughton's triumphant optimism—his dogged use of the future tense, his exhortative tone, and the speaker's air of absolute authority—by rejecting any form of temporality that claims to transcend the eventfulness of the present. Instead, the image of the 'horse without a rider' suggests that 'No Solution' favours a movement that is uncalculated, unpredictable, and even random. Gascoyne's emphasis on the purity of the moment's impulse indicates his adherence, throughout much of the early and mid-1930s, to the technique of unpremeditated, 'automatic' writing which Breton had advocated in his first *Surrealist Manifesto* (1924). The emphasis in 'No Solution' on 'Today', rather than on 'Yesterday' or 'Tomorrow', might also look back to Robert Desnos's declaration in a 1926 issue of *La Révolution surréaliste* that 'there is no difference between past and future; the only tense of the verb is the present indicative'.[25] Like Roughton's text, Gascoyne's poem builds towards a sense of revelation. However, in the case of 'No Solution' this epiphanic moment is not rendered in terms of an apocalyptic collapsing into each other of heaven and earth, but as the vision of a calm transcendent presence of 'white light above and below'. Surrealists on both sides of the channel invoked Sigmund Freud's suggestion that the unconscious existed in a state of 'unchangeableness' (*Unveränderlichkeit*) and 'indestructibility' (*Unzerstörbarkeit*), and the closing line of Gascoyne's poem can be seen to gesture towards the idea that Surrealist writing partakes of the undisturbed present of unconscious, dreamlike activity.[26] 'In the id there is nothing corresponding to the idea of time', as Read pointed out in his *Art and Society* (1937).[27]

[24] David Gascoyne, 'No Solution' [1935], in *Collected Poems 1988* (Oxford: Oxford University Press, 1988), p. 41.

[25] Robert Desnos, 'Confession d'un enfant du siècle', *La Révolution surréaliste*, 6 (1926), 18–20 (p. 20), my translation.

[26] Sigmund Freud, *Totem and Taboo: Resemblances Between the Psychic Lives of Savages and Neurotics*, trans. by A. A. Brill [1913] (London: Routledge, 1919), p. 157.

[27] Herbert Read, *Art and Society* (London: Heinemann, 1937), pp. 89–90.

While there was a strong political impulse in English Surrealism, the absence of a dominant figure like André Breton meant that the movement was always likely to fracture into an array of diverging artistic-political positions. Many poems by English Surrealists were taking the indirect route towards revolutionary action advocated in Gascoyne's 'Poetry and Reality' essay. They choose to register the decay of the material world—the physical withering-away of bourgeois society, as it were—rather than committing to the work of imagining a new social order or of describing the proletarian revolution. Among the most prominent instances of this tendency are the poems by Charles Madge, whose persistent fascination with the material detritus of bourgeois society can be seen to anticipate the documentary impulse of the Mass-Observation movement which he helped to found in the mid-1930s. The seismographic 'cold, trembling needle' of Madge's poem 'In Sua Voluntade' (1933) offers just such a picture of a disintegrating material world. The title of the poem alludes to a line from Dante's *Divine Comedy* ('In la sua voluntade è nostra pace') which Eliot had famously used to argue that it was necessary to share a poet's beliefs in order to attain a full appreciation of his or her poetry.[28] The automaton 'needle' of Madge's poem, however, recurs to Dante's verse mainly to register the demise of the Christian system of belief associated with it:

> I cannot have the round world in my hands
> I cannot join with the ascending light.
> . . . England is fallen. Home is gone. Time stands.
>
> Like the cold, trembling needle I write
> The stony, age-old words, and as I cease,
> The living, heavy downward flight
> Bears on with me. Life's flight is deathly peace.[29]

Madge's poem invokes the Christian language of salvation only to renounce the possibility of a revelatory vision from above. The 'heavy downward flight' associates the speaker with the fall of the rebelling angels, but Madge's poem also links this sense of eternal damnation with the dull ongoingness of everyday life in bourgeois society. Madge tended to attribute to writing a non-participatory, merely observing role, yet 'In Sua Volontade' also engages in a search for the deeper significance contained in the epiphenomena of social life. As I point out in the next chapter, the act of sifting through the fragments of a fissured social world in order to reveal

[28] See Eliot's footnote to the second section of his 'Dante' essay, in *Selected Essays, 1917–1932* (London: Faber and Faber, 1932), pp. 223–63 (p. 256 fn.).

[29] Charles Madge, 'In Sua Voluntade', in *Of Love, Time and Places: Selected Poems* (London: Anvil Press, 1994), p. 17.

hidden patterns of historical movement anticipates Madge's early artistic stakes in Mass-Observation. At the same time, the poem's hope that the archaic language of poetry—its 'stony, age-old words'—will somehow make it possible to stem the tide of history is at odds with Mass-Observation's sobered recognition that any such act of documenting and recording will continue to be premised on a bourgeois notion of authorship.

As the decade progressed, English Surrealism was drawn into the exclusionary rhetoric of the 1930s. 'In placing itself at the service of the revolution, surrealism can be allowed no political reservations', Madge warned in *New Verse*: Surrealism's artistic 'independence ought not to be extended into politics'.[30] Such rhetorical hectoring was partly designed to hide the slippages which existed between the diverging artistic and political meanings of the term 'revolution' and which found expression in the literary works of many English Surrealists, including outspoken communists such as Gascoyne, Roughton, and Madge himself. More often than not, English Surrealist texts illustrate that the politics of writing in the 1930s was an untidy affair characterized by overlapping modes of writing. The sturdy Marxism of Roughton's poems, for example, fails to conceal a deep irresoluteness concerning the means required to put the communist revolution into action. The closing stanzas of his 1937 'Building Society Blues' contemplate the new urgency which the thirties rhetoric of 'taking sides' took on after the outbreak of the Spanish Civil War in 1936:

> Dare you ask for a rifle and sign on the line?
> Remember the pain when you fractured your wrist.
> Could you bear the damp air in the grave,
> Or going to bed unkissed?
>
> Maneating [sic] plants have grown out of the bath,
> The pipes are about to burst through;
> Can you call for the plumber to help, with his soviet
> Grammar and sickle too?[31]

The poem addresses a strange combination of anxieties: an existential fear of 'the grave', the grotesque Surrealist fantasy of man-eating plants, as well as the middle-class dread of going over to the proletariat. The poem's insistent self-questioning is highly effective in magnifying the losses involved in leaving the Ivory Tower: 'Do you want to become an Insoluble Crime, | A lynching held in one of the parks?', an earlier stanza asks; and

[30] Charles Madge, 'Meaning of Surrealism', *New Verse*, 6 (December 1933), 14–18 (p. 14).

[31] Roger Roughton, 'Building Society Blues', *Contemporary Poetry and Prose*, 9 (Spring 1937), p. 45.

again: 'Will you cross your desires and your heart, | Finding reprieve in a suitable mass?' The wish to reach out to an extra-poetic realm of 'reality' is complicated by the poem's echoes of Eliot's 'The Love Song of J. Alfred Prufrock': 'And indeed there will be time | To wonder, "Do I dare?" and, "Do I dare?"': 'Do I dare | Disturb the universe? | In a minute there is time | For decisions and revisions which a minute will reverse.'[32] The rhetorical questions in Roughton's poem are intended to emphasize the necessity of radical political action, but they do not succeed in muting the hesitant and self-observing tone of Eliot's poem. Because 'Building Society Blues' implies that every moment is a border situation in time, a frontier between the past and an uncertain future, it can be seen to resist, almost despite itself, the overarching ideological narrative of a revolutionary struggle that leads on to a determinate political constellation. At the same time, the awkwardly phrased propagandistic vision of the 'plumber' equipped with 'grammer and sickle' participates in the kind of politicized language which Gascoyne had condemned as being concerned with 'strikes, factories, the armaments camp'.

The cases of Madge, Roughton, and Gascoyne illustrate the diversity of politicized writing among English Surrealists, though this diversity has largely been eclipsed by the confrontational rhetoric adopted by members of the far left, such as A. L. Lloyd. In what follows, I want to explore the historical reasons for the English Surrealists' uncertainties about the nature of the movement's revolutionary commitments. The trajectory of English Surrealism and its struggle to come to terms with the political pressures of the 1930s need to be understood in relation to the fraught political heritage which French Surrealism had brought with it across the Channel. Central to this legacy, I argue, was the so-called *affaire Aragon* of 1932 which set the stage for Surrealism's break with the Communist Party.

AGAINST COMMUNISM: ARAGON AFFAIR AND WRITERS' CONGRESS

Rod Mengham has observed that 'the British presentation of Surrealism was able to reflect the full range of concerns that had evolved in Francophone Surrealism over a period of a decade or more'.[33] The 'range of

[32] T. S. Eliot, 'The Love Song of J. Alfred Prufrock', in *The Complete Poems and Plays* (London: Faber and Faber, 1969), pp. 13–17 (p. 14).

[33] Rod Mengham, '"National Papers Please Reprint": Surrealist Magazines in Britain', in *The Oxford Critical and Cultural History of Modernist Magazines*, ed. by Peter Brooker and Andrew Thacker (Oxford: Oxford University Press, 2009), pp. 688–703 (p. 688).

concerns' inherited by English Surrealism was not limited to its artistic outlook, but also crucially included the French movement's complex political adjustments. Despite Breton's early pledge of allegiance to communism, French Surrealism had long been divided on the question whether its writing could be assimilated to the doctrines of the Communist Party. A particularly momentous realignment of Surrealism's political loyalties took place in the wake of the Aragon affair in 1932. Louis Aragon had been a founding member of the French Surrealist group, and he had joined the ranks of the Communist Party in 1927. A visit to the Soviet Congress of Revolutionary Writers in 1930 occasioned a change in Aragon's allegiances, and he became convinced of the incompatibility of Surrealism and Soviet-style communism. The decisive step towards Aragon's break with the Surrealists was taken with the publication of his poem 'Front Rouge' in 1931:

> They won't find the usual remedy
> and will fall into the hands of the rioters who will glue them to the wall
> Fire on Léon Blum
> Fire on Boncour Frossard Déat
> Fire on the trained bears of the social-democracy [. . .]
> I sing the violent domination of the bourgeoisie by the proletariat
> for the annihilation of the bourgeoisie
> for the total annihilation of that bourgeoisie [. . .]
> The bursting of gunfire adds to the landscape
> a hitherto unknown gaiety
> Those are engineers, doctors that are being executed
> Death to those who endanger the conquest of October
> Death to the traitors of the Fiveyearplan [sic]
> To you Young Communists
> Sweep out the human debris[.][34]

The poem employs a range of stylistic features which are recognizably Surrealist, but it utilizes them for essentially propagandistic ends. The poem's semantically self-contained lines, for example, are not used to signal an apparently random series of images and impressions but in order to combine a sense of revolutionary urgency ('Death to those who endanger the conquest of October | Death to the traitors of the Fiveyearplan') with a proleptic description of the violent rupture signified by the revolution itself ('The bursting of gunfire adds to the landscape | a hitherto unknown

[34] Louis Aragon, 'Front Rouge/Red Front' [1931], in *Complete Poems of E. E. Cummings, 1904–62*, ed. by George J. Firmage (New York: Liveright, 1991), pp. 880–97 (pp. 885, 889).

gaiety'). Aragon's 350-line paean of Soviet communism participated in the fierce rhetorical arms race that followed the break between the French Socialist Party, of which Blum and Frossard were members, and the communists. The subsequent debate in France and England about 'Front Rouge' raised the stakes for debates about the nature of 'revolutionary' art, and it notably led to an escalation of Surrealism's conflicts with the Communist Party which threatened to prise open a gap between the movement's artistic and political commitments.[35]

Breton initially sought to defend his old friend Aragon against the right-wing press in his pamphlet *La Misère de la poésie* (1932), one of the key texts of Surrealism in the 1930s. Breton's defence notes that 'the special feature of the problem raised by the inculpation of "Red Front" is that the problem, as I see it, offers two faces: a *social* face and a *poetic* face'.[36] Aragon's poem, I. A. Richards might say, requires only imaginative assent: we accept the author's beliefs only in so far as they help us to appreciate the quality of the poem. 'I say', Breton continued,

> that this poem, by its situation in Aragon's work on the one hand and in the history of poetry on the other, corresponds to a certain number of formal determinations which do not permit the isolation of any one group of words ('Comrades, kill the cops') in order to exploit its literal meaning, whereas for some other group ('The stars descend familiarly on earth') the question of this literal meaning does not come up. [. . .] The poem is not to be judged on the successive representations it makes.[37]

In his attempt to exculpate Aragon, Breton brashly subordinates the poem's declarative language, its 'literal meaning', to the procedures of Surrealist poiesis. As Svetlana Boym has pointed out, it is indeed possible to make a case for the poem's 'situation' 'in the history of poetry' rather than for its status as propagandist agitation. 'Front Rouge' can, for example, be read as a panegyric reprise of the incendiary poem 'Left March' (1918) by Vladimir Mayakovsky, whom Aragon had met in Paris in 1928.[38] Such a reading would seem to bracket the Agitprop aggression of

[35] For an overview of this process of estrangement, see Helena Lewis, *Dada Turns Red: The Politics of Surrealism* (Edinburgh: Edinburgh University Press, 1990), pp. 97–139.

[36] André Breton, 'The Poverty of Poetry: The Aragon Affair and Public Opinion' [1932], trans. by Richard Howard, in *What is Surrealism? Selected Writings*, ed. by Franklin Rosemont (London: Pluto, 1978), pp. 76–82 (p. 76), emphases in the original.

[37] Breton, 'The Poverty of Poetry', p. 77.

[38] Svetlana Boym, *Death in Quotation Marks: Cultural Myths of the Modern Poet* (Cambridge, MA: Harvard University Press, 1991), pp. 167–81. For an account of the meeting with Mayakovksy, see Louis Aragon, *Pour un réalisme socialiste* (Paris: Denoël et Steele, 1935), pp. 52–53.

Aragon's poem—or at least to put it at a further remove—by emphasizing its place in the 'tradition' of revolutionary poetry. However, it might be more precise to say that, instead of resolving the dilemma, the echoes of 'Left March' in Aragon's poem create a kind of anamorphic double effect that allows for the text to be read both poetically and politically. The co-existence of both significations also inflects the mode of address of certain English Surrealist poems which were written in a similar register, such as George Reavey's sonnet 'Bombs for All – In Memory of Mayakovsky' (1935): 'O give us poison, dagger or the bomb, | Swift bullets of the briefly speaking gun.'[39] The constitutive ambiguity of literary language—the possibility of reading it 'referentially' or 'rhetorically'[40]—is brought into sharp focus by the debates over Aragon's poem. Breton's reductive defence of 'Front Rouge' was resonantly dismissed by the communists, and only five days after the publication of *La Misère de la poésie*, the periodical of the French Communist Party, *L'Humanité*, issued a statement on behalf of Aragon which endorsed once more the views expressed in 'Front Rouge'. Breton's attempt to put the bellicose rhetoric of the poem in quotation marks collided with a politicized reading that was just as reductive of the text's ambiguities.

The Aragon affair quickly found its way into the pages of English left-wing periodicals. A translation of 'Front Rouge' by E. E. Cummings was published in the spring of 1933, and Gascoyne commented at length on the fallout between Breton and Aragon in his 1935 *Short Survey*. In *New Verse*, the magazine that had published several poems by English Surrealists, Stephen Spender devoted a whole article to the poem, condemning its 'superstitious belief in the necessity of murders and reprisals. [. . .] The reader of this poem should compare it with any speech by Hitler.'[41] The afterlife of the affair on the literary left—and in particular in the pages of *Left Review*—suggests that invoking Aragon became a short-hand way of asserting one's communist credentials and of dismissing the notion of pure poetry. The first number of *Left Review*, for example, opened with Nancy Cunard's translation of Aragon's communist poem 'Waltz' from his collection *Hourra l'Oural* (1934): 'Comrades the past is cracking | Where

[39] George Reavey, 'Bombs For All – In Memory of Mayakovsky', in *Nostradam* (Paris: Europa Press, 1935), p. 19.

[40] Jonathan Culler has remarked that 'the "openness" and "ambiguity" of literary works' are rooted in this structural ambivalence. They result 'not from vagueness but from the potential reversibility of every figure. Any figure can be read referentially or rhetorically.' See *The Pursuit of Signs: Semiotics, Literature, Deconstruction* [1981] (London: Routledge, 2002), p. 86.

[41] Stephen Spender, Review of Louis Aragon's 'Red Front', *New Verse*, 3 (May 1933), 24–25 (p. 25).

your powerful emblem stands.'[42] Sylvia Townsend Warner added to the affair's lease of life in the English communist press: 'Comrade, have you bled enough, | Are your wounds red enough?', noted one of her poems in *Left Review*. The title of the piece was 'Red Front!'.[43] From 1934 onwards, Aragon, the Surrealist-turned-communist, became a focal point of the myth of the uncompromisingly political 1930s on both sides of the Channel, and the Aragon affair fuelled the confrontational rhetoric that came to dominate much of the literary discourse of the decade.

Avant-garde modes of writing in particular could seem to be mired in a realm of mere poeticity. As far as Surrealism was concerned, Breton contributed his share to this popular critical conception. In *La Misère de la poésie*, he reminded fellow-Surrealists that his first *Surrealist Manifesto* had 'insisted [. . .] on disengaging the author's responsibility entirely in cases when certain texts of incontestably "automatic" character were incriminated'.[44] French Surrealist responses to the *affaire Aragon* frequently echoed Breton's arguments. René Crevel quoted with approval Breton's definition of 'pure psychic automatism' in the first *Manifesto* as a form of literary production 'dictated by thought, in the absence of any control exercised by reason, exempt from any aesthetic or moral concerns'.[45] Tristan Tzara agreed in his 'Essai sur la situation de la poésie' that, while it was important not to lose sight of the aims of communism, Surrealism was to 'follow the parallel activity of poetry'.[46] This common identification of Surrealism with a form of poetic purity culminated in 1935 with the 'International Congress of Writers for the Defence of Culture Against Fascism' in Paris.[47] The Congress, which ran for five days, was meant to formulate a response to the rising fascist threat, and amongst the 220 delegates from forty countries were Cecil Day Lewis and Rex Warner, as well as André Malraux, E. M. Forster, André Gide, Aldous Huxley, and Bertolt Brecht. The event was tightly controlled by the Soviet Communist Party which sought to propagate a more orthodox stance both in politics and in aesthetics. The tensions between communists and Surrealists escalated when Ilya Ehrenburg, Stalin's cultural representative at the

[42] Louis Aragon, 'Waltz', trans. by Nancy Cunard, *Left Review*, 1/1 (October 1934), 3–5.

[43] Sylvia Townsend Warner, 'Red Front!', *Left Review*, 1/7 (April 1935), 255–57.

[44] Breton, 'Poverty of Poetry', pp. 76–77.

[45] René Crevel, 'Le Patriotisme de l'inconscient', *Le Surréalisme au service de la revolution*, 4 (1932), 3–6 (p. 6), my translation.

[46] Tristan Tzara, 'Essai sur la situation de la poésie', *Le Surréalisme au service de la revolution*, 4 (1931), 15–23 (p. 23), my translation.

[47] For an account of the Congress, see Roger Shattuck, 'Having Congress: The Shame of the Thirties', in *The Innocent Eye: On Modern Literature and the Arts* (New York: Farrar, Straus and Giroux, 1984), pp. 3–31.

Congress, insulted the Surrealists as pederasts and Breton retaliated by slapping Ehrenburg in front of the Congress building.

Gascoyne was in Paris during the Congress in order to conduct research for his *Short Survey*. However, when the book was published later that year, it made no mention of the event—a conspicuous silence that is in keeping with Gascoyne's attempt to gloss over the most recent rifts between communists and Surrealists.[48] Nonetheless some of the poems which Gascoyne wrote around this time comment obliquely on the break between French Surrealism and the Communist Party. One of these pieces, 'Unspoken', was first published in *New Verse* in November 1935. Its first stanza reads:

> Words spoken leave no time for regret
> Yet regret
> The unviolated silence and
> White sanctuses of sleep
> Under the heaped veils
> The inexorably prolonged vigils
> Speech flowing away like water
> With its undertow of violence and darkness
> Carrying with it forever
> All those formless vessels
> Abandoned palaces
> Tottering under the strain of being
> Full-blossoming hysterias
> Lavishly scattering their stained veined petals[49]

At the most abstract level the poem's first stanza contemplates two distinct kinds of (verbal) signification: on the one hand, Gascoyne intimates that words, once they have been articulated, acquire agency in the real world and are capable of inflicting harm; on the other, the poem pictures the realm of unvoiced thoughts, associating this sphere with an untrammelled 'undertow of violence and darkness'. By foregrounding these themes, Gascoyne's poem reflects on the implications and impasses of one of Surrealism's original artistic aims. The technique of automatic writing, which Breton had propagated in the 1920s, had been designed to tap into the language of the unconscious; it was based on the assumption that the unconscious activity of the mind ran parallel to the mind's conscious processes and that

[48] By contrast *Left Review* covered the conference, printing Gide's speech in full and including a lengthy first-hand report by Christina Stead. See André Gide, 'The Individual', *Left Review*, 1/11 (August 1935), 447–52; and Christina Stead, 'The Writers Take Sides', ibid., 453–62.

[49] David Gascoyne, 'Unspoken' [1935], in *Collected Poems*, pp. 42–43 (p. 42).

this hidden language was not structured according to the same grammatical and semantic rules as the surface level of everyday speech. Gascoyne's poem, too, refers to the activity of the unconscious as a buried 'undertow', and the images with which 'Unspoken' opens—'The unviolated silence and | White sanctuses of sleep'—bring to mind the realm of undisturbed unconscious activity alluded to in 'No Solution'. However, instead of presenting Surrealist writing as an untainted 'parallel activity' and as fundamentally disconnected from the level of referential speech acts, Gascoyne's poem stresses the potentially destructive power of poetic language itself. The 'words spoken' by Surrealists do not exist in a discrete realm, he suggests. Instead, like the sentences of everyday speech, they are capable of inflicting damage which it is always too late to 'regret' as speech 'flow[s] away' relentlessly 'like water'. 'Unspoken' can thus be read as a response to the situation of Surrealim in the early 1930s. The second *Surrealist Manifesto*, issued in 1930, had claimed that 'the simplest Surrealist act consists in going out into the street, revolver in hand, and shooting at random as much as you wish into the crowd'.[50] Yet in the political fray of the mid- and late 1930s, the nature of such literary aggressions, the question of how far into the real world they were able to extend, was far from clear, and the case of 'Front Rouge' illustrated how easily the ludic aggressions of Surrealism could spill over into the realm of 'real' violence and political conflict.

'Unspoken' hints that it became difficult for many poets to separate the aggressive registers of Surrealist poetry from the violent language that came to dominate the political arena of the 1930s. In view of these difficulties, Breton's attempts to draw a *cordon sanitaire* around Surrealist poetry seem even more out of touch with historical realities. In a lecture delivered in Prague in 1935, Breton invoked Aragon's 'Front Rouge' as an example of the kind of poetry Surrealists needed to avoid. The talk sought to set up a hard and fast distinction between Surrealism's artistic and political revolutions. However, the expression 'revolutionary poet' turned out to be rich in ambiguities:

> This adjective ['revolutionary'], which hastily takes into account the indisputable nonconformist will that quickens [artistic] work, has the grave defect of being confused with one which tends to define a systematic action aiming at the transformation of the world and implying the necessity of concretely attacking its real bases. A most regrettable ambiguity results from this.[51]

[50] Quoted in René Wellek, *A History of Modern Criticism, 1750–1950, Volume 8: French, Italian, and Spanish Criticism, 1900–1950* (New Haven: Yale University Press, 1992), p. 92.

[51] André Breton, 'The Political Position of Today's Art' [1935], in *Manifestoes of Surrealism*, trans. by Richard Seaver and Helen R. Lane (Ann Arbor: University of Michigan Press, 1972), pp. 212–33 (p. 213).

Raymond Williams has argued that the opposition between the political and artistic meanings of the term 'revolution' mirrors deeper tensions within the language of modernist writing. Williams relates these conflicts to 'the double meaning of "sign" [. . .] as *signifier*, a unit within an autonomous language system, and "sign" in its very combination of "signifier" and "signified" as pointing both ways, to the language-system and to a reality which is not language'.[52] Such a contrast between the non-representational 'integrity' of poetic language and its contextual ties may seem too crude, but it helps to highlight the fact that in the mid-1930s discussions about Surrealism's political aims began to be embroiled in an exclusionary rhetoric which suggested that avant-garde art was incapable of making a genuine contribution to the political-revolutionary cause. 'The revolutionary artist', Read concluded in *Art Now* (1933), was 'not [. . .] to be identified with the revolutionary politician.'[53] These conflicts were half brought upon Surrealism by the Communist Party and half enforced by Breton. While Gascoyne's *Short Survey* passed over Surrealism's break with the Communist Party following the Writers' Congress in Paris, his notebooks register the pessimism to which the events of 1935 gave rise. On a blank page of his notebook, he noted in capital letters that 'THE REVOLUTION HAS NO NEED OF POETRY, BUT POETRY HAS GREAT NEED OF THE REVOLUTION'—a sentence which he repeated a few months later in his 'Poetry and Reality' essay. Some critics have taken Gascoyne's maxim as evidence that the Surrealist method could be used for political ends. In fact, however, the sentence translates verbatim a passage from Tristan Tzara's 'Essai sur la situation de la poésie' (1931) which anticipated the fear, central to the literary aftermath of the Aragon affair, that the 'activity' of poetry ran largely 'parallel' to politics.[54]

ENGLISH SURREALISM AND THE IDEA OF STYLISTIC 'PURITY'

Evidence of the break between French Surrealism and the Communist Party reached England in 1936 when André Breton's *What is Surrealism?* was published in the *Criterion* Miscellany series. *What is Surrealism?* was

[52] Raymond Williams, *The Politics of Modernism: Against the New Conformists* (London: Verso, 1989), p. 75, emphasis in the original. Williams elsewhere argues against such a clean division; see *Marxism and Literature* (Oxford: Oxford University Press, 1977), pp. 35–39.

[53] Herbert Read, *Art Now* [1933] (London: Faber and Faber, 1936), p. 13.

[54] DGP, Notebook from the mid-1930s, ADD 56040. See Tzara's remark: 'La Révolution sociale n'a pas besoin de la poésie, mais cette dernière a bien besoin de la Révolution' ('Essai', p. 23). Gascoyne himself does not attribute the quotation to this source.

the first of Breton's programmatic writings from the 1930s to be translated into English, and the text proposed a separate route for Surrealism, calling on artists to 'restore' the movement 'to its pristine purity' of the 1920s and advocating 'nothing less than *a rallying back to principles*'.[55] Breton's invocation of 'purity' harked back specifically to the first *Surrealist Manifesto* and its attempt to define Surrealism 'once and for all' as 'pure psychic automatism'.[56] *What is Surrealism?* left room for Surrealism's role as a supplement to the political revolution, but the pamphlet also unambiguously dissociated the movement from Soviet-style communism. 'An activity such as ours', Breton pronounced, 'owing to its particularisation, cannot be pursued within the limits of any one of the existing revolutionary organisations.'[57] A similar wish to restore Surrealism to its original 'purity', to an imagined state of ideological innocence that predated the political strictures of the 1930s, also animates many English Surrealist poems. For example, the same impulse of semantic disruption that runs through the famous Surrealist catchphrase from Lautréamont's *Les Chants de Maldoror* (1869) about 'the fortuitous encounter upon a dissecting-table of a sewing machine and an umbrella' is also written into Gascoyne's 'The Rites of Hysteria' (1935): 'The sewing-machine on the pillar condenses the windmill's halo | [. . .] And the ashtray balanced a ribbon upon a syringe'.[58] This tendency to maintain the movement's artistic purity could take the form of a belief in a Surrealist tradition which existed largely undisturbed by the economic and political forces of Marxist-Leninist history, but it could also be articulated through a reliance on particular methods of poetic production (such as automatic writing) or through an adherence to an established fund of Surrealist symbols.

Gascoyne's 'And the Seventh Dream Is the Dream of Isis', published in *New Verse* in 1933, has often been hailed as the first English Surrealist poem. The piece begins:

> white curtains of infinite fatigue
> dominating the starborn heritage of the colonies of St Francis
> white curtains of tortured destinies
> inheriting the calamities of the plagues of the desert
> encourage the waistlines of women to expand

[55] André Breton, *What is Surrealism?* (London: Faber and Faber, 1936), p. 72, emphasis in the original.

[56] André Breton, 'Manifesto of Surrealism' [1924], in *Manifestoes of Surrealism*, pp. 1–46 (p. 26).

[57] Breton, *What is Surrealism?*, p. 89.

[58] Comte de Lautréamont, *Les Chants de Maldoror* [1869], trans. by Guy Wernham (New York: New Directions, 1965), p. 263; David Gascoyne, 'The Rites of Hysteria' [1935], in *Collected Poems*, p. 56.

and the eyes of men to enlarge like pocket-cameras
teach children to sin at the age of five
to cut out the eyes of their sisters with nail scissors
to run into the streets and offer themselves to unfrocked priests
[. . .]
for the year is open the year is complete
the year is full of unforeseen happenings
and the time of earthquakes is at hand[59]

Gascoyne was conscious of his role as Surrealism's principal literary ambassador in England in the early 1930s, and certain passages in the poem read as if they had been written with the intention of providing English audiences with a quintessential sample of Surrealist *écriture*. The poem begins programmatically with a descent into the oneiric sphere of 'infinite fatigue', and while Gascoyne suggests that certain dreams can be 'calamities' he also hints at their ability to create an expanded perception of (sur-)reality as 'the eyes of men' 'enlarge like pocket-cameras'. The 'children' mentioned in the poem engage in a series of quasi-Surrealist activities: their unspecified acts of 'sin[ning]' challenge the Christian system of morality which offers a backdrop to much of the poem's satire; moreover, similar to the famous scene in Luis Buñuel and Salvador Dalí's film *Un Chien andalou* (1929), the act of 'cut[ting] out the eyes of their sisters' illustrates the transition from an embodied perception of the physical world to the quasi-spiritual vision craved by many Surrealists in the 1920s; finally, the children's impulse to leave the secure haven of their homes and to engage in public acts of moral perversity and disruption recalls Breton's notorious claim (quoted above) that 'the simplest Surrealist act' consisted 'in going out into the street' and running amok. The first stanza ends, appropriately for a poem that was intended to carry Surrealism into the pages of English periodicals, with three lines that are pregnant with foreboding. The imminent cataclysm and 'unforeseen happenings' predicted in the closing lines are the stuff out of which Surrealist art is made, but they also presage the momentous arrival in England of those Surrealist works themselves. Following the publication of 'The Seventh Dream Is the Dream of Isis', later issues of *New Verse* did indeed become an important early outlet for Surrealist work, including poems and criticism by Gascoyne, Sykes Davies, Madge, and Jennings. The key ideas and tropes of Gascoyne's poem—such as the celebration of sleep and the cutting up of eyes—signal its faithfulness to a putatively 'pure' Surrealist style whose most iconic tropes had been codified in the 1920s. Already in its opening words the poem reverts to a favourite accessory of the Surrealist unconscious. Curtains had been prominent items in the paintings of René Magritte (in his 'La Traversée difficile' from 1926, or in 'La Condition humaine' from 1933), as well as

[59] David Gascoyne, 'And the Seventh Dream Is the Dream of Isis' [1933], in *Collected Poems*, pp. 25–27.

in the poetry of Breton whose 'Rideau rideau' from 1932 felt nightmarishly locked into 'a kiosk of mirrors | On which a curtain of dew arose fringed with blood turned green'.[60]

The poem's second stanza begins with an emphasis on the present moment that anticipates Gascoyne's slightly later poem 'No Solution':

> today is the day when the streets are full of hearses
> and when women cover their ring fingers with pieces of silk
> when the doors fall off their hinges in ruined cathedrals
> when hosts of white birds fly across the ocean from america
> and make their nests in the trees of public gardens
> the pavements of cities are covered with needles
> the reservoirs are full of human hair
> fumes of sulphur envelop the houses of ill-fame
> out of which bloodred lilies appear

The mention of St Francis in the first stanza triggers a series of references to animal auguries such as the 'host of white birds fly[ing] across the ocean'. Indeed, nearly each line in the second stanza features an omen that forebodes a transformative, possibly apocalyptic event, from the 'pavements [. . .] covered with needles' to the 'fumes of sulphur' enveloping houses of ill repute. As in many of Gascoyne's later texts, the artistic revelation in this poem is modelled in part on the epiphanies of Christian religion, and the mention of 'ruined cathedrals' creates a sense that Surrealist poetry might even occupy the vacant position formerly held by religious faith. Animals, especially birds, are ubiquitous in the Surrealist imaginary of the 1920s and 1930s, and the bird augury in 'The Seventh Dream Is the Dream of Isis' can be read both as a premonition of some unspecified catastrophe and, similar to the first stanza's 'unforeseen happenings', as a token of the imminent arrival in England of Surrealism itself.[61] But the second stanza of Gascoyne's poem also draws on other popular Surrealist tropes. For example, the striking reference to 'reservoirs full of human hair' is not quite as idiosyncratic as it at first appears. In fact, hair had for some time been one of the prime objects of Surrealist erotic desire. The title of

[60] André Breton, 'Rideau rideau / Curtain Curtain' [1932], in *Poems of André Breton: A Bilingual Anthology*, ed. and trans. by Jean-Pierre Cauvin and Mary-Ann Caws (Austin: University of Texas Press, 1982), pp. 70–73 (p. 71). For further examples of visual art which may have served as an inspiration for Gascoyne's early poems, see Fraser, *Night Thoughts*, pp. 98–99.

[61] For the prominence of bird imagery in Surrealism, see Margot Norris, *Beasts of the Modern Imagination: Darwin, Nietzsche, Kafka, Ernst, Lawrence* (Baltimore: Johns Hopkins University Press, 1985), pp. 134–69; and Claude Maillard-Chary, *Le Bestiaire des surréalistes* (Paris: Presses de la Sorbonne Nouvelle, 1994).

Breton's collection *Le Revolver à cheveux blancs* (1932) had set a prominent precedent, but even an important early Surrealist poem like Breton's 1923 'Postman Cheval', which Gascoyne translated for *Contemporary Poetry and Prose,* could lustfully imagine 'Drawers of flesh with handsfull [sic] of hair'.[62] Furry erotica also figure in many other English Surrealist texts. Roger Roughton's 'Animal Crackers' featured hair in its climactic line ('Tomorrow REVOLT will be written in human hair'), and his poem 'Soluble Noughts and Crosses' (1936) was enraptured by 'the eyelash of a girl, | The most beautiful young girl of all' and found that 'love has grown up like a hair'; Gascoyne's own 'Automatic Album Leaves' (1937) similarly discovered that 'suffering has abundant hair and lives alone on a cliff'.[63] Not quite incidentally perhaps, the object that caught T. S. Eliot's eye when he visited the International Surrealist Exhibition in London was the fur-coated cup and saucer of Meret Oppenheim's 'Breakfast in Fur'.[64] A later line in 'The Seventh Dream Is the Dream of Isis' conflates this poetic obsession with hair with the Surrealist predilection for avian imagery: 'Her arms are like pieces of sandpaper | or wings of leprous birds in taxis | when she sings her hair stands on end'.

In a discussion of the Surrealist notion of artistic 'purity', Daniel Cottom has suggested that 'purity was the concern of a cultural movement that sought to extend its influence without losing its identity to the absorbing viscosity of the world': the 'enemy' of purity 'was not error but slackness, an absence of discipline that could take many forms'.[65] Surrealism's attempt to make an artistic law of the transgression of all laws, its adherence to what Eliot's *Criterion* dubbed 'systematic non-conformity', meant that the outlandish opacity of Surrealist imagery, its rhetoric of spontaneity and immediacy, could function as the movement's familiar literary code.[66] Walter Benjamin's formula—that the central tension in Surrealism

[62] André Breton, 'Postman Cheval' [1923], in David Gascoyne, *Collected Verse Translations*, ed. by Alan Clodd and Robin Skelton (Oxford: Oxford University Press, 1970), p. 4.

[63] Roger Roughton, 'Soluble Noughts and Crosses; *or,* California, Here I Come', *Contemporary Poetry and Prose*, 3 (July 1936), p. 55; David Gascoyne, 'Automatic Album Leaves' [1937], in *Collected Poems*, pp. 31–34 (p. 33)

[64] See Eileen Agar's recollection of the exhibition in *A Look at My Life* (London: Methuen, 1988), pp. 114–32 (p. 117).

[65] Daniel Cottom, *Abyss of Reason: Cultural Movements, Revelations, and Betrayals* (Oxford: Oxford University Press, 1991), p. 225. In this vein, Aragon had demanded that 'The purity of the dream, its purposelessness and uselessness: these need to be defended against the new wave of [literary] pen–pushing that is being unleashed' ('La pureté du rêve, l'inemployable, l'inutile du rêve, voilà ce qu'il s'agit de défendre contre une nouvelle rage de ronds-de-cuir qui va se déchaîner'). See his *Traité de style* (Paris: Gallimard, 1928), p. 186.

[66] Brian Coffey, Review of *A Short Survey of Surrealism*, *The Criterion*, 15 (April 1936), 506–11 (p. 508).

is between 'an anarchistic *fronde* and a revolutionary discipline'—would accordingly have to be reinterpreted as referring not to a political 'revolution' but to a certain poetic style which is held to be 'revolutionary' in the narrower realm of art.[67] Despite their insistent claim to open out to life—Rimbaud's call 'changer la vie' surfaces everywhere in Surrealist treatises and manifestoes—there is ample evidence that the poems by English Surrealists such as Gascoyne, Sykes Davies, and Roughton were making use of a specific repertoire of recurrent images and compositional rules, rather than being governed by pure 'chance, the openness of metonymic drift in language'.[68] It is indicative of the confusing admixture of political and poetic elements in English Surrealism that the poems of Gascoyne, one of the Surrealists who joined the Communist Party, are most responsive to the imagery of French Surrealism.

A further variation of this attraction to stylistic purity can be found in the works of Hugh Sykes Davies. Sykes Davies's Surrealist picaresque novella *Petron* had been published by Dent in 1935, and its short preface started with an eclectic list of the book's literary precursors. The book, Sykes Davies noted, had been written '[f]or those who used to enjoy Milton and Thomson's *Seasons* when they were at school [. . .] For those who have once read Poe. For those who have done a little novel-reading, and who like to be reminded now and then of the work of [Pétrus] Borel and [Eugène] Sue'.[69] The preface propounds a lineage of Surrealist forbears that had been rehearsed since the 1920s: Breton had celebrated Thomson's *The Seasons* and Poe's short stories as precursors of Surrealist writing, and Borel's novel *Madame Putiphar* (1839) was generally considered on a par with Lautréamont's *Les Chants de Maldoror* (1869) in terms of its proto-Surrealist qualities. Even so, the horrors which Sykes Davies's character Petron encounters on his journey ultimately owe more to the English traditions of Gothic and fantastic writing than to Surrealism's more profoundly disturbing attempts to discover the absurd within the patterns of everyday life. In *Petron* terrifying sights are usually revealed to have natural causes. After meeting an 'idiot' whose 'lower jaw, which hung down between his knees, bumped and banged on the road like a loose stick behind a cart, or broken harness on a runaway horse', Petron feels 'relief' upon discovering 'that the idiot's mouth is nothing more than the sunset, his throat is the

[67] Walter Benjamin, 'Surrealism: The Last Snapshot of the European Intelligentsia' [1929], in *One-Way Street and Other Writings*, trans. by Edmund Jephcott and Kingsley Shorter (London: New Left Books, 1979), pp. 225–39 (p. 225).

[68] Steven Connor, 'British Surrealist Poetry in the 1930s', in *British Poetry, 1900–50: Aspects of Tradition*, ed. by Gary Day and Brian Docherty (London: St. Martin's Press, 1995), pp. 169–92 (p. 181).

[69] Hugh Sykes Davies, *Petron* (London: Dent, 1935), p. vii.

gathering night, and the sounds that issue from it are those of roosting birds, newly-risen nightingales perched in the tips of his teeth'.[70] Similar to Gascoyne's 'The Seventh Dream Is the Dream of Isis', Sykes Davies's association of the Rabelaisian giant with birds functions as a token of the narrative's vague kinship with Surrealism, even as the text's conventionally omniscient narrative voice falls short of the systematic unsettling of traditional points of view that takes place in foundational Surrealist works such as Breton and Philippe Soupault's *Les Champs magnétiques* (1920). The 'archaising tone' of *Petron,* Peter Nicholls has remarked, 'finally has more in common with the fairy tale than it does with the urban narratives of the French writers'.[71] While it is true that *Petron* seems strangely distant from the improvised, experimental quality of 1920s Surrealism, Sykes Davies believed that the novella's relatively conservative narrative perspective and its preference for natural (rather than 'urban') settings signalled an allegiance to a set of older texts, all of which had recently been reclaimed as precursors of the Surrealist movement. One indication of the text's poetic craftedness is the handwritten glosses which Sykes Davies scribbled into the margins of his personal copy of *Petron.* These marginal notes point out that the opening pages of *Petron* contain 'a good deal of Lautréamont' and that a lengthy description of fantastic plants later in the novella offers 'Borel, Madame Putiphar. Almost literal trans.'.[72] Sykes Davies's scrupulous foregrounding of *Petron*'s literary models points to the cohesion effected by a shared Surrealist style. As Raymond Williams has observed, artistic movements develop 'a particular style' as an initial criterion of differentiation from other cultural 'formations'; this evolution of a recognizable set of discursive practices indicates a step towards artistic 'specialisation' in the field of literary production.[73] In a similar manner, the flaunting of *Petron*'s intertextuality in the preface and the reference to certain Surrealist ur-texts in Sykes Davies's handwritten notes serve to affirm the movement's fundamental unity and its ability to operate across geographical and linguistic boundaries.

The preoccupation with plants and bosky landscapes in *Petron*—for example in the passage lifted from *Madame Putiphar*—points to a widespread Surrealist fascination with organic forms, but it also resonates with the marked Surrealist preference for the colour green. *Petron* opens with the

[70] Davies, *Petron,* p. 22.

[71] Peter Nicholls, 'Surrealism in England', in *The Cambridge History of Twentieth-Century English Literature,* ed. by Laura Marcus and Peter Nicholls (Cambridge: Cambridge University Press, 2004), pp. 396–416 (p. 407).

[72] PSD, Excerpts from *Petron* with handwritten notes, 8/44. The original French passage is in Pétrus Borel, *Madame Putiphar* [1839], 2 vols (Paris: Léon Willem, 1877), II, pp. 26–27.

[73] Raymond Williams, *Culture* (Glasgow: Fontana, 1981), pp. 68–71.

vista of 'a landscape of interminable lawns, a tedious champaign diversified by groves, green savannah'.[74] Other English Surrealists joined in during the mid-1930s, for example Herbert Read whose *The Green Child* (1935) had been composed, Read claimed, as an exercise in automatic writing, or the painter John Banting who for much of the 1930s dyed his hair green (though he was 'not the only one' to do so, as his friend Eileen Agar later recalled).[75] Green, rather than the communist red, was the self-chosen colour of French Surrealism: Breton frequently donned green tuxedos and was wearing a bright green dinner jacket for the opening of the London Surrealist Exhibition in 1936; Breton's wife, Jacqueline Lamba, liked to paint her nails in the same colour ('There are also hands | long white hands with nails of fresh greenery', Benjamin Péret's 1934 poem 'Making Feet and Hands' recalled).[76] Green was also the colour which Roger Roughton chose for the cover of the 1936 'Surrealist Double Number' of *Contemporary Poetry and Prose.* And Gascoyne, too, contributed to this fascination: 'Have you ever paused to consider why grass is green | Yes greener at least it is said than the man in the moon', his poem 'Cubical Domes' from 1936 muses; and his piece 'The End is Near the Beginning' (1935) remembered 'the eglantine | Growing around the edge of the green lake'.[77]

There is reason to wonder whether English Surrealists were actually neurotically obsessed with hair, curtains, and greenery, or whether they had inherited this fixation from French Surrealism—an obsession, as it were, with the tropes of the movement rather than with the unconscious psychological mechanisms which generated them. The number and range of borrowings suggest that the works of many English Surrealists in the 1930s fed on a strong current of pre-established images. Rosalind Krauss has observed with a view to avant-garde 'styles' that the same rhetorical resources which function as the '*sign* of spontaneity' can be 'prepared for through the utmost calculation, and in this sense spontaneity [becomes] the most fakable of signifieds'.[78] To note the conspicuous recurrence of

[74] Sykes Davies, *Petron*, p. 3.

[75] David Thistlewood, *Herbert Read: Formlessness and Form* (London: Routledge, 1984), p. 22; Agar, p. 115.

[76] See Agar, p. 115; Benjamin Péret, 'Making Feet and Hands' [1934], in Gascoyne, *Verse Translations*, pp. 55–56 (p. 56).

[77] David Gascoyne, 'The Cubical Domes' [1936], in *Collected Poems*, p. 56; 'The End is Near the Beginning' [1935], in *Collected Poems*, p. 29.

[78] Rosalind Krauss, *The Originality of the Avant-Garde and Other Modernist Myths* (Cambridge, MA: MIT Press, 1985), p. 167, emphasis in the original. My chapter does not touch on the question of how 'spontaneous' French Surrealism had been in the 1920s or when it ceased to be so.

certain metaphors in poems by English Surrealists is not to insist that these works are the outcome of a deliberate, non-automatic construction process according to a set iconography or that certain poems are 'better' for their relative independence from such models. It does however help to bring into focus the internal workings of an established Surrealist style whose covert pressures English Surrealism was invariably encountering in the mid- and late 1930s. Like the river in Read's *The Green Child* which flows back towards its source, English Surrealism drew for some of its imaginative strength on the supposedly pure energies of the French Surrealist movement.

Like Gascoyne, Sykes Davies was striving for a Surrealist style that was particularly 'authentic', and one of the marginal notes in his copy of *Petron* states that a particular passage is 'presented very purely and well made'. However, the kind of stylistic 'purity' towards which *Petron* aspires also differs in some respects from that envisioned by Gascoyne. While Gascoyne took purity to reside in a particular method of composition, automatic writing, Sykes Davies believed that artistic purity could be achieved by locating the artwork in a distinct (Surrealist) tradition. Sykes Davies's poems in *Experiment* had drawn on Greek and Roman myth to create a similar sense of cultural continuity, and his attempt to cement the idea of a tradition of Surrealist writing culminated in his contribution to Herbert Read's edited volume *Surrealism* in 1936 which stated that contemporary Surrealist work was able to build on the writings of numerous English authors, ranging from Shakespeare through Milton and Wordsworth to T. S. Eliot.[79] Many English Surrealists were suspicious of Sykes Davies's 'well-made' type of Surrealism. Gascoyne, in a review for *New Verse*, thought that *Petron* was 'an ingeniously manipulated puppet, made to dance to a fantastic tune that Mr Davies once overheard in a library'.[80] John Davenport agreed that his friend Sykes Davies was playing a carefully rehearsed role: 'Have you seen *Petron*, published by Dent?', he noted in a letter to Julian Trevelyan: 'HSD as surrealist. N.v.g. [not very good].'[81] The process of artistic crafting that produced *Petron* is most conspicuously illustrated by one of Sykes Davies's shorter prose poems. First published in *Contemporary*

[79] Hugh Sykes Davies, 'Surrealism at this Time and Place', in *Surrealism*, ed. by Herbert Read (London: Faber and Faber, 1936), pp. 119–68.

[80] David Gascoyne, 'On Spontaneity', *New Verse*, 18 (December 1935), p. 19.

[81] JTA, Correspondence with John Davenport, Box 4, Uncat. letter from John Davenport to Julian Trevelyan, 15 November 1935.

Poetry and Prose in 1936, the text 'Poem' consists of six paragraphs, each of which rewrites, with some alterations, the same underlying sentence:

> In the stump of the old tree, where the heart has rotted out, there is a hole the length of a man's arm [. . .]
> in the stumps of old trees, where the hearts have rotted out, there are holes the length of a man's arm [. . .]
> in the stumps of old trees with rotten hearts, where the rain gathers [. . .]
> in the stumps of old trees where the rain gathers [. . .]
> in the stumps of old trees where the hearts have rotted out there are holes the length of a man's arm [. . .]
> in the stumps of old trees where the hearts have rotted out there are deep holes and dank pools [. . .][82]

The prose poem reads like a stylistic exercise, the deliberate poetic honing of a particular dream-vision, and it clearly runs counter to the idea of an unpremeditated 'automatic' writing.

It was the espousal of certain stylistic modes, rather than an inherent inability to engage with the pressures of the decade, which narrowed down the range of English Surrealism's rhetorical options. Gascoyne's adoption of the voices of Eluard and Rimbaud in his 1936 notebook in order to convey his own revolutionary enthusiasm is a case in point, but Sykes Davies, too, became aware of the internal pressures generated by established literary styles, of their gravitation towards a discursive realm of Ricardian pseudo-statements. In an essay from 1936 he upbraided Gertrude Stein for adhering to a dated kind of avant-gardism that belonged to the 1920s, rather than the 1930s. Particularly damaging, Sykes Davies noted, was Stein's refusal to 'accept the limitations of her own style'.[83] Her punctuation and distorted sentences 'gave pleasure' in the 1920s when they were 'used in prose with no rational end, for purely aesthetic purposes', but they were 'adapt[ing]' themselves 'very ill to the making of statements with meaning' in the new decade (755). Evoking Richards's stark dichotomy between the referential and poetic uses of language, these remarks associate the idea of poetic pseudo-statements specifically with a mode of high-modernist writing. In similar fashion a series of articles on 'Modern Poetry' which Sykes Davies wrote in 1933 while working on *Petron* registered English Surrealism's artistic belatedness as a significant limitation of its political-revolutionary reach, but it also contained some of the movement's most anxious reflections on the decade's new,

[82] Hugh Sykes Davies, 'Poem', in *Contemporary Poetry and Prose*, 7 (November 1936), p. 129.

[83] Hugh Sykes Davies, Review of Gertrude Stein's *Narration*, *The Criterion*, 15 (July 1936), 752–55 (p. 752).

politicized poetry. The second article in the series, entitled 'The Problem of Beauty and Sincerity', observes that 'the modern poet pursues simplicity and sincerity' rather than the aestheticist ideal of 'beauty': 'This stress on simplicity and sincerity is to be found in the critical writings of Mr. Eliot, of Mr. Yeats, of Mr. Read, and others', but it is 'especially' marked in 'the writings of Mr. Auden and the group of poets who have associated themselves with him, such as Mr. Day Lewis, Mr. Spender, Mr. Madge'.[84] Sykes Davies had been among the students who flocked to I. A. Richards's lectures in Cambridge, and in 1933 he became a Fellow of St John's College, located across the road from Magdalene College where Richards was teaching. The invocation of 'sincerity' in the *Listener* essay indicates Richards's influence, pitting stylistic 'simplicity' against the auto-referential system of a particular poetic style.[85] The other articles in the series frequently return to the idea of poetic 'sincerity'. Auden's 1930 *Poems* started a 'new movement', the fifth essay observes, and the 'results' of that movement

> are to be found in such anthologies as *New Signatures* and *New Country*. It is quite clear that Mr. Auden himself has moved rather away from Mr. Eliot's way of writing, and is rapidly becoming more easy to understand, likely to appeal to a wider public.[86]

Sykes Davies's *Listener* articles lack Gascoyne's awareness that Auden's 'sincerity'—with its hortatory addresses to the reader and its references to 'strikes, factories, the armaments camp'—was itself the product of careful rhetorical crafting. Instead, they identify the self-referentiality of poetic pseudo-statements exclusively with the modernist avant-gardes, placing Surrealist caprice in collective opposition to the political poetry of the decade.

Gascoyne's links to the *Experiment* circle in the early 1930s suggest that he was conscious of the kinds of problems posed by Richards's theories and of Sykes Davies's application of these ideas to the legacy of twenties modernism. And even while Gascoyne's writings do not generally indicate a strong inclination towards theoretical argument, the dilemmas which the *Listener* essays identified as affecting thirties avant-gardism have a bearing that extends well beyond Sykes Davies's own writings. A particularly clear recognition of the literary belatedness of English Surrealism and the problems to which this belatedness gave rise can be found in Humphrey

[84] Hugh Sykes Davies, 'The Enjoyment of Modern Poetry II: The Problem of Beauty and Sincerity', *The Listener*, 9 August 1933, 217–18 (p. 217).

[85] See the preceding chapter for a discussion of Richards's notion of poetic 'sincerity'.

[86] Hugh Sykes Davies, 'The Enjoyment of Modern Poetry VI: Reading the Modern Poets', *The Listener*, 20 September 1933, 435–36 (p. 436).

Jennings's review of *Surrealism*, Read's 1936 essay volume to which Sykes Davies had contributed. Jennings's review pointed to the ten-year gap that could make the aesthetic vanguard of the 1920s look, in the 1930s, like a literary passéism. Surrealism, he insisted, was slowly hardening into a manageable stylistic option. 'It is the next generation that *believes* the results' of an artistic movement, Jennings comments:

> So it is that the enduring statements of [the Surrealists] are due to their unquestioning acceptance of *all* the conditions of the moment: forgetting all 'beliefs' preceding the picture, which would deny the promise of the unknown. But so deadly agile is man's mind that it is possible, even easy, to form a series of 'truths' and 'loyalties' which produce imitations of the creative powers of non-selectivity; forgetting that Surrealism is only a means and believing in the 'universal truth' of it; or again, still relying on aestheticism to the rules of which Surrealism has now been added.[87]

One of Gascoyne's central aims in *Short Survey* was precisely to refute the idea that Surrealism drew on a set of canonical texts and a codified style: 'Surrealism is *not* a style', the book pointed out, 'Surrealism is by no means simply a recipe, or "specific method of creation".'[88] In a related vein, literary historians usually stress the alleged 'formlessness' of Surrealist writings and their ability to deal with the inchoate matter of history. Frank Kermode's distinction between the 'palaeo-modernism' of the 1920s and 'neo-modernist anti-traditionalism and anti-formalism' has proved particularly influential in this regard, as has Peter Bürger's parallel distinction between 'modernism' and the 'avant-garde'.[89] 'Avant-garde movements', Bürger states, 'did not develop a style. There is no such thing as [. . .] a surrealist style.'[90] Critics such as Ihab Hassan, Steven Connor, and Tyrus Miller have similarly affirmed that Surrealism is marked by an engagement with the entropic and the Bataillean *informe*.[91] And yet, as a late-comer to the scene

[87] Humphrey Jennings, Review of *Surrealism*, *Contemporary Poetry and Prose*, 8 (December 1936), 167–68 (p. 168), emphasis in the original.

[88] Gascoyne, *Short Survey*, p. 66, emphasis in the original.

[89] Frank Kermode, *Continuities* (London: Routledge, 1968), esp. pp. 8–16.

[90] Peter Bürger, *The Theory of the Avant-Garde* [1974], trans. by Michael Shaw (Minneapolis: University of Minnesota Press, 1984), p. 18. For a critical assessment of this position, see Andreas Huyssen's *After the Great Divide: Modernism, Mass Culture, Postmodernism* (Basingstoke: Macmillan, 1986), pp. 4–15.

[91] Ihab Hassan, 'Interlude: From "Pataphysics to Surrealism"', in *The Dismemberment of Orpheus: Toward a Postmodern Literature* (Oxford: Oxford University Press, 1971), pp. 48–79; Tyrus Miller, *Late Modernism: Politics, Fiction, and the Arts Between the World Wars* (Berkeley: University of California Press, 1999), esp. pp. 35–42; Steven Connor has commented on the 'terrifying formlessness' of David Gascoyne's poems ('British Surrealist Poetry', p. 172). See also Martin Jay, 'Modernism and the Retreat from Form', in *Force Fields: Between Intellectual History and Cultural Critique* (London: Routledge, 1993), pp. 147–57.

of experimental modernism, English Surrealism suffered the notoriously hard fate of literary belatedness, the 'ten-years-belated imitation of Paris' identified by Madge in an early number of *New Verse*.[92] For the English Surrealist group, as Julian Trevelyan noted in the 1950s, 'the tenets of orthodox Surrealism' could indeed be 'more of a bondage than a support'.[93]

'BRITTLE GHOSTS': ENGLISH SURREALISM IN THE LATE 1930s

Surrealism's perceived inability to support the political revolution had been the topic of intense debate ever since the late 1920s, and such publicity meant that the movement's difficulties in negotiating a radical political position during the 1930s came under greater scrutiny—and met with more hostility—than analogous attempts by other thirties writers. There is ample evidence that, in the eyes of many members of the literary left, politics and Surrealist writing were drifting apart. One instance of this trend is Surrealism's disappearance from the pages of *New Verse* in the second half of 1936, coinciding with the outbreak of the Spanish Civil War. *New Verse*'s 1936 Christmas number promised (under the title 'Honest Doubt') the publication of a questionnaire that had been sent out to major English Surrealist writers. The questions, penned by Auden under a pseudonym,[94] were divided into two discrete subsets, 'aesthetic' and 'political'. Most of the questions in the first category, concerning procedures of Surrealist literary composition, addressed familiar points: 'Is genuine surrealist writing always and absolutely automatic, and never consciously worked over? [. . .] [When] does it cease to be surrealist?' The second set of queries, by contrast, sought to clarify, once and for all, the relation of Surrealism to communism: if 'the surrealist rejects absolutely the use of reason and of the conscious faculties, [. . .] how does he square his position with communism?'. The 'authoritative answers' of the Surrealists were never printed 'owing to illness', and by the time the first issue of the New Series of *New Verse* was printed in February 1937 the project had been dropped. The 1936 Christmas number of the magazine had made the Surrealists the butt of one last literary joke. The number featured a few 'admirable results of surrealist method unconsciously used [. . .] by an ex-regular soldier, and used to advertise his boot and shoe business' as well

[92] Madge, 'Surrealism for the English', p. 14.

[93] Julian Trevelyan, *Indigo Days* [1957] (Aldershot: Scolar Press, 1996), p. 77.

[94] Monroe K. Spears, *The Poetry of W. H. Auden: The Disenchanted Island* (Oxford: Oxford University Press, 1963), p. 76.

as 'other documents from the same id'.[95] Six months into the Spanish Civil War and only seven months after the closing of the International Surrealist Exhibition in London, the English Surrealists had all but disappeared from the literary-political stage.

The Surrealist Exhibition, held in June and July 1936 in London, is frequently presented as a dashing display of Surrealism on English soil which signalled, in Raymond Williams's terminology, the emergence of an esoteric 'style' onto the stage of a 'collective public manifestation'.[96] But the veneer of the Exhibition concealed the fact that by 1936 Surrealism on both sides of the Channel was profoundly divided on its artistic and political goals. As Gascoyne recalled in the 1980s, the organizers of the Exhibition were careful to hide the 'beginning of the rift' that was fissuring French Surrealism. Eluard had sent a letter to the English Surrealists in April 1936 which announced his definitive break with Breton: 'The Eluards didn't arrive in London till half-way through the Exhibition to deliver a lecture. Few people realized at the time Eluard had broken with Breton after 18 years.'[97] The reason for Eluard's expulsion from the French Surrealist group had been his growing involvement in the French Communist Party, and while his exclusion at the hands of Breton was only made public in 1938, it was hardly a secret among the inner circle of Surrealists.

The official magazine of the Exhibition, the *International Surrealist Bulletin,* was published by the London Exhibition's organizational committee (Sykes Davies, Gascoyne, Jennings, Read, Roland Penrose), and it became instrumental to the staging of the Exhibition as a 'collective public manifestation'. The publication examined English Surrealism's potential for political intervention, but it remained silent about the recent artistic and political disputes within the movement. Calling for 'immediate activities', the introduction to the *Bulletin* ('The Situation in England') identifies fundamental social and political ills of English society such as the strong position of the Anglo-Catholic Church, 'Capitalism', and 'a tradition of individualism [. . .] among artists and intellectuals'. The article seeks to repoliticize Surrealism by presenting it as a form of collective action and it specifically takes issue with the 'English belief' that 'even the intelligent and revolutionary artists have been in the habit of thinking that they can best work alone, in a group of one': 'we shall put an end to individualistic anarchy'.[98] However, the article begs the question of how the

[95] 'A Terrible Battle Fought on the Fifty–Twelfth Day of Rotten Sticks, and Other Documents from the Same Id', *New Verse*, 23 (Christmas 1936), 1–7 (pp. 1, 7).

[96] For celebratory views of the Exhibition as a '*succès de scandal*', see *Visiting Picasso: The Notebooks and Letters of Roland Penrose*, ed. by Elizabeth Cowling (London: Thames & Hudson, 2006), pp. 24–25; and Michel Remy, *Surrealism in Britain* (Aldershot: Ashgate, 1999), pp. 73–100. For Williams's terminology, see *Culture*, pp. 68–70.

[97] DGC, Notebook 1985–87, 14/269.

[98] 'Situation in England', pp. 1, 4.

erratic energies of Surrealist writing can be tied to a political agenda, and it closes anticlimactically on a note of deferral: 'A constructive programme for immediate Surrealist activity is already taking shape. We shall explain our social and political position at the earliest possible moment. Numerous discussions and demonstrations will take place during the coming autumn.'[99] The ambitious plans to resuscitate the Marxist aspirations of English Surrealism following Breton's calls for artistic purity were stunted when the Spanish Civil War broke out only a fortnight after the closing of the Surrealist Exhibition on 4 July 1936.

The tendency to see the poetic and political impulses of Surrealist writing as opposed intensified during the early months of the Spanish Civil War as historical pressures seemed to make the taking of political sides inevitable. A few months after the outbreak of the war, Roughton was holding forth about the necessity of *engagé* art. 'There is no longer a fence for intellectuals to sit on', his editorial in *Contemporary Poetry and Prose* from October 1936 ('Fascism Murders Art') declared after the murder of Federico García Lorca by Spanish fascists: 'they must choose between fascism and anti-fascism; and magazines of modern poetry can no longer pretend that they are Something Apart. [. . .] Fascist or anti-fascist: which is it to be?'. The decade's mounting pressures came on too quickly for English Surrealism and they prevented the movement from putting forward a unified political stance which would transcend the diversity of opinions besetting it. Alick West's stricture in a *Left Review* issue of July 1936 is representative of a climate of opinion which advocated the use of literature as a weapon in the struggle against fascism. 'If the surrealists remain true to their negation of bourgeois society', West closed his spiteful 'Surréalisme in Literature', 'they must, like Aragon, become the poets and writers of Socialism.'[100] As Surrealism became immersed in the political antagonisms of the decade, the tension between its perceived inward-looking stance and outward-looking communism became ever more acute. Madge and Roughton were leaning towards orthodox communism in the mid-1930s, and Gascoyne went to Barcelona with fellow-Surrealist Roland Penrose in the autumn of 1936 to participate in the Republican propaganda effort. One year later Gascoyne was prepared to renounce the idea of poetic purity, declaring that there was going to be 'no more themeless improvisation, no more autonomous lyricism, no more "pure effect"' for him.[101]

[99] Ibid., p. 4.

[100] Alick West, 'Surréalisme in Literature', p. viii. T. A. Jackson, one of the longest-standing members of the British Communist Party, seconded West in the pages of *Left Review* one month later, 'Marxism: Pragmatism: Surrealism: A Comment for Herbert Read', *Left Review*, 2/11 (July 1936), 565–67.

[101] David Gascoyne, *Journal 1937–1939* (London: Enitharmon, 1978), p. 22.

The Communist Party's Popular Front policy which began to gain hold around 1935 and 1936 initially seemed to facilitate exchanges across ideological divides and to make communist ideology accessible to artistic formulations that lay outside the officially decreed aesthetic of socialist realism. However, in the words of George Orwell, 'by 1937 the whole of the intelligentsia was mentally at war. Left-wing thought had narrowed down to "anti-Fascism", i.e. to a negative'.[102] The stark binary rhetoric of the decade was largely pressed on English Surrealism from without, and it stalled the movement's efforts to cope with two conflicting demands: the endeavour to translate its writing into a form of propaganda and the attempt to sound the retreat into the Ivory Tower. Sykes Davies had recognized these inherent tensions and contradictions—between retreatism, on the one hand, and 'sincerity', on the other—early on in the decade, but the history of English Surrealism in the 1930s suggests the movement's inability to pull the two conflicting positions together in the medium of literary discourse. As Sykes Davies recalled later, Surrealism's latent contradictions came to the fore when the decade drew to a violent close. He had 'spent some time in reflection' in 1937 and 1938 'about Surrealism, the Spanish War, the even bigger war that was coming to us':

> When I found my friends still at their happenings, their private views at midnight and so on, I urgently wanted to warn them that the game was up, that playing with bright images was over. The images had turned around. The new *Ars Poetica* was to be the art of cursing, and we had to learn it.[103]

One of the poems (unpublished at the time) which Sykes Davies wrote in order to 'warn' his fellow Surrealists adopts a more colloquial and accessible tone than his densely allusive Surrealist pieces. The poem's rhymed stanzas offer a variation on the rhyme scheme and rhythm of Auden's *The Orators* (1932) and 'Letter to Lord Byron' (1937):

> I thought you talked too much, and found your verse
> A kind of Nero's fiddling, if no worse.
> Too plain, for you, the face of real danger.
> You wanted to stay pretty in your anger.
> I, waiting for some useful word to come,
> Grew taciturn at first, and finally dun.

[102] George Orwell, 'Inside the Whale' [1940], in *The Complete Works of George Orwell*, 20 vols (London: Seckler and Warburg, 1986–98), XII: *A Patriot After All, 1940–1941*, ed. by Peter Davison (1998), pp. 86–115 (p. 104).

[103] Hugh Sykes Davies, 'An Epilaugh for Surrealism', *Times Literary Supplement*, 13 January 1978, p. 34.

We came at last to noise, dirt, pain and fear,
And all these rank realities of war
Give body and savour to your prettiness
You'll raise some fine crops on this bloody mess
That yields me nothing, was already staled
With forethought, speeches and campaigns that failed.
[. . .]

You'll miss, my friend, these momentary gusts
Of solid impulse, but their brittle ghosts
Will hover between the paper and your pen –
The fighters, fitters, fettlers, solid men
And skilful women who grew hard and real
With common purposes in Iron and Steel.[104]

The poem taunts the English Surrealists for their complacent and 'pretty' romantic 'anger' which pales in the face of war's brutal realities. Moreover, the figure of the (presumably masculine) 'friend' addressed in the text recalls the central role which homosocial intimacy had played in sustaining the predominantly male groups of Surrealists in France and in England. The poem contrasts this idea of an intimate audience of like-minded 'friends', in which the policing of poetic purity could develop into a major concern, with a more diverse revolutionary collective of 'solid men | And skilful women' that moves beyond the strong masculine bent of Surrealist sociability. The 'brittle ghosts' of Surrealism—a reference to the movement's idiosyncratic fantasies as well as to the inherited elements of its style—are dispelled by the call for a more 'sincere' writing capable of addressing human suffering during wartime. Sykes Davies's wholesale dismissal of Surrealism after 1936 was partly the result of his own personal disillusionment, and it reflects an exclusionary thinking that was indebted to Richards's theories as much as to the ubiquitous left-wing rhetoric of 'taking sides'. His position glosses over the diversity of surrealist writing either before or after 1936, and it is precisely this kind of facile rejection of Surrealism as fundamentally apolitical that has shaped the still-dominant critical narrative about English Surrealism.[105]

Upon the outbreak of the Second World War, the remaining members of the English group issued a moving statement, titled 'Fight Hitler We Must':

> No dream is worse than the reality in which we live. No reality is as good as our dreams. The enemies of desire and hope have risen in violence. They have

[104] Ibid.

[105] Leo Mellor has also questioned this conventionalized narrative, calling it the 'teleology which we use to analyse' English Surrealism. See Leo Mellor, *Reading the Ruins: Modernism, Bombsites and British Culture* (Cambridge: Cambridge University Press, 2011), p. 93.

> grown among us, murdering, oppressing and destroying. Now sick with their poison we are threatened with extinction.[106]

'Life had caught up with Surrealism', Julian Trevelyan noted of this failure to salvage subjectivity from the crushing force of historical events.[107] The belief in poetry's ability to change society is as much part of the literary-historical myth of the 1930s as the demise of that belief in the wake of the Spanish Civil War and the outbreak of the Second World War. English Surrealists shared in the former, but the sobering recognition that (in Auden's oft-cited phrase) poetry might fail to 'be | A midwife to society' came to them earlier than to many other left-wing poets of the decade.[108] There is in the ranks of the Surrealists little of the clamant communism, the declarations of purpose, or the shrill republicanism that animate other texts from the 1930s. There is also no extreme political volte-face like that of Stephen Spender, who had chastised Aragon for the ferocious propaganda of 'Front Rouge' in *New Verse* in 1933, but was prepared to defend Aragon's adoption of hard-line communism in the same magazine only five years later on the grounds that it had been undertaken 'in public penance for his surrealist days'.[109] As I have pointed out, the political impetus of English Surrealism—its search for a mode of political intervention outside the confines of Agitprop art—was denigrated by more orthodox left-wingers. Yet English Surrealism's belatedness as an avant-garde movement, and its special difficulty in navigating a course between esoteric poetic play and the public manner of speech demanded by communism, also meant that it was more apprehensive of the ambivalences and of the dead-ends of the decade's high-strung political ambitions for poetry. The disillusionment which followed in the wake of the 1930s' high hopes for poetry was attenuated in the case of the English Surrealists by early doubts regarding poetry's political efficacy.

[106] 'Fight Hitler We Must', *London Bulletin*, 18–20 (1940), p. 1.

[107] Trevelyan, p. 80.

[108] W. H. Auden, *New Year Letter* (London: Faber and Faber, 1941), p. 19.

[109] Stephen Spender, 'The Left Wing Orthodoxy', *New Verse*, 31–32 (Autumn 1938), 12–16 (p. 15).

4

Social Facts and Poetic Authority

The Political Aesthetic of Mass-Observation

Mass-Observation functions as a focal lens in the context of thirties writing, reflecting some of the decade's central artistic and political ambitions and spelling out their inherent tensions. The project's conjunction of diverse strands of activity—artistic, sociological, and anthropological, as well as Marxist, democratic, and even (one critic has claimed) 'totalitarian'[1]—has been described as a 'confusion of methods and goals', albeit one that offers 'a complex example of the confusions of young intellectuals at the time'.[2] The anthropological motivation of Mass-Observation—most commonly associated with Tom Harrisson—has been amply documented and analysed. By contrast, the complexity of Humphrey Jennings's and Charles Madge's early artistic hopes for the movement has generally been neglected or belittled in critical accounts. Much recent scholarship has contributed to this trend by subordinating the enterprise's artistic motives to its stakes in anthropological analysis, on the one hand, and in spokesmanship on behalf of the masses, on the other. Departing from this trend, the present chapter examines the underlying hermeneutic problems of the project's early phase: questions concerning the scientific 'readability' of the gathered material as well as the relationship between a writing done by the (amateur) masses and an editorial reworking performed by the (professional) few.[3] It is against the backdrop of Mass-Observation's early artistic aspirations, I suggest, that the movement's anthropological and political interests begin to emerge more clearly. The plans for Mass-Observation predated the abdication crisis of 1936, and it is possible to reconstruct Jennings's and Madge's early vision of Mass-Observation's artistic reach by paying special attention to texts which are seemingly located on the

[1] James Buzard, 'Mass-Observation, Modernism, and Auto-ethnography', *Modernism/Modernity*, 4 (1997), 93–122 (p. 101).

[2] Samuel Hynes, *The Auden Generation: Literature and Politics in England in the 1930s* (London: The Bodley Head, 1976), p. 279.

[3] Tom Harrisson and Charles Madge, *Mass-Observation* (London: Muller, 1937), p. 41.

project's periphery and which often predate the movement's important book publications from 1937.

The ambiguous status of facts in Mass-Observation is at the centre of this chapter. Madge's early writings suggest that the concept of 'poetic facts'—closely linked to the elusive idea of a 'popular poetry' by, for, and about the people—was intended to bridge the gap between scientific description and poetic discourse, between statements and pseudo-statements. The central question for early Mass-Observation was how these facts ought to be collected and presented. In response to this problem, Jennings and Madge solicited 'day surveys' from volunteer Observers across the nation in the spring of 1937.[4] As I suggest, the anonymized reader reports which I. A. Richards collected from his students in his practical criticism lectures can be read as an early template for these day surveys. Richards's teachings provided a basis for Madge's and Jennings's early involvement in Mass-Observation, and they composed the terrain on which both could begin to formulate their own visions of the project. In contrast to Richards's venture, Mass-Observation was intended to authenticate, rather than to contest, subjective experience. Yet one corollary of the project's revolutionary ambitions was the impulse, inherited from Richards's *Practical Criticism* (1929), to subject the Observers' day surveys to a therapeutic editorial rewriting. Jennings and Madge were turning to modes of experience which had not been poeticized, but they were also reworking these experiences to fit extraneous political and aesthetic rationales, above all Jennings's Surrealist and utopian hopes for an emancipation of subjectivity from social constraints and Madge's socialist-realist attempt to make the present moment historically transparent. As a consequence, the examples of 'popular poetry' offered by Jennings and Madge privilege metaphorically over-determined facts over the messier data which Mass-Observation was trawling from the depths of English society, and they continue to be troublingly bound up with the bourgeois idea of the poet.

The general problems which beset criticism of Mass-Observation also apply to the present reading. Above all, the habit of Jennings, Madge, and Harrisson to sign letters and articles as if they had been produced jointly can make it difficult to determine the positions of the individual signatories. It seems clear, however, that such formal displays of unity

[4] Critics have acknowledged Mass-Observation's day surveys as the enterprise's major innovation in the field of auto-ethnography. See, for example, Jeremy MacClancy, 'Brief Encounter: The Meeting, in Mass-Observation, of British Surrealism and Popular Anthropology', *Journal of the Royal Anthropological Institute*, 1/3 (1995), 495–512. The term 'autoethnographic' has been given wider critical currency by James Buzard. For a rich theorization and wider application of the term, see his 'On Auto-Ethnographic Authority', *The Yale Journal of Criticism*, 16/1 (2003), 61–91.

never reflected a genuine consensus about the enterprise's methods or objectives. Jennings, for example, was irritated to find his name under the programmatic letter ('Anthropology at Home') which Madge and Harrisson published in the *New Statesman and Nation* in January 1937.[5] There is also the related difficulty of keeping Madge's and Jennings's views of Mass-Observation free from the propagandistic zeal with which Harrisson advertised the anthropological and sociological side of the project. This problem is compounded by the fact that Jennings, who thought about the enterprise's artistic potential more than anyone else, rarely wrote about his ideas in direct connection with Mass-Observation.

I. A. RICHARDS AND EARLY MASS-OBSERVATION: READER REPORT TO DAY SURVEY

Mass-Observation participated in wider thirties debates about the relationship between fact and fiction, objectivity and subjectivity, yet Jennings's and Madge's early approach to these problems can be seen specifically as a response to Ricardian assumptions about the nature of poetic language. Madge had come under Richards's influence well before he arrived at Cambridge. He had received *Principles of Literary Criticism* in January 1929 through his subscription to the *Times* Book Club, and the book had had an instant effect on him. A letter to his mother reports that 'the real event' of the day 'has been a mental one, the arrival, and by this time the partial consumption' of Richards's book. *Principles*, the letter records, 'engrossed me and stimulated a great deal of thought. [. . .] Not much work this evening, but how it sinks into significance [sic] compared with what I have been reading'.[6] The central distinction proposed in Richards's book—between the propositional-scientific and the emotive-poetic uses of language—continued to occupy Madge. One reason for his particular interest in Richards's theories, and for the puzzlement they were causing him, may be found in his biography: while still a student at Winchester College in the late 1920s, Madge thought that his true talents lay in science and was profoundly disappointed when his scientific career at Cambridge faltered; it was only at the recommendation of Richards, who became his tutor, that he decided to switch over to Moral Sciences and English literature.[7] Madge's unpublished diaries and notebooks from the 1920s and early 1930s indicate that Mass-Observation's attempt to import

[5] CMA, Ts autobiography, Box 2/1, pp. 68–71.

[6] CMA, Correspondence with Barbara Madge, Box 5/2, Uncat. letter from Charles Madge to Barbara Madge, 22 January 1929.

[7] CMA, Ts autobiography, Box 2/1, p. 33.

the factual language of science into the pseudo-statements of poetry cut across Richards's critical premises. Many of these reflections take the form of loose jottings: 'The important thing is that it should not be necessary for poets to make an absolute disjunction between poetry and science.'[8] But there are also more sustained thoughts about the Ricardian antinomy of poetry and science: a fifty-page long essay on Charles Darwin from 1936 observes that 'the great scientists have certain poetic faculties and the greatest poets have certain scientific faculties; the inferiority of lesser poets and scientists consists precisely in their lack of these complementary faculties.'[9] Darwin, Madge notes, was 'one of the great poet-scientists of materialism' who undertook 'the task of exposition not on behalf of science, nor on behalf of poetry, but on behalf of that expansion of humanity which I believe to be attainable through revolutionary marxism'. Madge's artistic ambitions of the mid-1930s were crucially informed by his communist convictions, and I will in a moment turn to his idea of a 'Marxist' style as the mediator between scientific description and poetic writing.

Humphrey Jennings had also come under the early influence of Richards. Even though Richards was away from Cambridge during Jennings's first year as an undergraduate, between March 1926 and September 1927, he later became his academic supervisor as Jennings embarked on doctoral work about Thomas Gray.[10] Jennings shared Madge's sense that the pseudo-statements of poetry were in need of fresh material from other domains of knowledge, and clues to his early interest in Mass-Observation can be inferred from his literary reviews and essays on aesthetic topics. In a *New Verse* review from December 1935, for instance, he complained about the self-involved and 'over-systematized' nature of Eliot's and Auden's writings: 'The problem now is how to present more of the world', the article exhorts Eliot and Auden, 'neither poet is presenting sufficient of "the known world" to justify men in the world regarding their works as of practical value of any kind.'[11] Jennings's dissatisfaction with the perceived mannerisms of French and English Surrealism is of special importance to his initial interest in Mass-Observation. A six-month stay in Paris in 1930 with his wife Cecily gave Jennings the longed-for opportunity to study Surrealist art at first hand. An early letter to his Cambridge friend Julian Trevelyan, suggests his disappointment with the movement's recent artistic output, as well as his hope for a new artistic departure: 'saw masses of paintings: as you will discover Surréalisme is dead already and the future

[8] CMA, Prose from the 1930s, Box 19/3, Undated ms notes [1935(?)].

[9] CMA, Essays from mid-1930s, Box 19/5, Uncat. ts essay 'Charles Darwin' [1936].

[10] Kevin Jackson, *Humphrey Jennings* (London: Picador, 2004), p. 68.

[11] Humphrey Jennings, 'Eliot and Auden and Shakespeare', *New Verse*, 18 (December 1935), 4–7 (pp. 5, 6).

seems to be ours.'[12] The hope to reform Surrealism by re-emphasizing the movement's attentiveness to the everyday, as well as its revolutionary and emancipatory potential, was carried over into Jennings's early involvement with Mass-Observation. Jennings and Madge's enterprise promised to open art onto reality, signalling a shift away from what they perceived to be the fixed stylistic 'purity' of Surrealism.

The day surveys produced by hundreds of Mass-Observers from February 1937 onwards can be read as a corrective to the reader reports which Richards had solicited from his students. Kevin Jackson has pointed out that it would have been 'uncharacteristically lazy and incurious' of Jennings not to take part in Richards's lectures on practical criticism.[13] And Madge, although he arrived at Cambridge too late to participate in the lectures, was certainly familiar with the collection of reader reports published in *Practical Criticism*. In analogy to Richards's student reports, Mass-Observation's day surveys were designed to offer close readings of the 'texture' (in Madge and Jennings's phrase) of social life.[14] At the same time, these surveys challenged the pedagogical methods put forward in *Practical Criticism*, especially Richards's spurious claims for textual objectivity which attributed ontological priority to the 'poem itself'. While Richards had solicited written responses from his students in order to show how they distorted and misread the poems in question, Mass-Observation's 'close-ups'[15] of contemporary society were meant to authenticate subjective experience. 'Feelings', Jennings reflected in his day survey of 12 April 1937, are 'part of the incident from my point of view'.[16]

Early Mass-Observation sought to put Richards's critical and pedagogical practice of close reading back onto its feet by stressing the subjective experience of social reality, rather than its 'objective' analysis by the trained expert. Madge had already been questioning the objectivist understanding of facts early in the 1930s. One unpublished essay faults 'modern science' with 'ignoring subjective consciousness',[17] while another piece, written

[12] JTA, Correspondence with Humphrey Jennings, Box 2, Uncat. letter from Humphrey Jennings to Julian Trevelyan, 20 July 1930. For Jennings's turn away from Surrealism, see David Chaney and Michael Pickering, 'Authorship in Documentary: Sociology as an Art Form in Mass Observation', in *Documentary and the Mass Media*, ed. by John Corner (London: Edward Arnold, 1986), pp. 29–46 (p. 39).

[13] Jackson, *Jennings*, p. 68.

[14] Humphrey Jennings and Charles Madge, 'They Speak for Themselves: Mass-Observation and Social Narrative', *Life and Letters To-Day*, 17/9 (Autumn 1937), 37–42 (p. 37).

[15] Humphrey Jennings, Charles Madge, and others, *May the Twelfth: Mass-Observation Day-Surveys 1937* [1937] (London: Faber and Faber, 1987), p. 90.

[16] MOA, Day Survey 360.

[17] CMA, Prose from 1930s, Box 19/2, English essay ['Isocrates, or, The Future of Enthusiams', 1934(?)].

around the time Madge was forming the idea for Mass-Observation, sheds some light on the broader theoretical premises of the enterprise. Commenting on the ontological status of facts, Madge asserts that 'we "know" facts in a limited way': they necessarily include 'a personal component', and 'are seen, or felt, to be partial structures, lacking finality or completeness'.[18] The scientific influences on Madge's views were diverse, and they included A. J. Ayer's *Language, Truth, and Logic* (1936), a book he later listed as a key influence on his thinking in the 1930s.[19] To 'say that a belief, or a statement, or a judgment, is true', Ayer wrote in defence of logical positivism, 'is always an elliptical way of ascribing truth to a proposition, which is believed, or stated, or judged'.[20] The idea that facts cannot be known independently of the way in which they are perceived—'believed, or stated, or judged'—departs markedly from Richards's positing of the basic textual fact of the 'poem itself'. Mass-Observation's accumulation of data is often seen as a manifestation of the decade's more widespread documentary impetus. While it is true that documentary artists in the 1930s rarely took a naïvely objectivist view of their ability to render reality, no other group of writers placed as much emphasis on the importance of individual experience in constituting a picture of social reality. Storm Jameson's essay 'Documents' (1937) is an example of the deliberately non-artistic, factual approach that Mass-Observation was departing from. The documentary writer, Jameson declared, 'must go for the sake of *the fact*, as a medical student carries out a dissection, and to equip himself, not to satisfy his conscience or to see what effect it has on him. His mind must remain cool'.[21]

Mass-Observation's initial valorization of the idiosyncratic elements in the day surveys came into conflict with its declared attempt to expunge the bourgeois prejudices that were inflecting the individual's experience of social reality. 'What has become unnoticed through familiarity', the early essay 'Poetic Description and Mass-Observation' notes, 'is raised into consciousness again.'[22] Jennings and Madge thought that the crisis which followed Edward VIII's unexpected abdication would unsettle habitualized ways of perceiving social reality. The idea that Mass-Observation would be able to support self-reflection was integral to the early phase of

[18] CMA, Undated Prose, Box 19/6, Uncat. essay 'The White Square: An Essay on Reason' [1934].

[19] CMA, Miscellaneous Jottings and Notes, Box 1/9, Uncat. Notebook [1970s].

[20] A. J. Ayer, *Language, Truth, and Logic* [1936] (London: Penguin, 2001), p. 85.

[21] Storm Jameson, 'Documents', *fact*, 4 (July 1937), 9–18 (p. 12), emphasis in the original.

[22] Humphrey Jennings and Charles Madge, 'Poetic Description and Mass-Observation', *New Verse*, 24 (February–March 1937), 1–6 (p. 3).

the project, and it can be understood as a continuation of Richards's attempt to cleanse his students' reports of 'stock responses' and 'irrelevant associations' which 'overwhelm and distort the poem'.[23] The rhetoric of the movement's early publications frequently invokes Richards's critical vocabulary. The opening paragraph of *Mass-Observation* (1937), the enterprise's first book publication, for example, claimed that the abdication crisis had 'at last' created 'a situation to which there was no stock response'.[24] Madge reiterated the idea in a notebook from the same time, asserting that 'intellectuals living away from the mass' could effectively discharge their 'prejudices and preconceptions' by becoming Observers.[25] The desire to cleanse subjective experience of bourgeois 'stock responses' entailed a critical and quasi-therapeutic reworking of the original day surveys. Mass-Observation thus brings into focus certain central tensions inherent in Richards's model, above all the conflict between an endorsement of subjective experience and the attempt to subject it to a corrective second-degree reading. Jennings and Madge revised the template laid out in Richards's *Practical Criticism*, but they also continued to occupy the role of the Ricardian censor. While Jennings's editing of the material in *May the Twelfth* (1937), the book-collection of day reports about the coronation of George VI in May 1937, sought to create a voice uninhibited by 'stock responses', Madge tended to subordinate the day surveys to broadly scientific rationales—at first that of Marxist-Leninist materialism, later that of anthropology. The social facts collected by Mass-Observation became the ground on which these diverging trends were contested.

THE ARTISTIC VISIONS OF EARLY MASS-OBSERVATION

Jennings, more so than Madge, believed that the overcoming of stock responses could enable the articulation of mass desires and that Mass-Observation's day surveys might constitute a form of collective poetry in its own right. A key essay in this regard is his 'The Theatre Today', first published in Geoffrey Grigson's 1935 volume *The Arts To-Day*. Jennings, who had been an avid stage designer and producer of theatre

[23] See especially Richards's chapter on 'Irrelevant Associations and Stock Responses', in *Practical Criticism: A Study of Literary Judgment* [1929] (London: Transaction Publishers, 2004), pp. 223–40 (p. 227).

[24] Harrisson/Madge, *Mass-Observation*, p. 9.

[25] CMA, Notebooks c.1931–51, Box 10, Uncat. notebook [1936]. One chapter in Richards's *Practical Criticism* had attacked 'inappropriate' 'critical preconceptions' (*Practical Criticism*, pp. 275–87).

plays at Cambridge, addresses the problem that since 'the seventeenth century, in England poetry and the theatre have gone in opposite directions'.[26] Jennings points out that this disjunction has left the theatre dull and predictable, catering to the audience's 'stock ideas' (211), while rendering poetry an increasingly private matter. What is needed, Jennings remarks, is 'something that nobody has seen in England: poetry *in action*' (212; original emphasis)—a poetry which understands silenced mass desires and is capable of directing them towards realization. The idea of poetry 'in action', Jennings goes on to explain, is 'derived from the following series':

> (*a*) Direct realization of desires in war, conquest and the apotheosis of the conqueror, which was once the action of Kingship.
> (*b*) 'Imitation' of above through the medium of the theatre by the poet (his desires not free) [. . .].
> (*c*) Realization of free desires through the medium of words only: regal action of poetry (Rimbaud).
> (*d*) Realization of free desires through the medium of the theatre: poetry *in action.* (213)

Jennings's list suggests that, following the breakdown of historical forms of kingship, the tasks of unifying and articulating mass feeling have fallen to the poet. As catalysts of mass desires, W. B. Yeats and Arthur Rimbaud are 'more completely the poet-king and less the poet-subject than others' (213). The critical step in Jennings's list is arguably the one between (*c*) and (*d*). It is not as clear as one might wish whether the move from the 'regal action of poetry' to theatrical 'poetry *in action*' signifies a genuine socialization of the poet's hermetic individualism, or whether it indicates an expansion of his subjective vision over the whole field of reality. The precise meaning of the transition depends on our understanding of 'popular' poetry: whether it is to be poetry 'for' and 'about' the masses, or whether it is also taken to be 'by' them. In other words, the question is whether the poet is presented as the passive mouthpiece of 'free [mass] desires' or whether he is thought of as actively shaping and manipulating them.

An earlier article on the poetry of Robert Herrick, published in the last issue of *Experiment* in 1931, helps to clarify the ideas in 'The Theatre Today'. Jennings chastises the exclusion of Herrick from the ranks of poets like Percy B. Shelley and Heinrich Heine on the grounds that the themes of his poetry are deemed 'trivial'. Jennings's defence of Herrick mounts an

[26] Humphrey Jennings, 'The Theatre Today' [1935], in *The Humphrey Jennings Film Reader*, ed. by Kevin Jackson (London: Carcanet, 1993), pp. 202–18 (p. 212).

attack against a restricted understanding of what constitutes poetry. 'The nineteenth century', he notes,

> failed to realize the nature of the experiences that can produce poetry, limiting them by a demand for naturalist statement: that philosophical poetry should sound like philosophy and natural description like nature. They found Herrick merely decorative because his experience fell outside their definition. [. . .] Herrick the flower-poet is largely the invention of people who like flowers and wish Herrick to have liked them too, because he mentions them.[27]

The essay suggests that Herrick's poems, rather than transcending the fullness of lived experience, dissolve the conventionalized boundary between life and art: they make 'a leap from metaphor into life' which 'is naturally connected with [Herrick's] interest in actual scenes of ritual where life seems to make a leap into metaphor'.[28] The 'Theatre Today' essay also looks for forms of collective experience outside the patterns of poetic tradition. Towards the end of the piece, Jennings notes that there 'are still certain things in England that have just not been culturized; examples: beer ads., steam railways, Woolworths, clairvoyants. [. . .] When the life has been finally veneered out of these, it really will be the end'.[29] Jennings's list of un-'culturized' items intimates that he aims for the disclosure of the total field of the everyday. For Jennings, the political motivation to let the silenced speak was connected to the aesthetic desire to open up uncharted areas of experience, and the day surveys of Mass-Observation offered a multiplication of such 'experiences that can produce poetry'.

Critics have emphasized the formative influence which Surrealism's turn towards everyday phenomena had on Jennings's early interest in Mass-Observation, but they have tended to neglect the extent to which his conception of the project's emancipatory potential was bound up with his Marxist sympathies.[30] The left-wing politics which supports Jennings's politicized aesthetic of the 1930s resonates most closely with the speculative materialism of Marx's early *Economic and Philosophic Manuscripts* (1844). The main point of Marx's analysis—that under capitalism labour has become reified and takes place under conditions of 'alienation' and

[27] Humphrey Jennings and J. M. Reeves, 'A Reconsideration of Herrick' [1931], in *Film Reader*, pp. 195–202 (pp. 196, 199). As Kevin Jackson points out, Jennings is to be credited as the principal author of the essay. See *Humphrey Jennings*, pp. 110–11.

[28] Jennings/Reeves, 'Reconsideration of Herrick', p. 200.

[29] Jennings, 'Theatre Today', p. 216.

[30] For Jennings's adherence to Surrealism, see especially Geoffrey Nowell-Smith, 'Humphrey Jennings: Surrealist Observer', in *All Our Yesterdays: Ninety Years of British Cinema*, ed. by Charles Barr (London: British Film Institute, 1986), pp. 321–33 (esp. pp. 323–26).

'estrangement'—is known well enough. More germane to my discussion, Marx argues that this process of alienation also entails an increasing 'self-estrangement of man from himself'—a process which he terms *Entwirklichung* (literally, 'de-realization').[31] What is needed, Marx argues, is a new relation of man to his environment: one that does not treat it as a world of reified objects but grasps it as man's '*inorganic* body', as the material result of his own 'life activity'.[32] This new and liberated life, according to Marx, will entail 'the complete *emancipation* of all human senses and qualities', and it will involve the realization (*Verwirklichung*) of man's fullest being:[33]

> Each of his *human* relations to the world – seeing, hearing, smelling, tasting, feeling, thinking, observing, experiencing, wanting, acting, loving – in short, all the organs of his individual being, like those organs which are directly social in their form, are in their *objective* orientation, or in their *orientation to the object,* the appropriation of the object[;] the appropriation of human reality.[34]

Marx's utopian vision of the reintegration of 'life activity' and 'human reality' presents reality as fluid and malleable—as a product of free and deliberate human agency. Jennings's view of the material collected by Mass-Observation and his editing of this material in *May the Twelfth* aim at a similar effect. By focusing on a moment of shock and crisis, *May the Twelfth* captured a moment when reified social relations seemed to be, for a short time, suspended. Jennings's understanding of Mass-Observation tends towards what Isobel Armstrong has called a 'radical aesthetic'. 'Radical', Armstrong points out, should not be understood in any immediately political sense but as reminder of the 'democratic [. . .] potential of aesthetic discourse'. Aesthetics is 'radicalized' by taking the term back to its root meaning of 'perception': 'the components of aesthetic life', Armstrong notes, 'are those that are already embedded in the processes and practices of consciousness – playing and dreaming, thinking and feeling.'[35] Such a project recalls Marx's insistence on the 'appropriation of man's essential powers' and the liberation of '*sensuous* consciousness'.[36] Jennings's interest in Mass-Observation was radical in a similar sense: it signalled a return to reality at the most elementary level by appealing to the individual and collective 'experiences that can produce poetry'. His insistence, in the

[31] Karl Marx, *Economic and Philosophic Manuscripts of 1844*, ed. by Dirk J. Struik, trans. by Martin Milligan (London: Lawrence and Wishart, 1970), p. 116.

[32] Ibid., p. 112, emphasis in the original.

[33] Ibid., p. 139, emphasis in the original.

[34] Ibid., pp. 138–39, emphases in the original.

[35] Isobel Armstrong, *The Radical Aesthetic* (Oxford: Blackwell, 2000), p. 2.

[36] Marx, *Manuscripts*, pp. 175, 176, emphasis in the original.

'Theatre Today' essay and elsewhere, on the 'realisation' of latent desires suggests a reversal of the Marxian process of *Entwirklichung* and the anticipation of a moment of 'human emancipation and rehabilitation'.[37]

Both Madge and Jennings expected that Mass-Observation would be able to change the masses' 'social consciousness' by cleansing it of stock responses.[38] Yet while Jennings thought that Mass-Observation might unearth deeper, communal structures of feeling, Madge's approach to the gathered data had a more doctrinaire inflection. Madge had been a member of the Communist Party of Britain since the early 1930s when he briefly took over as head of the Party's Cambridge bureau, and the poetry which he wrote early in the decade, prior to the founding of Mass-Observation, reflects his orthodox view of Marxism-Leninism. Acting on a recommendation from Richards, Michael Roberts had invited Madge to contribute to the left-wing anthology *New Country* (1933), and in December 1932 Madge set to work on 'Letter to the Intelligentsia', the only poem of his to be included in Roberts's volume.[39] The piece is a withering attack on the politics of the Auden clique, even as it recognizes Auden's greatness as a poet: 'we have left school now', it admonishes Auden's 'boys', 'we turn the pages | Of a larger atlas'. The 'Letter' is above all a political *cri de coeur* to Lenin ('Lenin, would you were living at this hour'). As Madge recalled in his autobiography, 'I felt myself in a position from which to admonish the English Communists from a strict Leninist point of view', and he was in effect 'inviting the "English Communist four"—Michael Roberts, W. H. Auden, Stephen Spender and C. Day Lewis—and others like them, to go a step further and follow me into the Communist party'.[40] For some time in the early and mid-1930s, Madge succeeded in fashioning himself as the most orthodox of the English left-wing poets.

For a poet so diligently immersed in Marxist-Leninist orthodoxy, the absence of a codified communist style was especially worrisome. It was only in 1935 that Madge encountered a body of ideas—socialist realism—which seemed to offer an artistic route by which the narrowly circumscribed language of Ricardian pseudo-statements could be overcome. The key text in this regard is Madge's review of *Problems of Soviet Literature*, a translation of the papers given at the 1934 All-Union Congress of Soviet

[37] Ibid., p. 146.

[38] The phrase features prominently in Madge's 'Press, Radio, and Social Consciousness', in *The Mind in Chains: Socialism and the Cultural Revolution*, ed. by Cecil Day Lewis (London: Muller, 1937), pp. 147–63; and in Harrisson/Madge, *Mass-Observation*, p. 47.

[39] Charles Madge, 'Letter to the Intelligentsia', in *New Country: Prose and Poetry by the Authors of 'New Signatures'*, ed. by Michael Roberts (London: Hogarth Press, 1933), pp. 231–33.

[40] CMA, TS autobiography, Box 2/1, p. 39.

Writers at Moscow. First published in 1936 in *Left Review*, the review applauds the doctrine of socialist realism promulgated at the Congress, and quotes approvingly from the speeches by Nikolai Bukharin, Maxim Gorki, Karl Radek, and A. A. Zhdanov. The article echoes Zhdanov's claim in the introduction to the volume that the artistic resources of bourgeois writing have been exhausted. Literature's retreat into 'the internal world, subjectivity and introspection', Madge suggests, has led to the ossification of bourgeois forms of expression, heralding 'the disintegration of the system of bourgeois wishes, ambitions, aims, sentiments' more generally.[41]

The review concurs in particular with the closing essay of the volume, Bukharin's lengthy disquisition on 'The Problems of Poetry in the U.S.S.R.'. Bukharin's contribution noted that bourgeois poets, because they were preoccupied with artistic models of the past, failed to grasp the historical significance of the present. Socialist realism by contrast would endeavour to make the present moment transparent: it would shed light on 'our own history, the history of late years, [. . .] comprehended in all its diversity'.[42] Bukharin called on writers to 'raise the level of poetic self-knowledge':

> There is a tremendous thirst to know everything, a tremendous desire to generalise, to rise on a new basis to an understanding of the process as a whole. [. . .] This period is the prelude to a phase in which poetry will summarise life, in which our epoch will be presented not in fragments of the whole, but [. . .] in all its connections and settings. (245)

The passage is uneasily lodged between an attention to the minute particulars of empirical reality—the desire 'to know everything'—and the wish to discern larger patterns of historical movement at the level of everyday life. The work of the modern poet, Bukharin declares, needs to anticipate the new social order by grasping 'to the full the historic place which we hold in the living stream of modern history' (244). Madge's review also understands the present as a critical historical moment whose significance the poet is required to 'summarise' and elucidate:

> In the capitalist countries, particularly in bourgeois England, one would expect these changes to take obscure and unclarified forms, since we lack the political and social guidance from which Soviet writers are able to benefit. To

[41] Charles Madge, 'Writers Under Two Flags', *Left Review*, 2/5 (February 1936), 228–30 (p. 230).

[42] Nikolai Bukharin, 'Poetry, Poetics and the Problems of Poetry in the USSR', in *Problems of Soviet Literature: Reports and Speeches at the First Soviet Writers' Congress*, trans. by H. G. Scott (London: Lawrence and Wishart, [1935]), pp. 185–258 (p. 243).

> make the unconscious response conscious, and to clarify the obscure symptoms of possible change, involves far-reaching analysis.[43]

Madge adopts a Freudianized rhetoric in portraying these latent historical forces and 'obscure symptoms', but he also espouses the idea of a therapeutic reading of contemporary society which puts the Marxist-Leninist critic into a position of inviolable interpretative authority. The review envisions a subtle kind of Marxist propaganda that resonates with Lenin's call (in his 1917 'April Theses') to avoid dogmatism and 'patiently to explain'.[44]

The quietly persuasive power of historical 'facts' was a widespread obsession on the literary left. Rex Warner's contribution to the communist anthology *The Mind in Chains* (1937) proclaimed that '[o]ur task is, in Lenin's words, "patiently to explain"': 'not only theory but the plain facts of contemporary history are becoming more and more obviously on our side.'[45] The most harmful thing, the Marxist economist Maurice Dobb had announced five years earlier, was 'a plain failure to explain'.[46] The fact-minded volumes of the Left Book Club, the Modern Books series, and the Hogarth Press Day-to-Day Pamphlets were thick with tables, graphs, and figures which predicted the demise of capitalism: from Dobb's beginner's *On Marxism To-Day* (1932) and John Strachey's *The Nature of Capitalist Crisis* (1935) to Sidney and Beatrice Webb's popular *Soviet Communism: A New Civilisation* (1935) and George Orwell's *The Road to Wigan Pier* (1937). All of these texts were fluent in what one book called 'the language of fact'.[47] The socialist-realist impulse to make the present moment decipherable also informed Dziga Vertov's scenario for an unrealized film that would record all events happening around the world within a single minute. 'This little minute', Vertov wrote, 'turns into the Minute of the World, into an instantaneous survey of the world, into a mighty document'.[48] Mass-Observation's focus on the present historical moment, in particular in the middle section of *May the Twelfth*, which collated day surveys to

[43] Madge, 'Writers Under Two Flags', p. 228.

[44] For Lenin's phrase, see 'The Tasks of the Proletariat in the Present Revolution' [= 'April Theses'] [1917], in *Selected Works*, ed. by Joe Fineberg, 12 vols (London: Lawrence and Wishart, 1936–39), VI (1936), pp. 21–26 (p. 22). For a discussion of socialist art's 'partisanship of objectivity', see Georg Lukács, 'Art and Objective Truth' [1954], in *Writer and Critic, and Other Essays*, ed. and trans. by Arthur Kahn (London: Merlin Press, 1970), pp. 25–60 (pp. 40–44).

[45] Rex Warner, 'Education', in *Mind in Chains*, ed. by Cecil Day Lewis, pp. 19–37 (p. 36).

[46] Maurice Dobb, *On Marxism Today* (London: Hogarth Press, 1932), p. 14.

[47] Dmitry Z. Manuilsky, *The Communist Parties and the Crisis of Capitalism* (London: Modern Books, [1931]), pp. 9–11.

[48] Dziga Vertov, 'A Minute of the World' [1944], in *Kino-Eye: The Writings of Dziga Vertov*, ed. by Annette Michelson, trans. by Kevin O'Brien (Berkeley: University of California Press, 1984), pp. 315–16 (p. 316).

offer an hour-by-hour account of the day, created the kind of concentrated vision of society for which Marxists like Madge were struggling.

INTERPRETATIVE AUTHORITY AND THE ROLE OF THE POET

Madge's intensely analytic optic differs from the emancipatory and utopian bent of Jennings's understanding of Mass-Observation. But Jennings's championing of Mass-Observation's creative potential also entailed a markedly different conception of history: while Madge's perception of the historical process belittled individual agency, Jennings tended to think of history as a process that was constantly being kept in motion by creative forces operative at the elementary level of everyday life. For him, history was not a reified object but a changeable ensemble kept in motion by the productive activity of human beings. Despite their differing perceptions of Mass-Observation's political and emancipatory potential, Jennings and Madge were both troubled by the question of how a new writing might be created out of the facts collected by way of the day surveys. Their texts sometimes advocate a 'popular poetry' written by, for, and about the masses, but they also share anxieties over the question whether the bourgeois role of the poet could finally be abandoned. In a letter from the 1970s, Madge insisted that he had never 'praised the people's art' and that 'it wasn't exactly that which I meant that Mass-Observation techniques would uncover'. The hundreds of reports which arrived at his Blackheath lodgings in London, he explained, presented 'realistic poetic descriptive statements relatively unvitiated by literary associations': they offered material for a new literature, but they were not themselves the new writing that thirties intellectuals were anxiously anticipating.[49] 'Popular Poetry' was Madge's working title for what was to become Mass-Observation, yet it is necessary to recognize the scepticism towards the idea that is revealed in Madge's letter as well as in many of Jennings's and Madge's writings from the 1930s.[50]

Madge's review of *Problems of Soviet Literature* had been doctrinaire in its assessment of socialist realism, but it had also been curiously deaf to the dilemmas articulated by the essays in the volume, most of which continued to advocate the distinct role of the poet even as they were enjoining

[49] CMA, Correspondence, Box 22/4, Uncat. ms letter to Valentine Cunningham, 5 December 1978.

[50] For Madge's comments on 'Popular Poetry', see Nick Hubble, *Mass-Observation and Everyday Life: Culture, History, Theory* (Basingstoke: Palgrave Macmillan, 2006), pp. 77–78.

communists to blend in with the mass. Maxim Gorki, for example, noted that the poet's role was far from being rendered obsolete: 'The idea, of course, is not to restrict individual creation, but to furnish it with the widest means of continued powerful development.'[51] Nikolai Bukharin's essay was similarly reluctant to let go of the idea of the individual artist. The 'quite definite conclusion' that was to be drawn, Bukharin noted, was that the 'entire diversity of life can and should serve as the material for poetic creation'.[52] The speeches at the Writers' Congress presented socialist realism as an expansion of the interests and occupations of the individual poet, rather than as the abolition of the role of the artist as such. Communist writing, *Problems of Soviet Literature* suggested, continued to be beset by the internal contradictions of bourgeois literature: by conflicts between the intellectuals and the masses, between a late-bourgeois preoccupation with literary 'style' and art's new communist 'content', between the language of poetry and the supposedly more factual language of science.

The articles which Jennings and Madge co-authored in the mid-1930s evince similar anxieties about the grip of bourgeois traditions on left-wing writing. The expectation that there was a popular poetry hidden in the structures of everyday life is stated most forcefully in an early *New Verse* essay, 'Poetic Description and Mass-Observation' (1937). The piece quotes three passages, from a 'contemporary novel', from a 'historical account of certain events that actually took place', and from 'a piece of observation by a Mass-Observer', and it alleges that the third textual sample dialectically weds poetic pseudo-statement and objective fact. The hard 'facts' of reality are made 'human' by being refracted through a subjective consciousness, becoming 'by implication, poetic'.[53] The result of this method is a supposedly more democratic aesthetic: 'the immediate effect of Mass-Observation is to de-value considerably the status of the "poet".'[54] The essay's insistence on 'poetic description' echoes Madge's claim, in another essay from 1937, that the data offered by Mass-Observation must be seen 'not as objective fact, but as poetic fact'.[55] 'Poetic facts' were intended to bridge the divide between poetic pseudo-statement and scientific description, between the view of poetry as an autonomous realm which was subject to the forces of poetic convention, on the one hand, and a widening of poetry's experiential base in everyday life, on the other.

'Poetic Description and Mass-Observation' is the most ambitious mission statement of the movement's early phase, but its vision of a more democratic and demotic art remains uneasy. The main piece of evidence

[51] Maxim Gorki, 'Soviet Literature', in *Problems of Soviet Literature*, pp. 27–69 (p. 64).
[52] Bukharin, p. 246. [53] Jennings/Madge, 'Poetic Decription', p. 2.
[54] Ibid., p. 3. [55] Madge, 'Press, Radio, and Social Consciousness', p. 151.

which the essay adduces to illustrate 'poetic facts' is a poem from Thomas Hardy's *Satires of Circumstance* (1914). As opposed to a 'prose anecdote', Jennings and Madge note, the 'metre and rhyme' of Hardy's 'poetic anecdote' help to focus 'the serious attention of the reader'.[56] Hardy's poem is intended to illustrate the possibility of pouring new content into bourgeois literary forms, but the appeal to Hardy generates a tension between the desire to abandon the role of the poet and a continued, albeit covert, adherence to it. The essay's sustained concern with questions of style might itself signal a late-bourgeois approach to poetry—one which remains attracted to the idea of poetic authority and writerly craftsmanship.[57] This emphasis on the mass-produced text as a literary artefact finds an echo in Jennings's insistence that poetry could only be 'constructed [. . .] from poetry'. Thomas Gray's poems, he remarked in a radio talk, present 'a perfectly contemporary scene, but in the language of poetry'.[58] What Madge's and Jennings's comments bring into focus is the indelible 'poeticity' of literary texts, and the difficulty of imagining a radically 'new' type of writing that would be performed by the amateur masses.

Jennings and Madge were warier of the limitations of a genuinely 'popular' art than the programmatic optimism of 'Poetic Description and Mass-Observation' suggests. Some of the enterprise's artistic anxieties can be traced back specifically to William Empson's *Some Versions of Pastoral* (1935).[59] In the first chapter of his book, Empson had insisted that 'proletarian literature' was a type of 'covert pastoral' because its eloquent portrayal of the voiceless working class was bound to take place at a remove from the life which it attempted to describe. '[T]o produce pure proletarian art', Empson explained with reference to Gorki's speech at the Writers' Congress, 'the artist must be at one with the worker; this is impossible, not for political reasons, but because the artist never is at one with any public.'[60] In bourgeois writing, Empson pointed out, the 'Worker'—like the masses courted by Jennings and Madge—tended to become a 'mythical cult-figure'.[61] The essay 'They Speak for Themselves', penned jointly by

[56] Jennings/Madge, 'Poetic Description', p. 5.

[57] This recourse to established literary forms is evident in Mass-Observation's 'Oxford Collective Poem', *New Verse*, 25 (May 1937), 16–19. For criticism of the poem's 'conservative aesthetic', see Valentine Cunningham, *British Writers of the Thirties* (Oxford: Oxford University Press, 1988), pp. 338–40.

[58] Humphrey Jennings, 'Plagiarism in Poetry' [1937], in *Film Reader*, pp. 247–50 (p. 250).

[59] Nick Hubble has pointed out that Empson's criticism was 'a significant catalyst for Madge's formation of Mass-Observation'. See Hubble, 'The Intermodern Assumption of the Future: William Empson, Charles Madge and Mass-Observation', in *Intermodernism*, ed. by Kristin Bluemel, pp. 171–88 (p. 176).

[60] William Empson, *Some Versions of Pastoral* [1935] (London: Penguin, 1995), p. 19.

[61] Ibid., p. 23.

Madge and Jennings, phrases the position of Mass-Observation in recognizably Empsonian terms:

> There is a general wish among writers to be UNLIKE the intellectual, LIKE the masses. Much 'proletarian fiction' is a product of this wish. But it is not enough for such fiction to be ABOUT proletarians, if they in their turn become a romantic fiction, nor even for it to be BY proletarians, if it is used by them as a means of escaping out of the proletariat.[62]

The passage invokes Empson's stinging comparison between proletarian fiction (which, Empson claimed, was structurally related to 'fairy stories' and 'ballads') and its pastoral blueprint: 'most fairy stories and ballads, though "by" and "for", are not "about"; whereas pastoral though "about" is not "by" or "for".'[63] Madge and Jennings's essay picks up two of Empson's prepositions, but it skirts the dilemma of the bourgeois poet who is facing a new audience and needs to find the right style 'for' them. Instead, 'They Speak for Themselves' implies that—given the right kinds of techniques and procedures—Mass-Observation will be made 'by' the masses themselves. Importantly, however, the text warns that such self-writing must not involve the wish of 'escaping out of the proletariat' because this 'escape' would mar the desired impression of authenticity. The passage paradoxically defends the social status quo by taking a placid view of class divisions, leaving Mass-Observation open to the charge which Empson levelled against Thomas Gray's 'Elegy Written in a Country Church-Yard' (1751): that the 'reader is put into a mood in which one would not try to alter' the situation of the lower classes.[64] 'They Speak for Themselves' opens with the radical aim of refuting Empson's injunction against proletarian fiction, but it ends anticlimactically by curtailing Mass-Observation's emancipatory and revolutionary potential. The essay's hesitations indicate a profounder uncertainty whether Mass-Observation's new writing might constitute a form of 'popular poetry', and the same dilemmas are also played out at the level of the movement's 'sociological' techniques and of its presentation of the day-survey material.

MAY THE TWELFTH AND THE LIMITS OF 'POPULAR POETRY'

May the Twelfth, Mass-Observation's first and most ambitious publication of day-survey material, provided a large-scale test for an aesthetic built on the experience of the hitherto inarticulate masses. The volume printed excerpts from more than two hundred anonymized day reports, most of

[62] Jennings/Madge, 'They Speak for Themselves', p. 37. [63] Empson, p. 13.
[64] Ibid., p. 12.

which had been sent in by volunteer Observers across the United Kingdom. The book's central section, relating events from the day of George VI's Coronation, is divided into four parts, all edited by Jennings: 'Preparations For May 12' (consisting of newspaper clippings about the lead-up to the Coronation), 'London on May 12' (comprising reports by a Mobile Squad of Observers stationed along the route of the procession), 'National Activities' (including reports of personal and collective celebrations), and 'Individual Reactions' (mostly responses by Observers who refused to pay attention to the day's events). The book closes with a 'Normal Day-Survey', edited by Madge, which draws on day reports from 12 February, 12 March, and 12 April 1937. Critics have pointed out that most Observers came from the lower-middle class—the *petite bourgeoisie* which Marxists were teaching themselves to despise. The failure to recruit working-class Observers limited the political scope of the project, but it has also more recently been understood as fundamental to the enterprise's larger aim of repoliticizing the everyday life of the *petite bourgeoisie*.[65] In what follows, I will not problematize the aims of Mass-Observation by focusing on the class affiliations of the Observers, but rather by investigating the underlying 'aesthetic' and artistic problems which the enterprise faced. Drawing on two foundational texts from 1937—Madge's contribution to *The Mind in Chains* and Jennings's editorial work in *May the Twelfth*—I assess Mass-Observation's attempts to import the experience of the mass into literature, as well as the ways in which Madge and Jennings moulded and misread the material which they claimed to be merely reporting or editing.

In *May the Twelfth*, newspapers figure as the most potent metaphor for the type of writing aspired to by early Mass-Observation. Madge's letter to the *New Statesman and Nation* from January 1937, announcing the founding of Mass-Observation, had opened the search for 'evidence of mass wish-situations';[66] and only a few months later, in the communist anthology *The Mind in Chains*, Madge declared that newspapers were the places where 'mass wishes' were rendered legible.[67] Madge, a former reporter for the *Daily Mirror*, noted that the journalist 'must be sufficiently sensitive to mass wishes to produce a formula which will sell his paper [. . .]. The fact that he is *selling* something gives to his work a reality, however lurid, which a more abstract or even a more altruistic approach could never attain' (158; emphasis in the original). This emphasis on the 'reality'

[65] See Tom Jeffery's *A Short History of Mass-Observation*, rev. ed. (Birmingham: Centre for Contemporary Cultural Studies, 1999).

[66] Charles Madge, 'Letter', *New Statesman and Nation*, 2 January 1937, p. 12.

[67] Madge, 'Press, Radio, and Social Consciousness', p. 157.

of the newspaper, on its ability to materialize mass wishes and thus make them readable, recalls Jennings's insistence on the realization of 'free' collective desires. However, Madge also suggests that newspapers illustrate the unfolding of a dialectical pattern: 'Even when ostensibly benevolent, capitalism cannot help being the bearer of evils; and even when, vice versa, it is simply out to win a big circulation, the newspaper cannot help being a good influence, and eventually an influence subversive of itself' (152). The claim owes much to Marx's argument about the ruse of capitalist reason by which industrial and scientific progress undermines the economic status quo that allows the bourgeoisie to exert its rule over the proletariat.

These orthodox convictions are also apparent in the example of 'popular poetry' which Madge offered in his contribution to *The Mind in Chains.* His essay closes with an article from the *Daily Mirror* which Madge presents as a crystallization of the 'mass wish':

> All day he sits huddled up in an old potting-shed in the Arboretum here – his secret retreat in a public park in the heart of Nottingham.
>
> All night he sleeps, trussed up in old raincoats and newspapers, between the roots of a tree in the forest.
>
> He is the human mole. He speaks to no one. For nearly two years he has lived the life of a nomad, shunning human society.
>
> And he does it so well that, although he is surrounded by houses and buses and cinemas, few people have ever seen him. To most he is just a legend of 'The Old Man of the Forest.'
>
> He is always washed and clean-shaved: his boots are always thick-soled and shining. He scorns alms and help.
>
> To-day I traced him down to his old potting shed.
>
> Summers is his name. He is an old soldier who has travelled most of the world, and was discharged with a disability pension. He had saved money to exploit an invention he had spent twenty years in perfecting. Then:
>
> 'For a time I wandered about in lodgings. Then I decided to exploit my invention. I needed more money, so I put the idea before a millionaire.
>
> 'He was impressed; said he would help me. But when I got home he sent a man to try to trick me into telling my secret.
>
> 'I swore that if my discovery was to be developed I would do it myself, without anyone's help.'
>
> His eyes shone and his voice rang as he added: 'And I mean it – no one but me shall get the honour of my invention. I have burned all my books. The secret is now in my brain, and if I die first . . .'
>
> He has set himself to live in utter poverty so that he can save the rest of his pension and one day launch his scheme. (161-62)

The story, Madge writes, fulfils 'all the requirements of popular poetry', and critics have correctly seen the piece as evidence of Mass-Observation's early interest in 'popular literature'.[68] This new type of writing, Madge points out in his commentary, will demote bourgeois poets to the role of observing 'Reporters':

> In this story the style and content are not only poetic, but have certain affinities with poetic tradition. It is given its peculiar force by the introduction of certain elements of unmistakable reality – the pottingshed 'in the heart of Nottingham', the newspapers in which the Mole wraps himself at night, and his thick-soled boots. Connecting the real world with this world of poetry fantasy is the Reporter, the anonymous and impersonal 'I' who tells the story.[69]

Madge admits that the story evinces 'certain affinities with poetic tradition', but his comment underplays the hold which assumptions about the metaphoricity of poetic language exercise over the story. The reprinting of the article in the communist volume *The Mind in Chains* invested it with a number of meanings which are not present when the piece is considered in the context of the *Daily Mirror*. In its new textual habitat, the story invites a determinedly ideological reading which presents the Human Mole both as a product and an allegory of social injustice. The weight which the news item places on class conflict—between the Human Mole and the millionaire—reads like a response to the call, in the volume's subtitle, for a 'cultural revolution'. The key figure of the story may even allude to Marx's 'old mole' of communism, with the closing phrase ('he can [. . .] one day launch his scheme') recalling Marx's idea that the 'mole' prepares the proletarian revolution by completing its subterranean 'preliminary work'.[70] Importantly, the point of view of the mole also encapsulates the earth-bound optic adopted by Mass-Observation and its reaction against the aloofness of the bird's-eye view that dominates much political poetry of the 1930s, most prominently that of Auden.[71] As Georges Bataille noted in 1930, Marx's 'old mole' had 'nothing to do with the heavens, preferred station of the imperialist eagles as of the Christian or revolutionary utopias. He begins in the bowels of the earth, as in the materialist bowels of proletarians.'[72] Madge's early poetry had been steeped in an Audenesque

[68] Hubble, *Mass-Observation*, pp. 77–78.

[69] Madge, 'Press, Radio, and Social Consciousness', pp. 162–63.

[70] Karl Marx, *The Eighteenth Brumaire of Louis Bonaparte* [1852], trans. by Cedar and Eden Paul (London: Allen and Unwin, 1926), p. 130.

[71] On this point see also Rod Mengham, 'The Thirties: Politics, Authority, Perspective', in *The Cambridge History of Twentieth-Century Literature*, ed. by Laura Marcus and Peter Nicholls (Cambridge: Cambridge University Press, 2004), pp. 359–78 (pp. 373–74).

[72] Georges Bataille, 'The "Old Mole" and the Prefix *Sur* in the Words *Surhomme* and *Surréaliste*' [1929–30], in *Visions of Excess: Selected Writings, 1927–1939*, ed. and trans. by Allan Stoekl (Minneapolis: University of Minnesota Press, 1985), pp. 32–44 (p. 35).

idiom, an influence which he tried to shake off as he became an 'empirical Marxist'.[73] One unpublished piece, 'Bird's-eye', written in December 1932, had eagerly proclaimed that 'We from our aeroplane gaze, high | In air from where white clouds roll', but the poem also felt uncomfortably reminded of the noisy proletarians shouting from below: 'dare | We join that chorus that laughs up?'[74]

In addition to these meanings, Madge's choice of the Human Mole story tenders a response to Empson's description of proletarian art as covert pastoral. Empson had proposed a strategy for countering sentimental bourgeois ideas about the working class: 'People who consider that the Worker group of sentiments is misleading in contemporary politics tend to use the word "romantic" as a missile; unless they merely mean "false" this is quite off the point: what they ought to do is to produce a rival myth.'[75] The Human Mole, spelled with capital initials in Madge's commentary, is just such a 'rival myth', as it pits a raw voice emanating from the lower depths against the reporter's bourgeois 'fantasising'. 'The creation of myths which are valid for the mass of people', Madge explained in the mid-1930s, 'is a special function of the imaginative artist.'[76] In the story of the Human Mole, Madge's commitment to Leninism-Marxism and its emphasis on the subterranean workings of economic history clearly gain an upper hand over the attempt to let the masses 'speak for themselves'. The article demonstrates how real-life 'facts' are transformed into poetic tropes, and Madge's adroitness at turning the Human Mole into a symbolic token of the communist future complicates the idea of a writing that relegates the poet to the position of an unobtrusive reporter. It also indicates that Madge and Jennings habitually underplayed the degree of editorial interference which their self-fashioned roles of reporter and editor entailed.

Jennings's reflections on the revolutionary potential of newspapers tended to be less ideologically laden than Madge's. His most extensive discussion of the principles undergirding his aesthetic came in a series of BBC radio talks (entitled 'The Poet and the Public') which was broadcast between April and June 1938. In the first broadcast, he observes that 'the two things that have got out of touch with each other are modern poetry and everyday life'.[77] Newspapers, he points out, have become more

[73] Julian Trevelyan, *Indigo Days* [1957] (Cambridge: Scolar Press, 1996), p. 82. None of Madge's Audenesque pieces from the early 1930s found their way into his published poetry collections. The unpublished poems are now in the Charles Madge Archive at the University of Sussex.

[74] CMA, Poems 1932–35, Box 16/2, Uncat. ts poem 'Bird's-eye' [December 1932].

[75] Empson, p. 20.

[76] CMA, Miscellaneous Prose, Box 19/3, Uncat. ts notes [1935].

[77] Humphrey Jennings, 'The Poet and the Public', in *Film Reader*, pp. 255–82 (p. 255).

intimately connected to the practice of everyday life—to acts of sympathetic identification, to the exercise of moral judgment—than poetry. 'Over the last three hundred years', Jennings observes, 'we have language going two ways: it's used for *news*, real news and romantic news, and it's used for *poetry*.'[78] News, as Richards might say, deals in the referential language of statements, while poetry has increasingly withdrawn into the semantic enclosure of pseudo-statements. At the same time, the unimaginative fact-mindedness of newspapers is also their particular weakness:

> We've seen the way in which newspapers and short stories help us to deal with the *outside* world, but what about our lives by *ourselves*? You see newspapers don't give us news about *ourselves*. Who is going to help us to show off ourselves to ourselves? – because that is what we need.[79]

The language which 'man' has invented 'to deal with *himself*', the radio talk explains, is poetry. As instantiated by *May the Twelfth*, Jennings's poetic 'news about ourselves' proposes a self-consciously poetic alternative to the 'science of ourselves' which Harrisson and Madge were variously advocating.[80] The central role of newspapers in *May the Twelfth* seems to justify Walter Benjamin's hope that they would dissolve the 'difference between author and public'. Because newspapers respond to the latent desires of a mass readership, their readers can be said to participate obliquely in the process of writing. The newspaper thus appears to demote the bourgeois author to a mere 'producer' in Benjamin's sense, 'forc[ing] us to re-examine the separation between author and reader'.[81]

The first section of *May the Twelfth* consists of press clippings which are intended to illustrate major drifts in mass opinion during the lead-up to the coronation. However, newspapers figure most significantly as metaphors in the book's central section, 'London on May 12'. At 6.20 a.m., one Observer detects a 'girl sitting on soiled newspaper' and 'reading *Daily Mirror*'; at noon, 'the sides of the road' along which the procession will pass are already 'covered in newspaper'.[82] Around the same time, Observer CM.1 discovers that 'there is an area of black mud strewn with pieces of torn newspaper', while the music is 'drowning the sound of rustling

[78] Ibid., p. 258, emphases in the original.

[79] Ibid., p. 260, emphases in the original.

[80] For the phrase see e.g. Tom Harrisson, 'Mass-Opposition and Tom Harrisson', *Light and Dark*, 2/3 (February 1938), 8–15 (p. 11).

[81] Walter Benjamin, 'The Author as Producer', trans. by Edmund Jephcott, in *Selected Writings*, ed. by Michael Jennings, Howard Eiland, and Gary Smith (Cambridge, MA: Harvard University Press, 1996–2003), II (1999), pp. 768–82 (pp. 771–72).

[82] Jennings/Madge, *May the Twelfth*, pp. 109, 122. References to this text will henceforth be given parenthetically in the text.

paper under people's feet' (124). Soon after, the same Observer notices that 'people are throwing balls of wet newspaper at one another' (139). As soon as the procession has passed and the crowd begins to disperse, the mass of clotted newspaper in the streets becomes inescapable: 'Along the East Carriage Drive', CM.1 writes, 'the side of the road is actually an inch deep in sodden newspapers' (144–45). The photographs which Jennings took on the day of the Coronation also show the streets and parks of London plastered with torn newspapers. Like these photographs, 'London on May 12' metaphorically transforms London into a spatial manifestation of the collective unconscious. 'London on May 12' is designed to suggest that the close-knit imagery of 'newspapers' somehow emerges from the day reports themselves: material reality itself, Jennings had written in 'The Theatre Today', would offer a '*solidification* of [subjective] imagery'.[83] The crowd's standing on and between the crumpled newspapers insinuates that they provide an outdated type of news which must be replaced by more adequate forms of self-knowledge. Viewed in this light, the task which Jennings envisions for 'London on May 12' is a doubly performative one: the imagery of the Observer reports visualizes—proleptically, as it were—the passing of the newspaper which *May the Twelfth* is intended to accomplish.

References to torn newspaper covering the streets lend 'London on May 12' an important degree of symbolic unity. However, the element of self-reflexivity implied by these references is much less central to the original day surveys—as a poetic 'news about ourselves'—than Jennings's heavily edited version suggests. Jennings had himself been a member of the Mobile Squad, and it is from his report, appearing in *May the Twelfth* as CM.1, that most of the references to newspapers are taken. Other Observers simply did not pay as much attention to the papier-mâché clinging to the streets. For instance, clotted newspaper does not appear at all in the photographs which Denzil Dunnett, Mobile Squad member CM.12, took at the Coronation and sent to Madge.[84] The marked-up version of Jennings's original typescript report reveals that he incorporated nearly all of it into the 'London on May 12' section—by far the greatest percentage taken over from any day survey. It has also gone unnoticed that most of *May the Twelfth*'s long, discursive footnotes refer to Jennings's own day survey. Another important case in point is the middle section's self-reflexive emphasis on different techniques of observing, on shifting angles and points of view.

[83] Jennings, 'Theatre Today', p. 214, emphasis in the original.

[84] MOA, Day Survey 274. By contrast, newspapers also figure importantly in the photos, inspired by Surrealism, which Henri Cartier-Bresson took on 12 May; for one of Cartier-Bresson's photographs, see Joel Meyerowitz and Colin Westerbeck, *Bystander: A History of Street Photography* (London: Thames and Hudson, 1994), p. 160.

More than any other Observer, Jennings paid attention to the diverse ways the Coronation was being watched, filmed, and photographed. His stint at the GPO Film Unit in 1934 might explain why his report is drawn to a detailed description of the routine of a 'G.B. camera man' panning over the crowd, refocusing his camera lens, and adjusting the viewfinder (142). Of particular importance to Jennings's report is the idea that the masses on Coronation Day were constantly watching themselves—an idea which reflects the hope that Mass-Observation would raise the masses to a new level of self-awareness and facilitate the eradication of stock responses. In Jennings's day survey, the central images for this continuous process of self-scrutiny are the cardboard periscopes which were being sold on numerous street corners on May 12.[85] Periscopes are used by people at the back of the crowd to catch a glimpse of the procession, or (in the words of one periscope seller advertising his products) to 'look how many's in front of ye' (110). As Steven Connor observes, the periscopes become 'an image of Mass-Observation itself, enabling one to look out over the mass and see the stammering King', as well as to see 'the mass itself, achieving a kind of tautological perspective on itself'.[86] The prosthetic device of the periscope symbolizes the enlarged vision which Jennings was expecting Mass-Observation to create.

This element of conscious poetic crafting is supplemented by less visible modes of editorial interference. Jennings's work of assembling passages from more than two hundred day surveys inevitably involved cutting out much of the material; however, a comparison of the original day surveys with the text published in *May the Twelfth* reveals that a main target of these excisions were the 'stock responses' which littered the reports. One such example is the report of CM.10, a twenty-three-year-old male. In the identifying questionnaire which prefaces his original report, the Observer declares that he sides with 'left politics', and Marxist sentiment runs more strongly in his day survey than in most other reports. Jennings decided to delete about a dozen lines in which political feeling was particularly intense, while quoting the surrounding text as a single paragraph (150). The excised lines describe a shop window displaying a miniature model of the royal family and the coronation ceremony:

> My immediate impression was one of irony: it is all right showing this middle age & Elizabethan stuff as a pageant in the Coronation procession. But once the stuff is offered for sale the mockery upon the poor who were gazing in

[85] See e.g. Jennings/Madge, *May the Twelfth*, pp. 109, 118, 139, 141.

[86] Steven Connor, '"A Door Half Open to Surprise": Charles Madge's Imminences', in *Mass-Observation as Poetics and Science*, ed. by Nick Hubble, Margaretta Jolly, and Laura Marcus, 52–62 (p. 60).

> this shop window becomes too blatant [. . .]. Makes one feel that the coronation has been bolstered up by powerful business men to keep the crowd contented. They seem to imply that England's history in the past when presented as a pageant will justify to the masses this amassing of wealth now.[87]

This kind of social and political bias was troublingly at odds with Jennings's vision of a subjectivity emancipated from ideological preconceptions, and he seems to have regarded the above observations as quasi-Ricardian 'irrelevant associations' which needed to be tacitly suppressed in the published text of *May the Twelfth*. The above passage is a particularly startling case of what is in fact a recurrent editorial practice. Madge had hoped that the day surveys would be 'unvitiated by literary associations', yet one of the most common 'stock responses' which the Observers (like Richards's students) brought to their analyses of the day's events was their knowledge of literature. A comparison between *May the Twelfth* and the original day-survey material reveals that Jennings deleted several such 'associations' from the body of the published text. CO.27, a twenty-five-year-old male Observer identifying himself as a 'Communist', responded to Madge and Jennings's question about the 'most peculiar incident' he encountered on May 12. The bulk of his response is reprinted in the section 'Individual Responses to May 12', with only his last association left out: 'I was reminded of Auden's "Surrealist Police"! I had never seen a Bobby looking under a lavatory door before.'[88] The passage suggests that CO.27's attention to the bizarre scene had been prompted specifically by his knowledge of Auden's poetry. The report of CO.32, a schoolmaster with left-wing sympathies, is even more strongly distracted by literary associations. Jennings decided to print a large portion of the original text in 'London on May 12', including one instance in which 'the drapery, the tiers of people, and the crush' at the procession route remind the Observer of the film *Ben Hur* (119). However, the selection from CO.32 leaves out several other literary allusions, most notably an extended reference to Edward Thomas's and A. E. Housman's '"doomed and young" poetry' that had been triggered by the cohorts of soldiers marching through London.[89] The overall effect of these excisions is to make the reports more straightforwardly and naïvely 'observing' than many of them actually are. The result of such acts of textual purging is that *May the Twelfth*—Madge's and Jennings's professed valorization of subjective experience notwithstanding—displaces or simply ignores the many ways in which Observers were making sense of the events of the day by resorting to familiar types of stock responses.

[87] MOA, Day Survey 405.
[88] MOA, Day Survey 538. See also *May the Twelfth*, p. 332.
[89] MOA, Day Survey 510.

The impression of Mass-Observation's emancipatory potential in 'London on May 12'—of a genuinely 'plural text', in Jeremy MacClancy's phrase—is carefully created, though this is not to say that the enterprise's capacity to transcend ingrained habits is purely illusory.[90] The dominant imagery of *May the Twelfth* serves to highlight a tendency among Observers to feel 'surprised' or 'struck' by the events of the day, and to see over-familiar realities in fresh and unaccustomed ways. Observer CL.25, for example, discovers that 'for the second time that day I was struck by the thought of how like sheep we humans really are. We just follow the flock' (116). The same Observer had earlier been bewildered by the willingness of the crowd to hold their ground in the rain, 'look[ing] at them in amazement and admiration' (115). Another Observer, CL.1, describing himself as a left-wing atheist, is 'surprised to find a lump in my throat and tears in my eyes' as the procession passes (131), while CO.32, a 'schoolmaster' of the 'inactive Left', is startled by 'how solemn everyone was, and thought it would be more appropriate if someone would sing' (119). It is these moments of self-reflection, littered across the handwritten reports, which Jennings's editing serves to foreground.

It has not been adequately understood how Jennings edited and modified the Observers' responses to the events of May 12. It seems clear, however, that the attempt to create a fusion of 'news' and 'poetry' was at the centre of his concerns. In the first of his BBC broadcasts, looking back to the ballads and broadsheets of Renaissance England, Jennings noted that 'once upon a time, it may be poetry and romance and news all managed to tie up together – and the poet was a kind of reporter'.[91] The phrase recalls Madge's vision of the future poet as a Reporter—a view which in turn resonates with Jennings's seemingly ancillary role as editor in *May the Twelfth*. Jennings and Madge did not ultimately succeed in doing away with the idea of poetic authority, and *May the Twelfth*, with its preference for structural complexity and metaphorical over-determination, can be seen to adhere to established principles of literary composition. Jennings's last radio talk effectively reinstated the poet, revoking the concept of a Reporter passively purveying 'news about ourselves': 'the idea of extracting an idea of "what I am"', Jennings notes, 'is a thing that the poet does for himself and especially it is a thing that he can do for the community; I mean he can try and tell them who they are.'[92] The idea that the poet ought to 'tell' the masses 'who they are' punctures Mass-Observation's hope that 'they' would 'speak for themselves'. Jennings's conviction (in 'The Theatre Today') that the poet had inherited from kingship the task of 'realizing' the

[90] MacClancy, p. 509.
[91] Jennings, 'The Poet and the Public', p. 260.
[92] Ibid., p. 282.

free desires of the masses found an unexpected parallel in the vacuum created after the abdication of Edward VIII. The analogy is borne out by *May the Twelfth* which focuses on the demotic periphery of the coronation ceremony while leaving the place of George VI himself conspicuously empty. The editor-poet temporarily occupies the place of the king as the catalyst of mass desires. The enduring centrality of the role of the bourgeois poet may be taken to signal the failure of one of Mass-Observation's central ambitions, but Madge's and Jennings's complex adherence to bourgeois literary tradition also meant that they never fully shared the optimism which some of the movement's more marginal figures, and many scholars, have been eager to invest in it. Mass-Observation, as David Gascoyne enthused, would 'debunk the professional poets': 'the poet is dead and it is in the people that we must seek to find what remains of the mysterious radiation of his soul.'[93] Madge's and Jennings's essays from the 1930s, as well as the editorial procedures that shape *May the Twelfth*, suggest a keener awareness that—societal conditions being what they were—any writing performed by the masses would continue to be troubled by the spectre of the 'dead' bourgeois poet.

THE READABILITY OF SOCIAL FACTS: MASS-OBSERVATION AS SCIENCE

Madge's attempt to conceptualize Mass-Observation as a quasi-scientific endeavour gained new momentum when Tom Harrisson joined the project. The pamphlet *Mass-Observation*, co-authored by Madge and Harrisson, was intended to popularize the view of Mass-Observation as a scientific enterprise, and it stated that the movement would 'put to the test the "readability" of material produced by amateur writers'.[94] By contrast, the particular strength of Jennings's work resides in its attention to moments when experience becomes opaque or unintelligible. In Jennings's report, for example, there is a constant obsession with signs that remain indecipherable—a tendency announced by the '[r]ed flag covered with Chinese lettering' (105) which appears towards the beginning of his day survey. And even the periscopes in CM.1's report fail to yield a stable perspective onto the mass: 'Some people are having trouble with their

[93] David Gascoyne, *Journal 1936–1937* (London: Enitharmon Press, 1980), p. 53. The second quotation is taken from the trilogy of prose-poems which Gascoyne composed after Jennings's death. See Gascoyne, 'Three Verbal Objects in Memory of Humphrey Jennings' [1950], in *Collected Poems* (Oxford: Oxford University Press, 1988), pp. 63–66 (p. 63).

[94] Harrisson/Madge, *Mass-Observation*, p. 41.

periscopes', Jennings's report notes, '"I keep seeing myself and looking quickly away!"—"It makes me giddy looking at this thing"' (118). 'London on May 12' often presents situations in which the crowds are unable to make sense of the events they witness: 'coming away from Hyde Park Corner the guns continue and a little boy with his mouth full of ice-cream asks his father: "What they firing the guns for? What they firing the guns for?"' (126). The crumpled paper in the streets symbolizes this chaos of observed facts, of destabilized points of view: 'every inch of street surface everywhere around', Observer CO.38 discovers on his way home, 'is coated with a sort of papier-maché [sic] paste of old newspapers, bags, flags, pieces of cloth' (153). These images serve as metaphors for Mass-Observation's difficulties in rendering legible the vast flood of subjective responses to the coronation. At the same time, the idea that the crowd is unable to determine the significance of the events in which they are participating presents a wry rejoinder to the breakdown of stock responses which Jennings and Madge were hoping for. The failure to couch events in familiar terms, Jennings implies, far from effecting an emancipatory bracketing of stock responses, can lead to a comprehensive failure to make sense, to a total breakdown of 'readability'. Jennings's important insight—that the data gathered by Mass-Observation might fail to be assembled into a coherent form—temporarily suspends the processes of signification and poetic bestowal of meaning which are otherwise central to his own editorial work in *May the Twelfth*.

Jennings's preoccupation with such moments of opacity is related to his Surrealist fascination with the disjointing effects of 'chance' and 'incidents'. For some of the sections in *May the Twelfth*, Jennings sent out questionnaires asking Observers to comment on the 'funniest', 'most peculiar', and 'most stirring incidents' of their days. As the film-maker Stuart Legg recalled, Jennings thought of such coincidences as 'knots in time' which revealed in flashes 'the meaning of a particular moment in historical time'.[95] However, the shock value of these 'incidents' constantly threatens to outstrip the 'meaning' which they are intended to convey. Jennings's day survey of 12 April 1937, reports a pertinent conversation with Charles Madge: 'Coming home we discussed "the incident": I watched for cars as we crossed several roads. Then Ch. said "I've got it" and made me jump as though it were a car.'[96] The scene is itself transformed into a kind of *mise-en-page* shock as it quite literally cuts short Madge's attempt to explain the conceptual significance of 'incidents'. The sense of incompleteness

[95] MOA, Miscellaneous material relating to Humphrey Jennings, Box 3, Uncat. interview with Stuart Legg by Robert Vas [1970s].

[96] MOA, Day Survey 360.

Fig. 1. Humphrey Jennings, Daubhill, Bolton, 1937.

that characterizes the passage from the day survey also animates Jennings's published Surrealist works from the decade. It is reflected, for example, in his 'Reports', a group of prose poems which were published in *Contemporary Poetry and Prose* in 1936.[97] These textual *objets trouvés* present what appear to be excerpts from longer historical or documentary narratives. Because they are pared down to a few descriptive essentials, the narrated events seem to be endowed with special meaning; yet at the same time, the absence of any explicatory context makes it impossible to grasp their unspoken significance. These prose poems test the limits of the decade's favourite literary genre, the documentary reportage: the failure of their mimetic strategies is paradoxically produced by their own myopic vision, by the fact that they are looking too closely to make sense of what they see.

The photographs of deserted streets which Jennings took during his stint as a Mass-Observer in Bolton in 1937 aim at a similar effect [Fig. 1 and 2]. They are notably removed from the anthropological interest of the densely populated scenes which Humphrey Spender was photographing in Bolton in 1937, or from the pictures in Bill Brandt's pioneering volume *The English at Home* (1936). The composition of Jennings's depopulated freeze-frames instead recalls a number of iconic Surrealist photographs,

[97] Humphrey Jennings, 'Three Reports', *Contemporary Poetry and Prose*, 4–5 (August–September 1936), 94–95.

Fig. 2. Humphrey Jennings, The Elephant Gate, Bridson's Bleach Works, Bolton, 1937.

such as the images which Jacques-André Boiffard contributed to André Breton's Surrealist novel *Nadja* [Fig. 3], or Eugène Atget's stills of empty Paris streets [Fig. 4].[98] Like Boiffard and Atget, Jennings took his photographs of Bolton early in the morning when the city was still deserted. The enigmatic images which resulted from this quasi-documentary approach give the impression of veering away from naturalist representation because they are so obviously devoid of action. They are the visual equivalents of Jennings's mock-historical 'Reports', but they also recall the confusing accumulation of facts in *May the Twelfth*.

[98] Eugène Atget died in 1927, but he was recognized as an ancestor by the French Surrealists who featured his work in flagship publications like *La Révolution surréaliste*.

Fig. 3. Jacques-André Boiffard, Wine merchant's shop, Paris, 1920s.

The painstaking exactitude of Jennings's texts and images is frustratingly at odds with their reluctance to engage in documentary explanation and analysis. The photographs which Jennings took on May 12 also do not debar the possibility of a politicized reading—one of the images even presents a close-up of a *Daily Worker* issue showing the face of Lenin—yet unlike Madge's story of the Human Mole they resist subsumption under an exhaustive Marxist rationale. Adopting Michael Sheringham's comments about Boiffard, we might say that Jennings's Bolton photographs capture a kind of degree zero of artistic activity—they anticipate 'the possibility of a future event', '[t]he sense of a stage on which something may be about to happen'.[99] His photos stage, in Richards's terminology, a 'complete' modernist 'severance' from '*all* beliefs' and from their own historical contexts:

[99] Michael Sheringham, *Everyday Life: Theories from Surrealism to the Present* (Oxford: Oxford University Press, 2006), p. 92.

Fig. 4. Eugène Atget, Rue Rataud at the corner of the rue Lhomond, Paris (Vth arrondissement), 1913.

they are directed towards a future that is radically undescribable in terms of what is familiar and known.[100]

Madge was more optimistic as far as the 'readability' of the day surveys was concerned. For him, Mass-Observation had always been, albeit in changing and inconclusive ways, a scientific enterprise. *May the Twelfth*'s 'Normal Day-Survey', which Madge edited, provides a telling contrast with the section arranged by Jennings: it categorizes the collected data in order to specify the 'social area of an Observer' and the kinds of personal interaction occurring in a single day. Madge's essay 'Magic and Materialism', first published in *Left Review* in 1937, attempts to fuse his earlier interest in 'scientific Socialism' with the anthropological impulse of Mass-Observation.[101] Both fields, Madge points out, rely on 'the clear light of materialism, fearlessly applied

[100] I. A. Richards *Science and Poetry* (London: Trubner, 1926), p. 64, emphasis in the original.

[101] Charles Madge, 'Magic and Materialism', *Left Review*, 3/1 (February 1937), 31–35 (p. 32).

to the elucidation of physical phenomena'. He notes that materialism has been applied to 'the study of the human animal itself' only recently, not least because 'bourgeois society demands that in that sphere the old darkness of magic and religion should continue to reign'. Because the notion of poetic autonomy is closely allied to the bourgeois illusion of a self-sufficient subjectivity, the encroachment of materialism on the realm of the self will also narrow down the autonomous space afforded to poetry: 'poetry deals, not with the inexplicable, but with what has not yet been explained. It lights up, by fitful flashes, a scene on which the full day of science will presently dawn' (32). The essay signals a decisive shift in Madge's thinking about Mass-Observation from aesthetic and artistic concerns towards the supposedly harder facts of science. The essay no longer contemplates the reconciliation, envisioned in the essay 'Poetic Description and Mass-Observation', between the pseudo-statements of poetry and the propositional language of science, but places the two in stark opposition.

In a 1940 memo to Madge, Harrisson wrote that 'M-O started from two main different sources, one mainly artistic and considerably subjective, the other mainly scientific and considerably objective'.[102] By the end of 1937 the attempt to arrive at a synthesis between these two poles had been abandoned, and the move towards a scientific formulation of Mass-Observation's goals was almost complete with the publication of *Mass-Observation* in 1937 and *First Year's Work* in March 1938. Madge and Harrisson co-authored *Mass-Observation*, and it can be difficult to decide which parts were written by whom. Some passages in the first chapter, however, contemplate the future of art, and these at least seem to have been written by Madge. They announce that the union between science and poetry—between statement and pseudo-statement—which early Mass-Observation had envisaged will have to be postponed until 'art descends again from the clouds which now hide it, and is once more generally intelligible'. 'In the meantime', Madge notes, poetry will 'have undergone a transformation into something more akin to science'.[103] Ironically, *May the Twelfth*, which took several months to be edited, was published only after *Mass-Observation*, even though it is in many ways the 'earlier' book. Both *Mass-Observation* and *First Year's Work* were determinedly statistical in their interpretation of facts, and in 1938 Harrisson could confidently announce the dead-end of Mass-Observation as a literary movement. In an article ('Mass-Opposition and Tom Harrisson') he mounted an attack on 'poets' who 'resent a "science of

[102] MOA, Miscellaneous materials relating to Mass-Observation in 1930s, Box 1/1, Memo from Tom Harrisson to Charles Madge, 18 January 1940.

[103] Harrisson/Madge, *Mass-Observation*, p. 27.

ourselves" because they have, for some time past, got away with claiming that title for their own work. Art has overstepped its bounds, into a pseudo-realism.' The 'facts' of sociology and the poetic statements of literature, Harrisson proclaimed, 'do not overlap to any appreciable extent'.[104] The essay scores a rhetorical victory over the artistic aims which Harrisson was seeking to exclude from Mass-Observation, but its cutting of the Gordian knot in favour of science is also its major shortcoming. Harrisson's insistence that art and science, pseudo-statement and statement, poetic and objective fact were incompatible quite simply ignored the circumstance that these were the fundamental dilemmas which Mass-Observation had initially set out to resolve. It was not true that Mass-Observation had started out in intellectual naivety and found itself, less than two years later, in a state of sobered disillusionment.

Madge's and Jennings's recognition of Mass-Observation's inherent contradictions in the mid-1930s was less sparing than critics have granted. The anxiety that the project's early artistic aspirations might founder was an integral part of the enterprise's Ricardian legacy and one of the defining conditions of its early phase. The peculiar strength of early Mass-Observation was that it did not assimilate its artistic interests too quickly to political or ethnographic rationales. On the contrary, its aesthetic concerns constituted the framework in which some of the enterprise's fledgling extra-poetic ambitions could be articulated. Both Jennings and Madge found it difficult to occupy the roles of reporter or editor which they had created for themselves. Instead, they assumed the fraught position of the Ricardian censor or critical judge—a role which Mass-Observation was continually struggling to repress. Jennings attempted to cloak the degree of his editorial interference in *May the Twelfth* by reducing his name to a cipher, 'CM.1', but the number associated with this alias inadvertently reflects the priority allotted to Jennings's own report. Mass-Observation's heightened consciousness of these artistic dilemmas reveals some of the tensions which invariably beset thirties writing but which tend to be silenced in the decade's more robustly revolutionary proclamations. The enterprise's fraught awareness of its own shortcomings produced one of the decade's most searching—and sobering—investigations into the possibilities of 'popular' art. The next chapter will turn to the communist writer Edward Upward to suggest that this element of self-interrogation and artistic self-doubt is also central to some of the most notoriously doctrinaire texts of the period.

[104] Harrisson, 'Mass-Opposition', p. 11.

5

Bad Dreams

Edward Upward and Marxist Prophecy

The trajectory of Edward Upward's literary career is usually held to be symptomatic of the artistic failures of thirties politicized writing more generally, and critics have insisted that Upward's literary output was marked by stylistic and qualitative hiatuses which coincided with his allegiance to doctrinaire communism. According to this established view, Upward's talent as a writer dried up with the transition around 1930 from his fantastic stories about the imaginary town of Mortmere to his politicized fiction. Yet despite these breaks, Upward's writings evince a remarkable continuity in terms of their underlying artistic concerns. Foremost among these is the effort to escape an empiricist understanding of history by discovering the abstract principles and patterns which govern history's course. Even Upward's attitude towards these views of history remained relatively stable: while he found the perceived nihilism of the empiricist position unacceptable, he admitted that the latter view (particularly in its Marxist-Leninist manifestations) could teeter on 'platitudinous abstractions'.[1] Upward's writings from the 1920s onwards struggle to come to terms with the artistic implications of this dilemma. His poetry from the mid-1920s is already drawn towards the question whether a higher and more abstract truth can be envisioned by poetic means, though it is only in the early 1930s that his search for moral and poetic authority finds ideological support in the doctrines of Marxism.

'Allen Chalmers', the pseudonym which Christopher Isherwood and Stephen Spender used to refer to Upward in their memoirs, has become (in Spender's phrase) the iconic 'case history' of thirties literature.[2] More than any other writer, 'Chalmers' was the figure onto whom politicized

[1] Edward Upward, *The Spiral Ascent* [1962–77], 3 vols (London: Quartet Books, 1977–79), I: *In the Thirties* (1978), p. 30.

[2] Stephen Spender, *World Within World* [1951] (New York: The Modern Library, 2001), p. 330. See also Stephen Spender, 'The Case of Edward Upward', *London Magazine*, 27 (1987), 29–43.

authors of the 1930s could project their artistic fears about going over to the Communist Party. John Lehmann, for one, scathingly observed that the 'imaginative gift in "Chalmers" [was] slowly killed in the Iron Maiden of Marxist dogma'—a view which later critics have shared.[3] Arguing against this reductive account, I contend that for Upward the problem of how literature might become political was not just a matter of holding the right opinions but of evolving the right kind of poetic voice. The attempt to distinguish between forms of literary 'fantasy' and 'prophecy' is central to Upward's literary output, and his works—from his early poetry and prose to his stories of the 1930s—negotiate these unresolved modes of signification over the artistic and ideological notion of 'dreaming'. I. A. Richards's association of literary discourse with the distinct realm of pseudo-statements led Upward to question literature's ability to intervene in social reality, and his texts notably fail to draw a line between the ideologically saturated dreams of communism and the 'bad' dreams of fantasy.

'FUTILE [. . .] DREAMS' AND ARTISTIC 'TRUTH': UPWARD'S EARLY POETRY

Upward's earliest surviving works, gloomy poems in a Symbolist and Decadent vein, were written between 1922 and 1924 while he and his close friend Christopher Isherwood were students at Repton School in Derbyshire. These poems characteristically doubt the reliability of their own artistic vision, and their scepticism is often associated, for instance in 'Nursery' (dated 'March '23' in Upward's manuscript version), with the ambiguities of poetic 'dreaming':

> The child whose hands grope for the skies
> Can never pass the window-glass,
> Nor near, for dreaming with grave eyes,
> The pleasant comfort of the stars.[4]

'Nursery' calls up the limitations inherent in any attempt to encompass the metaphysical 'comfort of the stars', and the idea of 'dreaming' is qualified by an adjective that serves as a reminder of the physical 'grave'. Another poem, 'Blood' (dated 9 September 1921), makes this association

[3] John Lehmann, *Autobiography*, 3 vols (London: Eyre and Spottiswoode, 1955–66), III (1966), p. 244. See also Samuel Hynes, *The Auden Generation: Literature and Politics in England in the 1930s* (London: The Bodley Head, 1976), p. 317; and Valentine Cunningham *British Writers of the Thirties* (Oxford: Oxford University Press, 1988), p. 213.

[4] EUP, Notebooks and poems from 1920s, ADD 72690, Uncat. ms 'Nursery'.

explicit by invoking urns 'loom[ing] like veering dreams of things, like graves | Of memories'.[5] In Upward's early poetry, dreams serve as metaphors for the loftiness of human aspirations and for their incompatibility with the intransigencies of human life. His poems frequently occupy a zone of indeterminacy, oscillating between Yeatsian vision and the merely delusional as in the following, untitled poem from 1924:

Lost on a world of dreams,
A moon-curved valley gleams,
Seven nights deep,
With gay words curled
About the leafy heart of the world
Tangled in sleep.

Darkly, wistfully,
Over the maze of the sky,
The grey stars wander in dream,
Die into dawn.[6]

Upward's unpublished notebooks and letters from the 1920s frequently comment on the influences which shape his early poems, and they register a particular literary obsession with the work of Rupert Brooke. Writing about one of Isherwood's poems in a letter from 1922, Upward detects in it a 'distinctly Brookean' tone: 'but I suspect that is', the missive continues, 'because I am so steeped in Rupert.'[7] Upward's later self-critical remarks, inserted from the 1930s onwards in the margins of his notebooks, also point to Brooke's influence.[8] Brooke's poems bear a special affinity to Upward's ambivalences about the visionary significance of dreams. Upward's poem 'Sleeper in Broad Daylight', for instance, written during a stay in Rouen in 1922, the year he matriculated at Cambridge, finds that the speaker's 'twilight dreams' are only chimeras, 'fashioned in illusion's land'.[9] The poem echoes lines from Brooke's similarly disillusioned 'Day That I Have Loved' which had first been published in his volume *Poems* (1911):

Beyond the shifting cold twilights,
Further than laughter goes, or tears, further than dreaming,
There'll be no port, no dawn-lit islands.[10]

[5] Ibid., Uncat. ms 'Blood'. [6] Ibid., Uncat. ms 'Lost On a World Of Dreams'.

[7] CIP, Letter from Edward Upward to Christopher Isherwood, 15 February 1922, 2288. Hynes has noted the special place of Brooke in the literary imaginary of the 1930s (p. 30).

[8] 'Too like R. Brooke', is a recurring comment (EUP, Notebook from late 1920s, ADD 72689 N).

[9] EUP, Notebooks and poems from 1920s, ADD 72690, Uncat. ms 'Sleeper in Broad Daylight'.

[10] Rupert Brooke, *Selected Poems* [1917] (London: Sidgwick, 1923), p. 7.

Such decadent pessimism about the visionary potential of dreams is present in many of Brooke's poems. The sonnet 'Love' from 1913 characteristically mulls over disenchanted lovers who 'are but taking | Their own poor dreams within their arms, and lying, | Each in his lonely night, each with a ghost'.[11] This conflicted usage of the term, which Upward inherited in part from Brooke, is marked by what Ernst Bloch has called the instability of 'anticipatory consciousness'. As described by Bloch, dreams (and especially daydreams) possess a dual character: they are 'open, fabulously inventive, anticipating', but they also constitute an undirected 'journey into the blue' in which 'real things' 'appear muted', and 'are often distorted'.[12] The necessity of 'dreaming' remains central to Upward's writing from the 1920s onwards, and it usually covers both of the meanings indicated above: 'dream' as fanciful delusion and as an index of utopian anticipation. Upward's early poems pick up the former, derogatory signification from Brooke's poetry, and it is only in the 1930s that he begins to invest the concept with greater authority and ideological force. Upward's attempt to overcome the Brookean pessimism of his poetry is already evident in his 1922 'Hymn to Truth'. Written the night before he left for Rouen, the text expresses Upward's hope for a new departure in his poetry: 'Stream onward still in Truth's infinitude. | [. . .] Fountain, arise from God with fluent streams, | Purge me of any futile loves and dreams.'[13] 'Hymn to Truth' is one of the few poems which escaped Upward's own harsh criticism in later years, and lines from it are quoted in the third volume of his semi-autobiographical trilogy *The Spiral Ascent* which recalls that 'Truth was invited [. . .] to purge me of all my futile poetic dreams', specifically 'dreams of a decadent kind'.[14] The reasons for Upward's defence of this particular poem lie in its affinities to the logic of abstraction which is also at work in his later Marxist works. Like his more explicitly political texts, 'Hymn to Truth' seeks to reach out to a manifest 'Truth' beyond the ambivalences of 'anticipatory consciousness'.

In the autumn of 1922, a few months after he had written 'Hymn to Truth', Upward went up to Corpus Christi College, Cambridge, where Isherwood followed him one year later. As Katherine Bucknell has noted, Upward attended I. A. Richards's lectures 'early in 1925', and the central theory which Richards propounded in those lectures—that literature conveys only psychological 'attitudes' and accordingly bears no direct connection to reality—'called into question the kind of poetry that Upward

[11] Ibid., p. 51.

[12] Ernst Bloch, *The Principle of Hope* [1938–47], trans. by Paul Knight, Neville Plaice, and Stephen Plaice (Oxford: Blackwell, 1986), pp. 88, 99.

[13] CIP, Edward Upward, Ms 'Hymn to Truth', 2276.

[14] Edward Upward, *The Spiral Ascent*, III: *No Home But the Struggle* (1979), p. 175.

was then trying to write'.[15] Richards's radical theories remained a source of artistic anxiety for Upward from which he and Isherwood were struggling to depart: 'if Mr Richards enormously stimulated us', Isherwood recalled in his autobiography *Lions and Shadows* (1938), 'he plunged us, also, into the profoundest gloom. It seemed to us that everything we had valued would have to be scrapped.'[16] Richards's theories dealt a blow to Upward's Brookean poetry, but they also confirmed his deeper suspicions regarding the immateriality of the illusions which literature has to offer. For Upward, it was far from self-evident that his early poems were able to convey the 'Truth' about the real world.

There was another reason why Upward felt the force of Richards's arguments as strongly as he did. Around 1923, some time before they attended Richards's lectures, Isherwood and Upward had begun to immerse themselves in the 'Other Town', a fictional world modelled on Cambridge. This hidden and esoteric universe owed its existence to an evening walk during which Upward noticed 'a strange-looking, rusty-hinged little old door in a high blank wall', and solemnly declared that it was the doorway 'into the Other Town'.[17] Over the course of the next two or three years Isherwood and Upward collaborated on short stories about this town, availing themselves of an ever expanding cast of grotesque characters. Mortmere, as Isherwood and Upward conceived of it, constituted a largely self-enclosed poetic world: what gave these stories their coherence as artworks was not, Richards's theories suggested, their tenuous reference to a shared world of external facts, but their internal artistic logic. One passage in Richards's *Principles of Literary Criticism* (1924), the book which first presented his theories about 'emotive' pseudo-statements to a wider audience, offered a particularly stinging rebuttal of Upward's search for 'Truth' outside literature's textual confines. 'The "Truth"' of a text, Richards noted,

> is the acceptability of the things we are told, their acceptability in the interests of the effects of the narrative, not their correspondence with any actual facts [. . .]. Similarly the falsity of happy endings to *Lear* or to *Don Quixote* is their failure to be acceptable to those who have fully responded to the rest of the work. It is in this sense that 'Truth' is equivalent to 'internal necessity' or rightness.[18]

[15] Christopher Isherwood and Edward Upward, *The Mortmere Stories*, ed. by Katherine Bucknell (London: Enitharmon, 1994), p. 19.

[16] Christopher Isherwood, *Lions and Shadows: An Education in the Twenties* [1938] (London: Methuen, 1985), p. 75.

[17] Ibid., p. 42.

[18] I. A. Richards, *Principles of Literary Criticism* [1924] (London: Routledge, 2001), pp. 251–52.

These comments relegate external claims to 'Truth' to the background of the literary text. At the same time, Richards's critical doctrines implied that the esoteric world of Mortmere, because it failed to speak to anyone apart from Isherwood and Upward, belonged in the 'lumber room of "private poetry" '.[19]

Upward had always been keener than Isherwood to maintain the secrecy of Mortmere and to defend it against the curiosity of relatives and friends. For him, the value of Mortmere lay in its hermeticism: the fantasy world took on a special place in his imagination precisely because its seeming self-containment allowed him to think through the relation of poetic discourse to the search for extra-literary 'Truth'. Amongst the problems which arose from Richards's condemnation of 'private poetry' was whether the fantasy of Mortmere, its ostentatious fictionality, could be reformed from within, or whether a completely new type of writing was required. The satiric intent of Mortmere maintained only an oblique connection to the world which it criticized, and Upward seems to have associated his fantasy stories increasingly with the distinct realm of fictional pseudo-statements postulated by Richards. The question which lay at the heart of these reflections and which haunted Upward with particular persistence was whether there was a way to go beyond the confines of literature—whether even Mortmere could be shown to have roots outside literature's narrowly discursive domain.

Katherine Bucknell has argued that 'the theories of Richards so shook [Upward] in the mid-1920s because [he] feared they might be true; for a time he could not see any connection between his imaginative writing and the real world.'[20] Isherwood contributed to the still-dominant critical narrative which asserts that Upward became disillusioned with his early poetry while at Cambridge and found a solution for his dilemma through his espousal of communism in the early 1930s. Upward, Isherwood observed in his memoir *Lions and Shadows*, sought to 'transform our private fancies and amusing freaks and bogies into valid symbols of the ills of society', finding the formula only 'at the end of a long and weary search [. . .] in the pages of Lenin and Marx'.[21] However, Upward's awareness of the rift between the internal discursive 'Truth' of a text and the 'Truth' of its statements about reality clearly predated his encounter with Richards's theories, and the profound ambivalence which resulted from this tension continues to make itself felt in his later Marxist writings.

[19] Isherwood, p. 75.

[20] Katherine Bucknell, 'The Achievement of Edward Upward', in *W. H. Auden: 'The Language of Learning and the Language of Love': Uncollected Writings, New Interpretations*, ed. by Katherine Bucknell and Nicholas Jenkins (Oxford: Clarendon Press, 1994), pp. 165–86 (p. 171).

[21] Isherwood, pp. 168–69.

Upward's strenuous attempts to articulate a reliable vision of 'Truth' in his works of the 1930s are anticipated in particular in the poem 'To a Historian', written in the spring of 1924. Like Isherwood, Upward had entered Cambridge with a scholarship to read history, but he soon grew dissatisfied with the way the subject was taught there. In Upward's eyes, the academic analysis of history amounted to a meaningless agglomeration of historical detail. What made him hate 'history as it was presented at Cambridge' was, he recalled later, 'its fact-grubbing passionlessness'.[22] 'To a Historian'—written, as Isherwood notes, 'at the height' of their Mortmere phase [23]—attacks 'fact-grubbing' history because it puts up a barrier to Upward's newly professed quest for 'Truth':

> You who must ponder cause and act,
> Historian, from the quag of fact
> Search out, propound a cause for this –
> The cross of life we bear who miss
> Life's truth, and grope with baffled hands
> About a stage none understands.
> [. . .]
>
> We should be glad of nature's laws,
> And take unquestioning this crust
> Of various life, this peak of dust.
> We should have mind to mark the gleam
> In the chaos of time's stream,
> And in this hubbub and this night
> Glimpse the unapparent light.
> We are God's purblind fools, it seems,
> Who hunt the moon with shafts of dreams[.][24]

The historian's sense of mastery is disrupted by the vision of a teeming miscellany of historical 'facts', and the poem associates the historian's futile 'dreams' with the empiricist failure to grasp the immanent patterns of historical movement—those 'laws' which are all the more real because they underlie, and remain unaffected by, the 'chaos of time's stream'. The 'quag of fact' pictured in the poem becomes a central test case for Upward's search for 'Truth', and one of eminent importance to his literary career in the 1930s. Both Upward's preoccupation with the hidden world of Mortmere and the later assimilation of Marxist doctrines into his writing are fuelled by a desire to reach through the 'hubbub' of history and to disclose

[22] Upward, *No Home But the Struggle*, p. 179. [23] Isherwood, p. 43.

[24] The poem is reprinted in *Lions and Shadows*, pp. 43–44. The manuscript version gives 'January 1924' as the time of composition (EUP, ADD 72690).

the deeper significance concealed within it. A letter to Isherwood from 1932 gives expression to Upward's hope that Mortmere and Marxism were not worlds apart: 'Mortmere is literally the realisation of what was after all not merely the daydream of two warped collegians but a profound understanding of the *substructure* of our times.'[25]

FROM MORTMERE 'FANTASY' TO MARXIST 'PROPHECY'

From the late 1920s onwards, Upward was searching for a poetic voice capable of articulating the seriousness and intensity of his search for the subtext of social life. He found a tentative solution to this problem in the work of E. M. Forster. He had read *Howards End* (1910) in 1925, and by the end of the year had bought all of Forster's available novels.[26] 'Forster's the only one who understands what the modern novel ought to be', Upward instructed Isherwood: instead of 'trying to screw all his scenes up to the highest possible pitch, he tones them down until they sound like mothers'-meeting gossip'.[27] While Upward was the one who 'discovered' Forster and theorized profusely about his aesthetic, Forster's novels had a more instant and sizable influence on Isherwood. As Peter Parker points out, Isherwood's next literary project, provisionally entitled *Seascape with Figures* and begun only a few days after he had read *Howards End*, was modelled on Forster's novel.[28] Over the course of the following years, Forster became one of the most important guru-figures in Isherwood's life—a writer who praised Isherwood's work and whose own writings were in turn absorbed by his eager disciple. By contrast, Upward's works are never at home with the casual tone of Forster's 'mothers'-meeting gossip', and his writing caught up with Forster's influence only after some delay, with the publication in 1927 of *Aspects of the Novel*, a series of lectures which Forster had given at Cambridge earlier that year. Upward had left Cambridge in 1925, and he did not hear Forster's lectures when they were first delivered. Even so, the publication of *Aspects of the Novel* came at a pivotal moment in Upward's life: he was profoundly unhappy with his position as a private tutor in Cornwall which he had taken up after leaving university, and he had done almost no literary work for two years. One reason for Upward's silence was that he felt increasingly uneasy about the fantasy

[25] CIP, Letter from Edward Upward to Christopher Isherwood [1932], 2314, emphasis in the original.

[26] I am grateful to Ed Maggs for this information.

[27] Isherwood, p. 107.

[28] Peter Parker, *Isherwood: A Life* (London: Picador, 2004), pp. 130–31.

writing which he and Isherwood had practised at Cambridge. Mortmere appeared to put him out of touch with reality; in order to be able to write again, he had to 'purge' his style 'of fantasy, make it truer to life'.[29]

Aspects of the Novel spoke immediately to Upward's concerns. Following the book's famous analytic chapters on 'Character' and 'Plot', Forster presented the interpretative and speculative centre of his study: two chapters titled 'Fantasy' and 'Prophecy'. Forster's lectures suggest that these two categories represent the extremes of a continuum along which storytelling takes place. 'Fantasy', Forster notes, 'asks us to pay something extra': it superimposes onto everyday reality a layer of extravagant artificiality, thus highlighting the story's status as fictional artefact, as artful illusion.[30] 'Fantasy' draws additional attention to the fact that 'a work of art is an entity' which 'has its own laws which are not those of daily life' (103). This ostentatious craftedness lends 'fantasy' its 'improvised air', its 'force and charm', but it also diminishes its ability to inquire into the inner nature of the things which it describes: 'the power of fantasy penetrates into every corner of the universe, but not into the forces that govern it' (105). 'Prophecy', by contrast, stays focused on 'the universe, or something universal'. As Forster observes, his concept of 'prophetic' fiction excludes 'the narrow sense of foretelling the future', locating 'prophecy' instead in a particular 'accent in the novelist's voice' (116). Because 'we are not concerned with the prophet's message' (123), the peculiar authority of prophetic narratives resides in the act of signification itself rather than in the things and events which are being predicted. Forster's argument inadvertently blurs the distinction between the two elementary types of narrative which it propounds. In his account, 'prophecy' can appear as immaterial as 'fantasy' because it is not directed towards historical facts, but towards a future that has not yet materialized.

Forster's lectures held out a tentative alternative to the fantastic style of Mortmere, as well as a new approach to the Ricardian gap between factual statements and fictional pseudo-statements. Prophecy, as Forster presented it, was able to talk about the laws which Upward wanted to discover underneath the 'hubbub' of life, and it managed to do so without falling into the flat propositional statements of scientific discourse. Upward's fiction from the late 1920s onwards is anxious to evolve a particular mode of prophetic signification, but its 'prophetic accent' is beset by the tensions which lie dormant in Forster's explication of the term. 'Fantasy', Antonio Gramsci explained in 1932, can only conceive of the future as an inversion of the present: it is 'basically the present turned on its head

[29] Upward, *No Home But the Struggle*, p. 24.

[30] E. M. Forster, *Aspects of the Novel* [1927] (London: Penguin, 2005), p. 104.

which is projected into the future'.[31] Prophetic fiction, by contrast, insists on a radical break between present and future, but it too needs to resort to the imperfect language of its own historical moment in order to talk about things to come. The constitutive instabilities of Upward's fiction derive from the difficulties he encountered in distinguishing between a prophetic and a fantastic vision of the future. Even the most Marxist and future-oriented of Upward's prophetic fictions continue to be haunted by the bad daydreams of fantasy.

Upward's last Mortmere story, 'The Railway Accident', is not really about Mortmere at all. Written in 1928, after three years of almost complete artistic unproductiveness, the story narrates a train ride to Mortmere, but only the very last paragraphs actually take place in the fantasy world itself. Nevertheless, 'The Railway Accident' is firmly rooted in the lore of the 'Other Town': its characters appear in several earlier stories by Isherwood and Upward, as do certain parts of the landscape through which the train passes. The story's protagonist, Edward Hearn, shares a compartment with Gustave Shreeve, the headmaster of a boys' school in Mortmere. During their conversation, Shreeve draws Hearn's attention to the fact that a fatal collision took place on the same route a few years earlier. According to Shreeve's account of these events, the earlier accident was preceded by a number of ominous signs. Hearn's nervous imagination is instantly captivated by Shreeve's story, and in the course of their journey he becomes convinced that signs for another impending crash are beginning to emerge. The predicted second accident duly takes place towards the end of the story, killing most of the passengers on the train; following one last omen, Shreeve and Hearn manage to jump free only seconds before the crash. 'The Railway Accident' is the first text by Upward to rehearse a Forsterian 'prophetic accent'. The story is 'tense with visionary excitement', although it does not yet locate its predictions within the more narrowly ideological matrix of dialectical materialism.[32] Rod Mengham has argued that the 'constant desire for the random' in Upward's fantastic fiction 'is in fact a sign of its attempt to stem the advance of the [. . .] irrevocable', 'of the descending weight of a fixed pattern from which it is always struggling, with only small success, to escape'.[33] The place of 'The Railway Accident' in Upward's artistic development may also hint at a contrary agenda. The story tries to rule out the possibility of insignificance, of the

[31] Antonio Gramsci, *Selections from the Prison Notebooks*, trans. by Quintin Hoare and Geoffrey Nowell-Smith (London: Lawrence and Wishart, 1991), p. 175 fn.

[32] Bucknell, p. 168.

[33] Rod Mengham, 'Smithereens: *The Railway Accident* and *The Orators*', *Ideas and Production*, 4 (1985), 25–43 (p. 28).

merely accidental, countering it with statements about the inevitability of future events.

The first paragraphs of the story show Hearn in the company of one Donald Gunball, waiting for the departure of the train to Mortmere. While he is contemplating the inside of the railway station, Hearn abruptly drifts off into a 'daydream':

> Through the roof panes the sun froze in whey-white on steam columns from the waiting engines. Other insignia of the bogus, curt and modern cathedral ceremony which in my daydream, induced partly by the cold, I had begun to arrange were the reverberating stammer of slipping driving-wheels on suburban trains and the fussing haste of porters loading the guard's van with wooden crates.[34]

The dream presented in these sentences recalls the metamorphoses in Upward's and Isherwood's Mortmere stories whereby Cambridge was turned into the esoteric Other Town. When the train arrives, it represents the waywardness of its destination, Mortmere: 'my impression of most details in the design of this train was that they were unnecessary or, if necessary, belonging to a world in which I should have felt [. . .] wholly disoriented' (39). 'The Railway Accident' invokes such daydreaming only to replace it with Hearn's paranoid vision. A prophetic accent enters the story through the narration of Shreeve who points out that an ominous 'fisherman dressed in green standing among the rhododendrons and winding his reel' had been glimpsed by travellers a few years earlier before their train crashed on the same line. Hearn comes to believe that he has had a similarly portentous vision of Harold Wrygrave, a character familiar from other Mortmere stories, standing up in a convertible car. Hearn convinces himself that Wrygrave is 'a different kind of fisher in green', and Shreeve enthusiastically supports this theory: 'Yes. Yes. That's it. An omen, a warning in the quiet of the day, a visible prefiguration it may be of death as we comfortably roll through the frozen countryside' (54). Further intensifying the story's paranoid vision, Shreeve recounts how a tunnel on the same route collapsed, burying a whole train and killing all of its passengers:

> Why did the tunnel collapse in two places almost simultaneously ten years ago? A minute error in trigonometry. [. . .] You could pretend to accept that explanation, like the coroner. But if you'd stood as I have done for many hours among those terrible ruins it might have occurred to you to wonder whether after all it was an accident, an error, that the distance between the

[34] Edward Upward, 'The Railway Accident' [1928], in *The Railway Accident and Other Stories* (London: Penguin, 1972), pp. 33–70 (p. 36).

two collapsed sections of the tunnel almost exactly corresponded to the average length of an express train. (56)

The story's vision of the inevitable is upset by Shreeve himself who confesses to sabotage just before he and Hearn jump free of the train. Although Shreeve retracts his confession immediately after they have landed in the reed bushes beside the rail tracks, the story intimates that Hearn may have been fooled by Shreeve—that his vision of imminent disaster is only another fantastic daydream.

Hearn's inability to distinguish between prophecy and fantasy is partly explained by his status as an outsider in the world of the Other Town. Upward's and Isherwood's list of Mortmere characters explains that he is only a 'visitor': a supposedly real-life *Doppelgänger* of Upward and Isherwood who fails to determine whether the omens he witnesses are not after all part of an extravagant and elaborate delusion.[35] 'The Railway Accident', although it frequently approximates a sense of imminent revolutionary cataclysm, ultimately hesitates to make the rhetorical transition into the register of the prophetic. Upward attempted to turn away from the poetic self-containment of his early fantasy stories in the 1930s, but he never quite abandoned the possibility that his dreams, even at their most ideological and prophetic, might be mere fictions. His stories are marked by a similar refusal to privilege either of the two narrative modes—fantasy and prophecy—over the other. As he reflected in a letter to Isherwood from 1939, even his most overtly political stories 'still have and always will have a foot in Mortmere'.[36]

Upward rejected attempts to 'over-intellectualize' Mortmere by stressing its affinities with Freudian theory.[37] The influence of psychoanalysis on Upward's writing was indeed more localized than critics have assumed, and it certainly did not extend to Sigmund Freud's more complex theories regarding the subconscious. The specific ambiguities of Upward's prophetic accent in 'The Railway Accident' appear to be derived from a few select passages in the contemporary psychoanalytic literature which Upward was reading at the time. One point of reference is Freud's *Introductory Lectures on Psycho-Analysis* (1917) which Isherwood had given to Upward as a gift on 4 April 1926.[38] Freud's book returns several times to the fears triggered by railway travel, pointing out that the

[35] Isherwood/Upward, p. 31.
[36] CIP, Letter from Edward Upward to Christopher Isherwood [1939], 2456.
[37] CIP, Letter from Edward Upward to Christopher Isherwood, February [1926], 2341.
[38] The personal inscription in Upward's 1922 copy of the book states that it had belonged to Isherwood in 1925 who passed it on 'to E. F. Upward' one year later. I am grateful to Ed Maggs for this information.

common fright of dying in a train accident is an instance of neurosis set in motion by 'a general apprehensiveness, [. . .] a "free-floating" anxiety': 'We call this condition "expectant dread" or "anxious expectation".'[39] Hearn's premonition of the accident is, on this reading, not a prophetic prediction but merely a nervous phantasm triggered by an overpowering 'expectant dread'. Some of Freud's arguments had been anticipated in England by Havelock Ellis, the champion of sexology and of the psychoanalytical interpretation of dreams. Ellis had been another favourite author of Upward and Isherwood, who read his works aloud to each other while at Cambridge. In his *The World of Dreams* (1911), Ellis had suggested that the phrase 'prophetic dreams' was only a metaphor for a widespread psychological phenomenon: 'the subsequent "recognition" of things or persons seen in dreams', he noted, 'is due to the emotional preparation of the dream, and the concentrated expectation.'[40] Freud's and Ellis's theorizations of 'expectant dread' and 'concentrated expectation' were demoting prophecy to a form of acute neurosis, and the precariousness of Upward's prophetic voice in 'The Railway Accident' is governed by a quite similar set of ambivalences: depending on our point of view, Hearn's prescience appears either as an accurate prediction of events or as a hallucination prompted by emotional strain.

Upward's attempt to see in the story's 'premonitions' (a keyword in 'The Railway Accident') more than just immaterial daydreams also led him to engage anew with Richards's theories about the discursive effects—the internal 'Truth'—of literature. In the early 1930s, he drew up a list of 'Fifty Pointed Questions to Mr. I. A. Richards'.[41] His notes, which quickly dwindled down to thirty questions, fill an entire notebook without ever reaching a degree of completion. Many of the questions are in fact thinly disguised statements relating to Upward's own fragmentary theory of literature. They are directed at Richards but also at Upward himself: 'Isn't it plain', Question 17 notes, 'that your distinction between thoughts which have objects and feelings which have no objects is [. . .] fundamentally unsound?' Upward's questions reveal the unease he felt at Richards's critical doctrines: the theory of pseudo-statements, he writes, threatened to 'cut the legs off poetry'.[42] In his notebooks, Upward set out to define a set of poetic rules and axioms which posit a link between the pseudo-statements of literature and the external world. Yet the fragmentary state

[39] Sigmund Freud, *Introductory Lectures on Psycho-Analysis* [1917], trans. by Joan Riviere (London: Allen and Unwin, 1922), p. 332.

[40] Havelock Ellis, *The World of Dreams* (London: Constable, 1911), p. 93.

[41] CIP, Letter from Edward Upward to Christopher Isherwood [1931], 2420.

[42] EUP, Notebook from the early 1930s, ADD 73689 X, Uncat. ms 'Fifty Pointed Questions to Mr. I. A. Richards'.

of the questionnaire suggests that his attempts to refute Richards's theories remained frustratingly inconclusive.

Critics have sometimes written about Upward's espousal of communism as though it happened with the abruptness of a conversion.[43] As Katherine Bucknell has observed, however, Upward's was a long struggle for ideological conviction. The 'important frontier' which he needed to cross was the 'internal' one 'between vision and disillusion, past self and present self, bourgeois self and Marxist self, continually rediscovering and reanimating his developing political and poetic convictions and thereby charting the relationship between them'.[44] While Upward's adoption of communism signifies a crucial biographical divide, the relatively prolonged segue from one set of artistic convictions to the other also means that Upward's works from the 1920s and his politicized stories from the 1930s have a number of salient features in common. 'The Railway Accident' is perhaps Upward's most remarkable transitional story, as it attempts to assemble a prophetic accent out of the fantastic materials of Mortmere. Upward's decision to reprint the text (as the only one of his Mortmere stories) in the Penguin edition of his writings already indicates that its prophetic accent has more in common with his later, Marxist work, than with his fantasy stories from the mid-1920s. After 1927, Upward's goal was to give prophecy a more solid grounding in social and historical fact, and he found support in the teachings of Marxism, especially in Lenin's *Materialism and Empirio-Criticism* (1909), a book which argued—against Richards, as it were—that emotions reflected the real world. Marxism opened up new ways to think about the status of poetic dreams. If 'fantasies', as Brian Finney suggests with a view to Mortmere, are 'dreams' through which 'we seek to avenge ourselves on a world that stubbornly refuses to conform to our ideas of what it should be like', the 'dreams' of Marxism seemed to consist of more accurate and objective predictions about the course of history.[45]

As a system of thought rooted in the dubious science of dialectical materialism, Marxism was suspicious of most types of ideological and literary dreaming. 'The Marxist tradition', as Ruth Levitas observes, 'has for the most part been strongly antipathetic to utopianism.'[46] Yet one of the most

[43] For example Anthony Arblaster, who contrasts Upward's 'leap of commitment' with his contemporaries' 'ambiguity' about joining the CP. See Arblaster, 'Edward Upward and the Novel of Politics', in *1936: The Sociology of Literature*, ed. by Francis Barker, 2 vols (Colchester: University of Essex, 1979), II, pp. 179–96 (p. 181).

[44] Bucknell, p. 169.

[45] Brian Finney, 'Laily, Mortmere and All That', *Twentieth-Century Literature*, 22 (1976), 286–302 (p. 287).

[46] Ruth Levitas, *The Concept of Utopia* (London: Philip Allan, 1990), p. 35.

influential and most widely read expositions of Marxist-Leninist doctrine, Lenin's *What Is To Be Done?* (1902) had given a resonantly affirmative reply to the question whether 'a Marxist' had 'any right at all to dream'. 'We ought to be dreaming!', Lenin began his discussion, quoting with approval a passage from the nineteenth-century radical thinker Dimitri Pisarev:

> 'There are differences and differences', wrote Pisarev concerning the difference between dreams and reality. 'My dream may run ahead of the natural progress of events or may fly off at a tangent in a direction in which no natural progress of events will ever proceed. In the first case the dream will not cause any harm; it may even support and strengthen the efforts of toiling humanity. [. . .] Divergence between dreams and reality causes no harm if only the person dreaming believes seriously in his dream, [. . .] and if he works conscientiously for the achievement of his phantasies [. . .].' Now of this kind of dreaming there is unfortunately too little in our movement.[47]

In an analogous way, Marxism allowed Upward to 'dream' in the conviction that history was on his side. Here was a way to move beyond Forster's injunction that 'fantasy penetrates into every corner of the universe, but not into the forces that govern it'. Forster's phrasing is in fact echoed in Upward's most important statement about the nature of politically motivated writing, the 1937 'Sketch for a Marxist Interpretation of Literature', as if to signal the accomplishment of a move into literary prophecy: 'The greatest books are those which, sensing the forces of the future beneath the surface of the past or present reality, remain true to reality for the longest period of time.'[48] Upward's works from the 1930s incorporate Lenin's crucial distinction between prophetic dreams, which 'run ahead of the natural march of events', and fantastic dreams, which 'fly off at a tangent'. However, his stories almost always undermine the tidiness of these categories rather than naturalizing them successfully into the medium of fiction.

FANTASIZING MARXIST HISTORY: 'THE COLLEAGUES' AND 'SUNDAY'

Upward joined the Communist Party of Britain in 1932, a step into political commitment which he had been contemplating for at least two years,[49]

[47] V. I. Lenin, *What Is To Be Done?* [1902], in *Selected Works*, ed. by Joe Fineberg, 12 vols (London: Lawrence and Wishart, 1936–39), II (1936), pp. 25–192 (pp. 180–81).

[48] Edward Upward, 'Sketch for a Marxist Interpretation of Literature', in *The Mind in Chains: Socialism and the Cultural Revolution*, ed. by Cecil Day Lewis (London: F. Muller, 1937), pp. 41–55 (pp. 46–47).

[49] CIP, Letter from Edward Upward to Christopher Isherwood, 4 April 1930, 2403.

and his letters and notebook jottings from this time frequently display a dogmatic certainty about the course of history: 'I suppose there really will be a revolution quite soon', a letter to Isherwood from July 1931 confidently predicts.[50] Less than a year later, Upward was on his way to Moscow and Kharkov to witness the unfolding of Marxist history at first hand. On his journey back to England, Upward stopped off for a few days in Berlin to meet up with Isherwood, who introduced him to Stephen Spender. According to Spender, it was Upward who converted him to communism, and Spender's recollections of their meeting in his memoir *World Within World* (1951) have almost single-handedly set the picture of 'Allen Chalmers' as an unflinching doctrinaire hardliner.

The inscription of Chalmers into the myth of the 1930s has served to erase Upward's own more complex presence from the literary contexts of the decade.[51] Spender remembers in particular Chalmers's rebuttal of the popular view that 'the future remains always uncertain': 'I could not think that in 1931 a war which would take place eight years later existed within the structure of events. [. . .] This Berlin contained within a pattern.'[52] Spender was impressed with the internal coherence and the prediction value of Upward's Marxist worldview. As he recalls, Upward's political convictions also shaped the outlook of a novel which he was planning to write at the time:

> a novel in which the virtuous and sympathetic characters would be capitalists and the unpleasant ones Communists, but which would show that nevertheless the Communists were 'right' because they were 'on the side of history' – [this] seemed now a parable of our time: a parable, though, whose moral I took in the sense opposite to that intended by Chalmers.[53]

Upward was seeking a utopian or 'providential realism' which did not simply describe the way things were (the documentary art of the decade: Orwell's, the GPO Film Unit's, the proletarian writers', would take care of that), but the way they were going to be.[54] Lenin's remarks had implied

[50] CIP, Letter from Edward Upward to Christopher Isherwood, July 1931, 2417.

[51] For the origins of the Chalmers label and Upward's difficulties in inhabiting the role, see also Benjamin Kohlmann, '"A Foot in Mortmere": Christopher Isherwood and Edward Upward', in *The American Isherwood*, ed. by Jim Berg and Christopher Freeman (Minneapolis: University of Minnesota Press, forthcoming 2014).

[52] Spender, *World Within World*, p. 147. [53] Ibid., p. 276.

[54] I am borrowing the term 'providential realism' from Fredric Jameson who uses it to describe a mode of writing in which 'the reality principle' is 'joyously discredited', but which 'outwit[s] sheer wish-fulfilment and daydream'. Such realism, Jameson points out, is one of the 'figures of the political'. See Jameson, 'The Experiments of Time: Providence and Realism', in *The Novel*, ed. by Franco Moretti (Princeton: Princeton University Press, 2003), II, pp. 95–127 (pp. 125, 112).

that such realism was by its very nature prophetic: 'Socialist realism dares to "dream" and should do so, basing itself on real trends of development', Nikolai Bukharin announced at the 1934 Writers' Congress in Moscow which decreed the aesthetic tenets of socialist realism.[55] The artistic dimensions of Upward's espousal of communism are complicated by his persisting doubts about the nature of such ideological 'dreaming'. His literary and critical works from the 1930s betray a set of underlying ambiguities that are not primarily rooted in the nature of his political commitment, but in the attempt to find literary forms which might convey the sincerity of that commitment.

If one looks for a founding document of the politicized literature of the 1930s, *New Country* (1933), the volume of politicized poetry and prose edited by Michael Roberts, is a likely candidate, both in its dogmatic excesses and in its earnest longing for new modes of writing. The book brought together contributions by some of England's leading left-wing writers, including Auden, Isherwood, Day Lewis, and Spender. Upward contributed two short stories: 'The Colleagues' and 'Sunday', and both texts fitted the book's agenda well because they could be seen to capture the very moment at which Upward crossed the ideological border into communism. 'The Colleagues', which Upward had written in 1929, features two characters, the bourgeois schoolmaster Lloyd and his diffident colleague and proto-communist *Doppelgänger* Mitchell. The story falls neatly into three sections: the first begins with a description of the school grounds from the point of view of Lloyd, the second consists of a dialogue between the two colleagues, and the third describes Mitchell's growing recognition of school life as a foolish and meaningless charade. The story's narrative structure suggests a stark opposition between Lloyd's and Mitchell's interior monologues, but it also implies a dialectical forward movement which works to subvert Lloyd's liberal-humanism by contrasting it with Mitchell's growing awareness of the hollowness of school ritual. The third section in fact begins anticlimactically with Mitchell's reprimanding himself for abiding by the school rules and for agreeing to a meeting with Lloyd whom he detests for his bourgeois smugness. Mitchell's frustration leads him to doubt whether his attempts at resistance will ever amount to more than 'the same daydream plans for evasion'.[56]

Mitchell's self-indictments bring about a mental crisis that also effects a temporary disintegration of his field of vision. This crisis is conveyed

[55] Nikolai Bukharin, 'Poetry, Poetics and the Problems of Poetry in the USSR', in *Problems of Soviet Literature: Reports and Speeches at the First Soviet Writers' Conference*, trans. by H. G. Scott (London: Martin Lawrence, 1935), pp. 185–258 (p. 253).

[56] Edward Upward, 'The Colleagues' [1933], in *Railway Accident*, pp. 71–78 (pp. 77).

through the breakdown of the story's narrative into disconnected descriptive vignettes: 'In the tool-shed well-oiled sacking covered the motor-mower. Bast hung from a nail on the open door. There was a smell of grass seed or weed killer. Oblongs of sacking protected the lavatory windows from frost' (77). The fragmented descriptions index Mitchell's failure to attain a reassuringly stable vision that will enable him to square his reluctant entanglement in bourgeois society with his latent desire to revolt against it. Mitchell subsequently experiences an epiphany that seems to remedy his mental crisis. Watching his colleague Lloyd play rugby with the students, Mitchell observes:

> He sprang, he raced towards the tennis courts. Bucking, heavily agile with jerking shoulders. Baboon or antelope. Going all out, broadbacked in a tight sweater. How terrific. How electrically vile. He plunged, he touched down, stumbling among tree roots. It's a vision. I am palpably standing here. There are no other witnesses. If there were they would have nothing to report except that a young preparatory schoolmaster has kicked a football. I have seen a horror which no one else here would have been privileged to see. For an instant I must have been authentically insane. [. . .] I've had an hallucination. (78)

In an important sense this epiphany fails to move beyond the terms of the original dilemma. Instead of precipitating the decision to embrace communist action, it offers a bifocal optic that combines a view of the school as a functioning institution with a recognition of its moral preposterousness. Mitchell's vision is not achieved by any kind of open rejection, nor does it entail a turn towards revolutionary action. By placing sentences of realistic description and flashes of grotesque fantasy side by side in this passage, Upward instead indicates that the vision has been achieved precisely by virtue of Mitchell's conformism with bourgeois society: Mitchell's thorough immersion in school life and its outdated rituals has made it possible for him to recognize their absurdity.[57] The force of the story's closing epiphany depends on the recognition that what appears to be a chimerical dream-vision—nothing more than 'an hallucination'—is not merely Mitchell's private fantasy, but that this hallucination corresponds to the phantasmal structure of bourgeois ideology itself. Social rituals, Upward suggests, are only a thin veneer concealing the historical forces which are at work underneath it; it is in this sense that the illusion of a harmonic and progressive society is essential to the continuation of bourgeois-capitalist

[57] For a more detailed discussion of Upward's belief that a degree of conformity offered a viable path towards communism, see my 'Edward Upward, W. H. Auden, and the Rhetorical Victories of Communism', *Modernism/Modernity*, 20/2 (2013), 287–306.

ideology. Mitchell's brief fit of madness possesses cognitive value because it reflects the 'insan[ity]' of the system in which he lives.

The story's closing sentences oscillate between an anticipation of communist action and a promise of momentary repose: 'An award of power. This is only the beginning. A genuinely religious delusion. I am very glad' (78). Instead of offering a vision of the communist future, 'The Colleagues' suggests that at the present historical stage a degree of acquiescence in bourgeois society offers a more promising route towards a genuinely communist consciousness than violent resistance. 'The Colleagues' thus propounds a distinction between two kinds of fantasy: on the one hand, the deceptive fantasy of social cohesion that is projected by bourgeois society, and, on the other, the tutor's meaningful 'hallucination' which exposes bourgeois false consciousness. The story does not close by describing a fully developed and internally coherent communist consciousness, but by positing the co-existence of two radically opposed points of view which are in their turn symbolic of the split consciousness of the bourgeois on the cusp of going over to communism.

The second story published in *New Country*, 'Sunday', is also closely connected to Upward's Marxist search for patterns of historical development. The story consists largely of the interior monologue of an unnamed protagonist who saunters home to his lodgings for Sunday lunch. The speaker is presented as a neurotic who fears 'discrimination' by his bourgeois environment and finds hope only in 'elaborat[ing] his fear into something monumental'.[58] Instead of seeing a measure of conformity as a starting point for a radical political attitude, however, 'Sunday' begins by imagining the pleasures of nonworking time: 'The whole afternoon and evening will be free. Realize that, realize what I could do. All the possibilities of thinking and feeling [. . .], emerging with Lenin, foreseeing the greatest of all eras' (80). By contrast, work is presented as a dulling routine of 'drug-taking' from which leisure offers a temporary release (80). Besides being determined negatively, free time also creates space for the life of the mind, and it can become the site of potential social critique: reading Lenin, the protagonist hopes, will constitute the beginning of a communist consciousness. Illustrating the narrator's belief in the liberatory potential of free time, the story's opening paragraphs feature the same form of hallucinatory double vision that occurs at the end of 'The Colleagues'. As the tutor pictures crowds of bourgeois flocking to the city streets, he anticipates that '[e]veryone will appear quite at ease, fairly well-dressed, comfortably married, not at all furtive or sinister.

[58] Edward Upward, 'Sunday' [1933], in *Railway Accident*, pp. 79–84 (pp. 79, 81).

Nothing will visibly suggest that they are all condemned, that what they stand for is already dead, putrescent, stinking, animated only by preying corpse-worms' (80). However, 'Sunday' also indicates that the double vision attained in the final paragraphs of 'The Colleagues' can in its turn become a form of bad dreaming once the material reality of bourgeois society is neglected in favour of the penetrating vision of the communist. In other words, the very attempt to identify the deep structure of history can disable the will to engage with social reality itself: 'Day after day you have walked . . . trying to dismiss the office buildings as an inconvenient dream, as a boring abstraction, as something neither pleasant nor unpleasant, without colour or shape or substance, finally as nothing at all' (83). Once the bourgeois world is dismissed as mere fantasy, it ceases to be seen as a set of historical determinations that need to be changed through revolutionary action.

'Sunday' suggests that the false comfort afforded by the Marxist vision provides the story's protagonist with a way of escaping his 'monumental' fears vis-à-vis the constraints of bourgeois society. The story indicates that the only way to overcome this dilemma and to attain a genuinely communist perspective is to reject the special status attributed to individuality in liberal-bourgeois societies. The protagonist begins to realize that '[i]t's no use pretending you are splendidly or redeemingly or even interestingly doomed' (82)—and like 'The Colleagues' 'Sunday' culminates in an epiphany. This time, however, the subjectivist emphasis of the coda of 'The Colleagues' ('I am very glad') is replaced by a supposedly more objective account of historical movement. The fear that history might only be an extravagant subjective fantasy, an immaterial pseudo-statement, is deflected by rooting it in the 'real' things and locations which make up the story's narrative space: 'History', the narrator insists, 'is living here', it 'is here in the park, in the town' (83). With the help of such deictic pointers, the text hints that history does not come to rest in the abstract evolutionary patterns envisaged by dialectical materialism, but that it is a social process firmly embedded in the activity of living.

In order to convey the crisis of the liberal subject, Upward engages in a series of narrative manoeuvres which work to destabilize the story's point of view. The first of these abrupt shifts occurs halfway into the story, as the narrative moves from first-person into second-person narration:

> Aren't we becoming a little extravagant, almost metaphysical? Don't you think so? [. . .] Don't you suspect that after all they may have been right, that history is nothing more than a convenient figment, an abstraction, and that only concrete things like motor coaches and duplicators and ultimately electrons [. . .] are real? (83)

The change in perspective signals the transformation of a subjective account of events into moral exhortation, but it also serves to intimate the troubled self-questioning of the bourgeois-turned-communist. While writing the story, Upward complained in his diary that 'My monologue, "Sunday", is no advance. It is still self-negating, tortured, bourgeois' (3: 5 November 1931).[59] The ending of the story attempts to move beyond the protagonist's anxious self-exhortations by shifting into the more detached mode of authorial narration:

> He will go back to his lodgings for lunch. He will read the newspaper, but not for more than a quarter of an hour. He will look out of the window and see the black hats and rolled umbrellas, but he will no longer be paralysed by disgust or apprehension. He will go out into the street and walk down to the harbour. He will go to the small club behind the Geisha Café. He will ask whether there is a meeting tonight. At first he may be regarded with suspicion [. . .] He will have to prove himself, to prove that he isn't a mere neurotic, an untrustworthy freak. It will take time. But it is the only hope. He will at least have made a start. (84)

The closing sentences of the story signify a rebuttal of subjective fantasy, and the move into third-person narrative is intended to articulate the Marxist insight that individual lives are governed and transcended by larger forms of historical movement. 'The Colleagues' had suggested that Mitchell's fantastic double-vision was 'only a beginning', and the sudden shift into the future tense in 'Sunday' signals an effort to supplement the grotesque vision of a decaying bourgeois world with a prophetic anticipation of the communist future.

'Sunday' marks Upward's attempt to dispel the fear that history is only 'a convenient figment, an abstraction'. Even so, the force of the ending of 'Sunday', like the epiphany of 'The Colleagues', is strangely deferred; it offers only a dim presage of the future, instead of an actual description of the events which it so anxiously anticipates. Upward's diaries suggest that the story did not offer the right literary form for his new political convictions. 'The trouble with "Sunday"', Upward noted in December 1931, 'was that it was too abstract. "Sunday" was disingenuous' (3: 20 December 1931). The tone of 'Sunday'—its tenuous dreaming, its unsure expectation of things to come—recalls the inconclusive omens of 'The Railway Accident', and the sudden shift from a subjective, first-person viewpoint towards an objective recognition of historical necessity reads more like a

[59] The seventy-six diaries which Upward kept between 1924 and 2002 have been in an uncatalogued collection at the British Library since Upward's death in 2009. Quotations from the diaries will be followed by the volume number and date of the entry.

rhetorical trick than a convincing ideological triumph. 'The Colleagues' and 'Sunday' ultimately fail to imagine history as something which can attain immediate presence in the experiential realm.

MAKING A COMMUNIST VOICE: 'THE ISLAND' AND 'SKETCH'

'The Island' was published in the January 1935 issue of *Left Review*, and the story constitutes Upward's most determined attempt to go beyond the fantastic visions—the 'self-negating, tortured, bourgeois' tone—of his earlier work by moving into the rhetorical register of prophecy. 'The Island' begins with an extended address to a 'you' that is intertwined with a description of the island itself, a place of consummate leisure so perfect that it resembles a daydream. The possibility that this island might only be an extravagant escapist fantasy is instantly refuted: 'this island can't be a flood-lit cloud, can't be a daydream through which you'll slip to find yourself back on the job and under the poisonous eyes of a bullying foreman'.[60] The opening of the story offers a view of leisure-time that is even more celebratory than the one offered in 'Sunday'. At the same time, Upward subtly unsettles the reader's sense regarding the story's mode of address: the 'you' is alternately used to refer to an individual and a collective addressee, and it includes both workers (who long to escape from the 'bullying foreman') as well as members of the middle class. The flexibility of the personal pronoun suggests that it is intended to gesture towards a kind of universal social subject, a classless utopia that is anticipated in the experience of leisure.

Like the two *New Country* stories, 'The Island' attempts to articulate a dialectical forward movement. Similar to 'Sunday', the unmasking of illusion begins with the recognition that the utopia of leisure offers only a temporary reprieve, a 'two or three days' holiday' (226), from work in capitalist society. In sharp antithesis to the utopian register of the story's opening, the narrative voice insists that the island idyll is only 'morbid bunk': 'This is the result of indulging in freakish fantasies and getting above yourself' (227). The 'you' now seems to include the narrative voice as it struggles to cleanse itself of the vision of 'that sickly dreamland, that paradisial island of culture and everlasting joy' (227). A lengthy description of the cliffs' geological strata and the remains of ancient settlements serves as a reminder of 'past struggles, of gradual developments and cataclysmic changes' (226), and it gives way to the realization that today, too,

[60] Edward Upward, 'The Island', in *The Railway Accident*, pp. 221–30 (p. 221).

the island is fissured by social conflict and 'preparations for a world-wide war' (229). The explosion of false 'daydreams' is a common rhetorical gesture in Upward's stories and it correlates with the Marxist aim to demolish bourgeois false consciousness. However, the narrative movement of 'The Island' does not terminate in a call for temporary acquiescence (as in 'The Colleagues') or in a detached recognition of historical necessity (as in 'Sunday'). Instead, the story gestures towards a prophetic vision that manages to sublate the wish-fulfilment fantasy of the opening pages into a more mature vision of the communist future:

> And yet there is something worthwhile here, something that is not poison, some freedom, some joy, some leisure, something that you cannot easily abandon for a life of grim revolutionary struggle, some beauty that seems to invite your trust and your love. (229–30)

In the diary which Upward kept while working on 'The Island' he recorded that the story was intended as 'a reasonable Utopia' (4: 7 April 1934). The transformation of fantastic illusion, of daydreaming, into a collective vision of the island—'the strength of the certainty of a real place, the island as it can be, a place fit for men and women, as it must be, as it will be' (230)—gives full vent to the speculative impulse of Upward's prose even as it recognizes the inevitability of the revolutionary struggle. For its prophetic accent the story draws on the utopian energies of a vernacular English tradition, rather than on the more conservative dogmas of Soviet aesthetic theory: 'The real justification of the dream', Upward commented, 'is that like Morris's *News from Nowhere* it gives a picture of the future. Shows what life might be – and also what it is' (5: 14 May 1935). Echoing Morris's conclusion to *News from Nowhere*—'if others can see it as I have seen it, then it may be called a vision rather than a dream'—Upward's story rejects the idea of bad dreaming and instead announces a shared prophetic vision.[61] 'The Island' comes closer to prophecy than any other of Upward's fictions, yet Upward believed that this story, too, was beset by fundamental artistic anxieties. Surveying his short fiction of the early and mid-1930s while composing 'The Island', Upward noted that 'in these short prose pieces there can be no paragraph, no sentence almost, which is a one-way street, which doesn't contain within it the struggling forces' (4: 2 April 1934). Indeed, 'The Island' closes with a reminder that its utopian vision might after all be nothing more than a pure fiction, a 'convenient figment': it is revealed that the view of the island has been worked up into

[61] William Morris, *News from Nowhere*, ed. by David Leopold (Oxford: Oxford University Press, 2009), p. 182.

a utopia by a narrator who only saw it at a distance, observing it 'from the steamer today' (230).

The leaps into Marxist faith towards which Upward's politicized writings invariably move are haunted by similar sets of problems. Upward was keenly aware of the inconclusiveness of many of his story endings, investing their narrative climaxes with an element of hesitancy and self-doubt which has rarely been given due consideration by critics. The particular paradox of the ending of 'The Colleagues', for instance, resides in the fact that it has recourse to a rhetoric of religious revelation in order to articulate Mitchell's 'conversion' to atheistic Marxism. The epiphany of the story is supplemented by a quasi-religious vision, and the hybrid result of this conflation is a climax which is both 'genuine' and a 'delusion'. However, Upward's political convictions did not make him oblivious to the differences between his real-life commitment to communism and its fictional representations. The late Frank Kermode, one of Upward's most adamant defenders, proposed a distinction between 'myths' and 'fictions' which can help us to understand the terms underlying Upward's dilemma. Myths, Kermode notes, are characterized by a degree of ideological closure that is alien to fictions:

> Fictions can degenerate into myths whenever they are not consciously held to be fictive. In this sense anti-Semitism is a degenerate fiction, a myth; and *Lear* is a fiction. Myth [. . .] presupposes total and adequate explanations of things as they are and were; it is a sequence of radically unchangeable gestures. [. . .] Myths call for absolute, fictions for conditional assent.[62]

Kermode's critical vocabulary recalls Richards's ideas about literature's discrete coherence and the 'imaginative assent' which it requires.[63] The doctrinal 'Truth' of Marxism is incommensurate, Richards might say, with the emotive truths of fiction. But the passage also questions Richards's categories: if fictions can 'degenerate into myths', Kermode implies, myths might also regress to the status of fictions. Upward's difficulties in organizing his literary writings along the lines of his political convictions indicate similar overlaps and slippages between 'myth' and 'fiction', doctrinal statement and poetic pseudo-statement.

Shortly after completing 'Sunday', Upward commented in his diary: 'I have written. But what I have written – with the exception of the questions

[62] Frank Kermode, *The Sense of an Ending: Studies in the Theory of Fiction* [1966] (Oxford: Oxford University Press, 2000), p. 39.

[63] For Richards's idea of 'imaginative assent', see e.g. his essay 'Belief' [1930], in *Complementarities: Uncollected Essays*, ed. by John Paul Russo (Manchester: Carcanet, 1976), pp. 24–36.

to Richards – is not worth preserving' (3: 5 November 1931). Upward felt that his stories would only stand the test of time if they had a solid footing in Marxist theory. Upward's search for a 'new style' (in his 'Sketch for a Marxist Interpretation of Literature') and a 'new technique' (in *Journey to the Border*) was complicated by the fact that he was writing in a vacuum of English Marxist aesthetics: the most important Marxist criticism of the decade—Ralph Fox's *The Novel and the People* (1937), Alick West's *Crisis and Criticism* (1937), and the bulk of Christopher Caudwell's aesthetic writings—was only published in or after 1937. Lacking such support, Upward felt understandably hounded by the fantastic ghosts of Mortmere, and in 1932 he opined that even his most outspokenly political writings sounded 'wrong and very like Cambridge'.[64] Such self-doubts had much to do with personal psychology, but they are also indicative of a further structural ambivalence. After all, Kermode's neat discrimination between myth and fiction, much like Forster's between prophecy and fantasy, is itself only a simplifying fiction (though one which might in its turn become a critical myth). Upward, because he wanted the teleological myth of Marxism to provide a pattern for his literary writings, tried to convince himself that there existed a hidden connection between the two. However, his prose never quite manages to repress the possibility that the Marxist doctrines which he so rigorously defended might themselves only be fictions disguised as quasi-objective myths. While Upward's political commitment remained largely unaffected by such worries, they notably fail to be contained in his literary works.

Upward's most significant attempt to shake off the anxiety of influence which reached him through the fantasy writings about Mortmere and through Richards's theories was his 1937 'Sketch for a Marxist Interpretation of Literature'. The essay was first printed in *The Mind in Chains*, the volume which brought together critical and sociological articles by emerging Marxist intellectuals, including Rex Warner (writing on 'Education'), Anthony Blunt (on 'Art under Capitalism and Socialism'), Arthur Calder-Marshall (on 'The Film-Industry'), Charles Madge (on the current state of 'Press, Radio, and Social Consciousness'), and Cecil Day Lewis (who edited the volume and penned the introduction). Upward's piece is in many ways at the centre of the book—not only because most contributors were themselves literary authors, but because the essay attempted to define the terms on which communist writing in England would have to be premised.

The 'Sketch' rephrases the Forsterian distinction between prophecy and fantasy as a conflict between an ideologically saturated form of social

64 CIP, Letter from Edward Upward to Christopher Isherwood [1932], 2435.

dreaming which has a basis in historical fact and a delusional form of day-dreaming. The essay rejects the latter, pointing out that 'a modern fantasy cannot tell the truth' because 'fantasy implies in practice a retreat from the real world into the world of imagination': 'a modern fantasy might be a more or less truthful imitation of past fantasies, but it could not be as true to the life of our own time as the work of earlier fantasy-writers was to the life of their times.'[65] It was of course far from clear in what sense fantasy-writing might be 'true to life', and Upward's essay is troubled by the blurriness of the categories on which its argument is constructed. 'For the Marxist', it notes, 'a good book is one that is true to life.' 'If', however,

> a novel were to be written describing with complete faithfulness the surface of life in England to-day [. . .] such a novel would be untrue to life. It would show one side of the picture only, and not the most important side; it would be pessimistic, would represent militant socialism as a comparatively insignificant movement having not more than a few thousand adherents; it would distort the future and misinterpret the past; it would tell us almost nothing about the real forces at work beneath the surface of life.[66]

The passage appeals to the familiar idea of artistic verisimilitude, linking it to the problem of translating Marxist prophecy into the medium of fiction. While communist literature needs to pay attention to its own historical moment, Upward suggests, it must also offer a distinctly future-oriented view of reality. Communist writing, in this account, is marked by an anticipatory imagination that looks at the present from a projected point of view in the future. Rather than offering a recognizable depiction of the present, narrative acts of this kind rewrite reality, moulding it into a proleptic vision—or fiction—of things to come. Upward's 'Sketch' exposes the structural ambiguity of communist art's mimetic strategies: while the crudely fact-minded aesthetic of naturalism offers a 'pessimistic' account of society, the future anterior of communist fiction—inserting a knowledge of what will have happened into a description of contemporary society—can just as easily look like a 'distorted' rendering of the present.

Upward's argument illustrates the conceptual slippages between what Frank Kermode calls 'myth' and 'fiction', as well as between the two types of 'dreams' described in Lenin's *What Is To Be Done?*. As Nikolai Bukharin warned in an essay published in English in 1935, the categories of dialectical materialism could not be easily translated into prophetic fictions: 'The strict knowledge of the objective laws of social development is a long way from presupposing in Marx [. . .] any kind of "destiny" or "fate". The forecasts of Marx [are no] "prophecy" or "promises". [. . .] All these

[65] Upward, 'Sketch', pp. 48–49. [66] Upward, 'Sketch', p. 46.

analogies are playing with words.'[67] There was always the possibility that the revolutionary future could look, from the limited point of view of the present, like a fantasy—like a fiction rather than a myth. This is one source for the disabling irony of the ending of 'The Colleagues' with its anticlimactic surrender to a late-bourgeois 'religious delusion'. The predictions of Marxism, whose basis in historical fact was sometimes difficult to discern, could look like the ultimate pseudo-statements.

These unresolved tensions culminate in the closing paragraphs of Upward's essay which contemplate the possibility of a prophetic style. 'The writer's job', Upward notes, 'is to create new forms now', but 'speculation about future literary forms is idle unless it is accompanied by the realisation that already now the old forms can no longer adequately reflect the fundamental forces of the modern world'.[68] The 'new style', this passage suggests, is itself only a necessary fiction, a projected fantasy whose exact form is impossible to predict. Calls for a 'new' artistic style were of course common on the literary left. Michael Roberts's Preface to *New Country*, for instance, called for 'the evolution of a style which [. . .] will make the revolutionary movement articulate'.[69] The dilemma which Upward's essay ponders was also a familiar one for Marxist writers of the 1930s. John Middleton Murry's popular volume *The Necessity of Communism* (1932) couched it in terms strikingly similar to Upward's:

> An agonizing spiritual issue is being fought to the death, or to the life, in the world to-day; but the true nature of this issue is hard for us to apprehend. This difficulty is inevitable, for on those who are most conscious that a spiritual struggle is being waged the temptation is almost irresistible to formulate it in terms that are already familiar and blunted. But this formulation of the struggle in familiar terms [. . .] has the dangerous consequence of blinding us to the fact that the world is in travails of something new.[70]

The failure to picture such newness is not 'owing to any individual failure of imagination', as Fredric Jameson has pointed out, but evidence of our 'constitutional inability' to grasp the future.[71] The literary and political contexts of the 1930s, with their revolutionary predictions of an impending social apocalypse, multiplied opportunities for such 'failure[s]

[67] Nikolai Bukharin, 'Marx's Teaching and its Historical Importance', in *Marxism and Modern Thought*, trans. by Ralph Fox (London: Routledge, 1935), pp. 1–90 (p. 34).

[68] Upward, 'Sketch', p. 54.

[69] Michael Roberts, 'Preface', in *New Country: Prose and Poetry by the Authors of 'New Signatures'*, ed. by Michael Roberts (London: Hogarth Press, 1933), pp. 9–21 (p. 18).

[70] John Middleton Murry, *The Necessity of Communism* (London: Cape, 1932), p. 19.

[71] Fredric Jameson, *Archaeologies of the Future: The Desire Called Utopia and Other Science Fictions* (London: Verso, 2005), p. 289.

of imagination'. Apprehensions about the future are indeed endemic in left-wing literary and critical discourses of the 1930s, and they fall into the class of emotions which Ernst Bloch has labelled 'expectation affects'. As Bloch points out in *The Principle of Hope* (a book written over the course of the 1930s and 1940s), 'expectation affects' differ from 'filled affects' like greed, envy, or love, because they aim not at an individual object but at the 'configuration of the world in general'.[72] 'Expectation affects' of this kind, Bloch remarks, are highly ambiguous. They combine a powerful attraction towards the future with a wariness of its radical novelty, oscillating between the anguish and exhilaration of revolutionary upheaval.

The hesitations which beset Upward's political writings from the 1930s point towards the wider climate of artistic anxiety which emanated from the desire for a radically new beginning. It was certainly easier to gloss over such ambivalences in the doctrinally robust medium of criticism and theory than in that of literary fiction. Day Lewis's 'Letter to a Young Revolutionary' (1933), for example, temporarily managed to repress such waverings: 'the certainty of a new life', the 'Letter' admonishes young communists, 'must be your starting-point.'[73] The polemics of Upward's 'Sketch' is designed to silence such ambiguities, and the essay has in fact been advanced as proof of the strident dogmatism and alleged ideological extremism of thirties Marxist literary criticism. Upward's fiction gives a voice to the anxieties which are sometimes suppressed in the more confident communist tracts of the decade. To remark on the profound instabilities in Upward's prose, then, is not to question the seriousness of his political commitment. It does, however, help to bring into focus the complexity of the revolutionary sentiments that animate much left-wing literature of the 1930s.

'MIXED FEELINGS': PROPHECY IN *JOURNEY TO THE BORDER*

Journey to the Border was published by the Hogarth Press in 1938, but Upward had been working on the short novel for most of the decade. The opening pages of Upward's text announce the tutor-protagonist's search for a 'new technique' of 'thinking and feeling', and they read like a direct continuation of the themes and concerns of 'Sketch for a Marxist

[72] Bloch, pp. 108–13. See also Fredric Jameson, *Marxism and Form: Twentieth-Century Dialectical Theories of Literature* (Princeton: Princeton University Press, 1971), p. 127.

[73] Cecil Day Lewis, 'Letter to a Young Revolutionary', in *New Country*, ed. by Michael Roberts, pp. 25–42 (p. 27).

Interpretation of Literature'.[74] The plot of the story concerns a nameless tutor, a little-concealed *Doppelgänger* of Upward himself, who has become dissatisfied with his work.[75] He loathes the Parkin family for whom he works, and reviles their upper-middle-class lifestyle and adherence to a dying bourgeois culture. As the story progresses, the tutor's 'new technique' takes on a variety of forms. In the opening pages, the tutor (rather like the unnamed protagonist of 'Sunday') indulges in escapist dreams which demote his daily life with the Parkin family to the level of insubstantial 'fantasy': 'he had disliked them because he had wrongly taken them, not for freaks belonging to the same order of reality as the characters in a Grimms' fairy story or a cinema film, but for ordinary living people' (86). The passage signals an oblique attempt to discard Mortmerean fantasy by showing its inadequacy as a 'new form'. The protagonist of the story recognizes that these 'desperate fantasies', these 'fairy tale acrobatics', constitute only 'a day-dream victory' (92–93). They have only served to rationalize his over-assimilation to the Parkins's bourgeois life and to justify his imaginative retreat into an extreme form of Romantic subjectivity: his 'resolution', the tutor discovers, 'had become a dream from which he had been jerked awake by the ordinary noises of daytime' (96). Apprehensive of this flaw, the tutor is now able to move into closer proximity with 'reality'. Arriving at a racecourse with Mr Parkin, he meets a number of people at a crowded marquee, including his love interest Ann (who, he learns, is now distributing pamphlets for the CP) and her relative MacCreath. The tutor has abandoned his fantastic 'fairy tales', yet still the only solution to his plight seems to be running away: he asks Ann to elope with him to Reykjavik even though he realizes that this is just another 'dream of escape'. When she refuses, the tutor is again afloat in the crowd, lacking a way out of his oppressive situation.

After these initial events, the story's dialectical movement gains momentum. Through MacCreath, the tutor meets Gregory Mavors—a duplicitous character who comes to represent everything Upward finds despicable about liberalism. The figure of Mavors is a caricature of Auden, but it may also be modelled in part on the English educator and spiritualist Gerald Heard whom Auden idolized and whose books Upward and Isherwood were heatedly discussing in their letters of the mid-1930s.[76] Auden had

[74] Edward Upward, *Journey to the Border* [1938], in *Railway Accident*, pp. 85–220 (pp. 86, 87, 92, 107, and *passim*).

[75] Upward noted in his diaries that '[t]here is no real division of outlook between myself as the writer and the tutor as the actor' (5: 12 January 1936).

[76] On Auden as a model for Mavors, see my 'Edward Upward, W. H. Auden, and the Rhetorical Victories of Communism', pp. 301–2.

introduced Isherwood to Heard in 1932, and Isherwood joined his group of 'mystics' during his American exile in the 1940s and 1950s. More importantly for Upward, the closing pages of Heard's *Substance of Religion* (1931), the exemplary statement of his speculative anthropology, rejected the collectivist ideology of communism in favour of a radical individualism. In *Journey to the Border*, Mavors propounds a crudely Freudian understanding of Desire (spelled with a capital initial in the text) that seems to be derived from Heard's teachings: 'Disease is a result of disobedience to the inner law of our own nature, which works by telling us what we want to do and has no use for "don'ts".' 'There is only one sin', Mavors goes on to explain, 'and that is disobedience to our desires' (156–57). Mavors's *faux-naif* belief that 'Desire creates life; only reason brings death' is rendered dubious through an anecdote about the past of another character, Tod Ewan. Ewan, who is introduced to the tutor by MacCreath, is presented as a former colonialist who sadistically killed a Nigerian during his time in Africa (165). Like Mavors, Ewan is essentially an allegorical figure. As Upward recalled in his semi-autobiographical fiction *The Spiral Ascent*, he and Isherwood often used 'Tod', the German word for death, as a metonymic shorthand for the psychoanalytic theories of Sigmund Freud.[77] In similar fashion, the character 'Tod' in *Journey to the Border* corresponds to the Freudian death drive, providing the destructive complement to Mavors's extreme belief that 'unrepressed Desire is always gay and friendly'. The story of Tod Ewan, who is also revealed to be an anti-Semite, divulges the malignant face of liberalism—an excessive selfishness that would rather countenance the destruction of others than submit to their desires. The tutor learns that the primacy of personal happiness preached by Mavors places disproportionate emphasis on the Ego and that it ignores the individual's life in and obligations to society.

Intuiting the need to abandon his Ego, the tutor realizes that he is now redeemingly in touch with reality: 'He would be drilled, given no rest, bawled at or kicked whenever he tried to begin to dream'. But the tutor is also 'on the point of going mad' (184–85). Caught between the discarded illusions of bourgeois liberalism and the not-yet-fulfilled dreams of a communist future, he can no longer retreat into his Ego, nor can he at this point abandon it in favour of a classless, collectivist society. It is at this transitional point where 'nothing exist[s]' that unexpectedly 'out of nothing something was born. A noise, a voice. Ghostly and distinct, it came from high up among the fir trees. It spoke into his left ear' (190). Following a long, quasi-catechistical exchange, the disembodied

[77] Upward, *In the Thirties*, p. 187.

voice strengthens the tutor's decision to join the workers' movement. One of the central passages in this argument concerns the validity of the tutor's earlier 'dreams'—the element of Mortmere fantasy which runs, with remarkable consistency, through Upward's own writing. Joining the communist cause, the tutor fears, 'might [. . .] also destroy the things I have valued and loved':

> '. . . What things?'
> 'I cannot easily explain. Poetic dreams. The splendour and the joy.'
> '. . . Dreams of escape. Twisted fantasies. Unhealthy substitutes for the action you should have taken.'
> 'Quite true. But they were something more than that. They may have been a substitute for action, but at the same time they were themselves a form of action. They may have been fantastic but at the same time they contained within them elements of something other than fantasy. Unreality was not their essence: it was foreign to their essence, a taint, a disease that had invaded them. I can explain now what they were. They were my attempts to find a significance in the life I was leading, to build up my experiences into a coherent, a satisfying pattern. [. . .] [S]urely my attempt was better than nothing, was a sign of life, a form of action, was better than allowing myself to sink into apathy.' (200)

The deflection of the fantastic energies of Mortmere takes on an almost ritualistic aspect in Upward's fiction of the 1930s. However, his attempts to pass off the fantastic elements in his writing as mere daydreams and to place them in opposition to the prophetic dreams of Marxism occlude the fact that more often than not fantasy and prophecy occur alongside each other in his work.[78] In the passage quoted above, Upward is closer to embracing the presence of fantasy in his writing than at any other point in his post-Mortmere writings. The passage looks for prophecy within the fictional patterns of fantasy rather than upholding a crude distinction between the two. Ernst Bloch's remarks about the double nature of daydreams, quoted towards the beginning of this chapter, help to illuminate Upward's defence of his 'twisted fantasies' and 'dreams of escape'. Such dreams, Bloch points out, include an element of fantastic escapism, but they are also active, effecting a '*utopian strengthening*' of the 'anticipatory consciousness'.[79] Daydreams, Bloch specifies, rehearse the basic structures

[78] Critics have often mistaken *Journey to the Border* for a 'conversion narrative'. See, for example, Patrick Quinn, 'At the Frontier: Edward Upward's *Journey to the Border*', in *Recharting the Thirties*, ed. by Patrick Quinn (Selinsgrove: Susquehanna University Press, 1996), pp. 233–46 (p. 238); W. H. Sellers, 'Edward Upward: An Introduction', *The Dalhousie Review*, 43/2 (1963), 163–74 (p. 174).

[79] Bloch, pp. 91–92, emphasis in the original.

of utopian thinking not by offering up an alternative world but by defamiliarizing everyday reality. An unpublished semi-autobiographical story by Upward envisions a very similar process of defamiliarization: looking back to the narrator's espousal of communism in the 1930s, the story notes that 'if it had not been for the poets and the contrast between their world and the actual world [. . .] I might never have questioned the rightness of the actual world'.[80] Fantasy, because it so obviously denaturalizes social reality, can be the starting point for a reflective and critical stance towards it.

However, the view of fantasy which emerges in *Journey to the Border* remains ambivalent. As Upward recalled later, the question was still how he could go on from this 'negative kind' of writing 'to the new positive kind I needed to write'; fantasy might be able to offer a corrective to reality, but it could not serve as an affirmative guide to revolutionary action.[81] Despite its comparably benevolent attitude towards the tutor's poetic 'dreams of escape', the ultimate aspiration of the passage I have just quoted is to cleanse 'dreams' of the 'taint', the 'disease that had invaded them', in order to lay bare the 'elements of something other than fantasy' which they contain. Dreams which become real and take on the certainty of fact had been one of the aspirations of Upward's art since 'The Railway Accident'. Towards the end of his exchange with the 'voice', the tutor recognizes that he will have to pass through 'an intermediate period, a dreamless and fallow period' (203). The 'voice' informs the tutor that the dreams which follow this 'intermediate' phase will finally be purged of the 'taint' and 'disease' of fantasy: he 'will be allowed to dream and think' again after he has joined the workers' movement. As the story closes, the tutor decides that

> [h]e would begin tutoring again, but with a difference. Perhaps he would be able to do propaganda work in the village, among the agricultural workers. His decision to join the workers' movement would lead to difficulties. But he would at least have come down to earth, out of the cloud of his fantasies; would have begun to live. [. . .] The tutor reached the road and began to walk down the hill. (220)

Upward's closing paragraphs once more hesitate over the reliability of their vision of the future. The only thing they can imagine with any certainty is

[80] CIP, Ms of 'Beginners' [1960s/1970s], 2270. The archive gives the date of composition as 1926. This is obviously wrong, not least because of the story's considerable critical leverage on literary 'fantasy'. Other evidence, such as Upward's handwriting and the confessional tone of the story, might suggest a date in the 1960s or 1970s when Upward was at work on his fictionalized autobiography.

[81] Upward, *In the Thirties*, p. 183.

the tutor's 'difficulties' in crossing the metaphorical 'border' indicated by the story's title. Like almost all of Upward's stories from the 1930s, *Journey to the Border* resorts to conditionals and to the subjunctive mood in talking about the events which it so anxiously anticipates. Like his 1931 letter to Isherwood, Upward's narratives 'suppose there really will be a revolution quite soon', but they do not quite dare to imagine what this new order will look like.

Even though Upward, unlike many others, did not fall away from active communist politics in the late 1930s, the endings of his stories invariably articulate a sense of deferral or even disappointment. This is true as much of *Journey to the Border* as of 'Sunday' ('But it is the only hope. He will at least have made a start'), 'The Colleagues' ('This is only the beginning. A genuinely religious delusion'), and 'The Island' ('a place fit for men and women, as it must be, as it will be'). Upward's hesitations can well come as a surprise, given the rich theoretical disquisitions by English Marxists about the nature of the imminent communist world revolution. John Strachey's *The Theory and Practice of Socialism* (1935), one of the most influential expositions of communist doctrine to be published in English in the 1930s, is a notable example of such revolutionary optimism:

> The test must be, as usual, one of prediction value. If this really is the pattern of history, exhibited in coil after coil, in spiral after spiral, of ascending development, it must surely be possible to predict the general character of the next phase? [. . .] It is upon this ability to foretell the general direction of historical development, that dialectical materialism bases its claim to proved validity.[82]

If one was unsure where history was tending, one only needed to look to Russia. There, Maurice Dobb (and many others) believed, 'history is moving at a faster rate, probably, than ever before'.[83] Upward's stories fail to be so convinced. They especially flinch from the Romantic pathos which communist writers like Alick West associated with the proletarian revolution. West's *Crisis and Criticism* specifically urged a return to 'sentimental' writing because it would help to create a post-capitalist 'feeling of social solidarity'.[84] Upward's stories, by contrast, give expression to what Frank Kermode has called 'mixed feelings', a class of emotions that also

[82] John Strachey, *The Theory and Practice of Socialism* (London: Gollancz, 1935), pp. 387–88.

[83] Maurice Dobb, *In Soviet Russia, Autumn 1930* (London: Modern Books, 1930), p. 3.

[84] See West's chapter on I. A. Richards in *Crisis and Criticism and Selected Literary Essays* (London: Lawrence and Wishart, 1975), pp. 54–65 (esp. p. 56). For Richards's influence on West and artistic 'sentimentality' in the 1930s, see Roy Fuller, *Owls and Afterlives: Oxford Lectures on Poetry* (London: Deutsch, 1971), pp. 27–43.

includes Bloch's 'expectation affects'. His writing is at the same time drawn towards and troubled by the revolutionary apocalypse which it tries to imagine; its dominant affect consists 'of a consciousness of extraordinary novelty and deep anxieties about loving the unknown'.[85]

There were of course precedents for Upward's hesitations in what I have called the 1930s' climate of artistic anxiety. Beginning with the *Communist Manifesto* (Section III: 'Socialist and Communist Literature'), there existed a critical, iconoclastic strain within Marxism which maligned detailed imaginative renderings of the communist future. Friedrich Engels himself had stressed that 'Socialism' was 'scientific' rather than 'Utopian'. Arguing against representations of the future in works by Saint-Simon, Robert Owen, and Charles Fourier, he had proclaimed that 'these new social systems were foredoomed as Utopian; the more completely they were worked out in detail, the more they could not avoid drifting off into pure phantasies'.[86] Such elaborate 'phantasies'—far from offering accurate predictions about the revolutionary future—would result in 'a mish-mash allowing of the most manifold shades of opinion'.[87] Engels's arguments were taken up and given new force by English Marxist critics. Most prominently perhaps, Christopher Caudwell's posthumous collection of essays, *Studies in a Dying Culture* (1938), pointed out that 'Marx [. . .] wasted no time in planning beautiful Utopias'. Attacking 'the bourgeois dream-Utopias' of H. G. Wells, Caudwell claimed that 'thought visualising the future and divorced from action, can do no more than project the disheartening poverty of the present into the richness of the future'.[88] Upward's suggestion, in *Journey to the Border*, that the tutor 'will be allowed to dream and think' once he has embraced 'action' also finds an echo in Caudwell's essay on Wells:

> as for what this world will be when social relations no longer press on man blindly but he is truly free – how can we children of a collapsing world, in all the ruin wrought by our outworn social relations, ourselves *exactly* predict? [. . .] Action [. . .] brings into birth what our limited thoughts cannot to-day conceive, and by doing so makes possible those richer thoughts we would long to think but cannot, those dreams we only dream of having. (89–90; original emphasis)

From the limited viewpoint of the present, the communist future appears like a doubly removed fantasy: one of the 'dreams we only dream of

[85] Frank Kermode, *History and Value* (Oxford: Clarendon Press, 1988), p. 53.

[86] Friedrich Engels, *Socialism: Utopian and Scientific* [1880], trans. by Edward Aveling (London: Allen and Unwin, 1892), p. 12.

[87] Ibid., p. 27.

[88] Christopher Caudwell, *Studies in a Dying Culture* (London: John Lane, 1938), pp. 90, 88.

having'. Upward's stories, which usually break off at the moment of epiphany, are regulated by similar ideological strictures, and the weight of these injunctions stymies the speculative impulse of Upward's fiction by closing off its desired field of reference. Upward's writing is burdened by an undescribed (and indeed undescribable) future—the revolutionary action towards which it gravitates must take place outside, and after, the fiction.

As I have suggested, Upward felt that his espousal of communism in the early 1930s necessitated a comprehensive rejection of the fantasy world of Mortmere. At the same time, the renunciation of Mortmerean fantasy made the search for a new style all the more urgent. The tortuous course of Upward's struggle for a prophetic style and the tormented inconclusiveness of his search stand in marked contrast to the uncompromisingness of Upward's political opinions.[89] Upward's works raise the question of how fiction copes with the extraneous demands that are imposed on it by political ideologies. On the one hand, they require us to think about the politics of writing not in the sense of a writing successively absorbed into a distinct realm of political action, but of a doctrinaire viewpoint altered, and made more ambiguous, as it is being transposed into the medium of fiction. The literary text, as Jonathan Culler has remarked, 'is a structure of signifiers which absorbs and reconstitutes the signified'.[90] Frank Kermode has argued with a view to these processes of ambiguation that if literary works

> carry messages about history they do so in a medium which diffuses or ironizes the messages; [. . .] *good* poems about historical crises speak a different language from historical record and historical myth. [. . .] [T]he poems about history we continue to value tend to be complicated, ambiguous, and if only in that respect deviant from any official and any popular view of their occasions.[91]

And yet, when reading Upward's texts, we are constantly confronted with the problem of their 'total seriousness'.[92] The peculiar strength of his writings is that—in spite of their ineradicable ambiguities—their tone of moral and ideological conviction fails to conform to constricting literary standards which elevate ambiguity to a token of artistic value. As Upward

[89] This inconclusiveness is not identical with farce or self-parody, the 'comedy of dogma' which Andy Croft has detected in some thirties left-wing writing. See Croft, *Red-Letter Days: British Fiction in the 1930s* (London: Lawrence and Wishart, 1990), pp. 288–92.

[90] Jonathan Culler, *Structuralist Poetics: Structuralism, Linguistics and the Study of Literature* [1975] (London: Routledge, 2002), p. 191.

[91] Frank Kermode, *Poetry, Narrative, History* (Oxford: Blackwell, 1990), pp. 67, 50, emphasis in the original.

[92] Arblaster, p. 190.

pointed out in a response to Virginia Woolf's scathing anti-1930s essay 'The Leaning Tower' (1940), it 'is doubtful whether any of the "leaning tower" writers, in spite of their hostility towards the old and their sympathy for the new, can be called "great"'.[93] There is something programmatic about this failure, or tenacious refusal, of literary eminence. Upward's works from the 1920s and 1930s converge on what remains properly unspeakable within the discursive realm of fiction. Caught between a commitment to historical particularity and a search for the vaster subtext of historical development, the tonal ambiguities of Upward's works from the 1930s effect not a disengagement from but a more thorough immersion in the profoundly conflicted political commitments of their decade.

[93] Edward Upward, 'The Falling Tower', *Folios of New Writing*, 3 (Spring 1941), 24–29 (p. 26).

Coda

The intensity with which many thirties authors criticized the idea of politicized writing after 1939 has become one of the iconic volte-faces in twentieth-century British literary history. But the years after 1939 also afforded other literary figures—self-styled moderates like George Orwell and members of the twenties modernist establishment like Virginia Woolf—an opportunity to reassert their credentials. In his essay 'Inside the Whale' Orwell condemned left-wing writing root and branch: 'on the whole the literary history of the thirties seems to justify the opinion that a writer does well to keep out of politics.'[1] According to Orwell, only a few writers, such as Henry Miller, stood apart from the 'orthodoxy-sniffers' of the 1930s because they seemed to 'belong to the twenties rather than to the thirties'.[2] Virginia Woolf conceded in her essay 'The Leaning Tower' that there might well be some thirties writers 'whom posterity will value most highly', but these, she hastened to add, were bound to be the ones who had resisted political commitment and who 'could not fall into step, as leaders or followers'.[3] These statements come from two writers who were in many respects located at opposite ends of the artistic and political spectrum, yet both authors share the sense that 'good' writing was at last beginning to re-emerge after having been in retreat for a long, dishonest decade.

One literary platform that helped to propagate the idea that modernism was once again on the rise was Cyril Connolly's literary magazine *Horizon*. Connolly had been emphatic in his praise of 'Mandarin' writing throughout the 1930s, and his programmatic early editorials in *Horizon*, starting with the publication's first number in 1940, voice his relief that the political side-taking of the 1930s is a thing of the past: 'We believe that a reaction away from social realism is as necessary now as was, a generation

[1] George Orwell, 'Inside the Whale' [1940], in *The Complete Works of George Orwell*, 20 vols (London: Seckler and Warburg, 1986–98), XII: *A Patriot After All, 1940–1941*, ed. by Peter Davison (1998), pp. 86–115 (pp. 105).

[2] Orwell, 'Inside the Whale', p. 86.

[3] Virginia Woolf, 'The Leaning Tower', in *The Moment, and Other Essays* (New York: Harcourt Brace, 1948), pp. 118–54 (p. 140).

ago, the reaction from the Ivory Tower'.[4] The revolt against Mandarin high modernism, Connolly notes, led to a conflagration in which 'many green young saplings have been damaged'.[5] The pages of *Horizon*, to extend Connolly's horticultural metaphor, were tasked with weeding out the excess growth that was thirties writing and to nurse 'the best writing' back into bloom: 'Our standards are aesthetic', the first issue announced, 'and our politics are in abeyance'.[6] In Connolly's opinion, this enterprise of recovery and restoration also necessitated a reeducation of readers whose tastes had been exposed to the literary atmosphere of the previous decade. One of Connolly's editorials states that '[s]ince the Marxist attack ten years ago' good writing 'has been lost sight of, and it is our duty gradually to reeducate the peppery palates of our detractors to an appreciation of delicate poetry and fine prose'.[7] The opening numbers of *Horizon* advocated an artistic return to the 1920s, but only a few numbers later the attention of Connolly's 'Comments' was once more forced towards historical events as the world war gained destructive momentum.

On the face of it, the idea that modernism would enter a second blossoming after the literary wasteland of the 1930s was only a reversal of the anti-modernist rhetoric that had ostensibly dominated the 1930s. As I have suggested, however, thirties anti-modernism had itself been a response to an influential myth about high modernism that had emerged in part during the debate between Eliot and Richards. As the radical energies of the 1930s began to fade during the war and the postwar years, this tenacious older myth about the status of literary language came to the fore once again. The development was hastened by Richards's move to Harvard in 1939 which helped to bolster a New Criticist outlook that posited the possibility of a largely self-contained writing. In the 1940s, the 'reeducation of the peppery palates' envisioned by Connolly was taking on concrete institutional shape as practical criticism became the dominant axiom underpinning pedagogic and scholarly activity in Anglo-American academe.

Recent exponents of neo-formalism, in particular Susan Wolfson, have shown that the New Criticism was less naively text-centred and more keenly attuned to the extra-literary dimensions of poetic language than its later antagonists have granted.[8] Even so, there is a degree of proximity between the central themes of the Eliot-Richards debate and certain tenets

[4] For the idea of 'Mandarin' writing, see Connolly's *Enemies of Promise* [1938; 2nd ed. 1948] (Chicago: University of Chicago Press, 2008).

[5] Cyril Connolly, 'Comment', *Horizon*, 1 (1940), pp. 68–71 (p. 70).

[6] Connolly, 'Comment', *Horizon*, 1 (1940), pp. 5–6 (p. 5).

[7] Connolly, 'Comment', p. 70.

[8] See especially Susan J. Wolfson, *Formal Charges: The Shaping of Poetry in British Romanticism* (Princeton: Princeton University Press, 1997), pp. 1–23.

of the New Criticism. For example, Cleanth Brooks observed in his now-classic *The Well Wrought Urn* (1947) that '[s]ome modern poetry is difficult for the reader simply because so few people, relatively speaking, are accustomed to reading *poetry as poetry*'.[9] Both Brooks's phrasing ('reading *poetry as poetry*') and the title of the chapter in which the sentence occurs ('What Does Poetry Communicate?') look back to the language used by Richards and Eliot in the mid- and late 1920s. As Alan Filreis has pointed out, a significant portion of literary scholarship in the 1950s was characterized by a desire for an 'immaculate modernism' which was 'conceived as a direct, unsullied continuity from the 1910s and 1920s'.[10] This return to '*poetry as poetry*' entailed the dismissal of much thirties left-wing writing. One influential American critic, Stanley E. Hyman, harangued the 'Marxist absolutism, ignorance, and parochialism of the '30s'. Hyman singled out Edward Upward as a particularly embarrassing specimen who in his 'Sketch for a Marxist Interpretation of Literature' had 'achieved what is probably the most stupid single piece of Marxist criticism ever written'.[11] According to these post-war accounts, the attempt to politicize literature betrayed a profound lack of understanding regarding the actual nature of poetry: for the poet as a 'public performer', as the New Critic William K. Wimsatt remarked in 1954, poetic language is 'a complex and treacherous medium'.[12] The persistence with which committed writers like Upward continue to be excluded from the literary canon today indicates that our own standards of critical evaluation are still more deeply embedded in the anti-thirties discourse of the 1940s and 1950s than we commonly admit.

The tendency to instrumentalize the 1930s in cultural debates over the past decades has played up to the diverse interpretative paradigms, or 'myths', established by thirties authors themselves. Few decades have been 'rewritten' and 'revised' as often as the 1930s, and the titles of prominent critical publications on the decade—with their rhetoric of 'reading' and 're-reading', 'charting' and 'recharting'—signal the convention of seeing thirties writing as divisible into two antagonistic and complementary critical options: from *The Thirties: A Dream Revolved* (1960), *Recharting the Thirties* (1996), and *Rewriting the Thirties: Modernism and After* (1997) to *And*

[9] Cleanth Brooks, *The Well Wrought Urn: Studies in the Structure of Poetry* (New York: Harcourt Brace, 1975), p. 76, emphasis in the original. I have discussed the idea of reading 'poetry as poetry' in detail in chapter one.

[10] Alan Filreis, *The Counter-Revolution of the Word: The Conservative Attack on Modern Poetry, 1945–1960* (Chapel Hill: University of North Carolina Press, 2008), p. 94.

[11] Stanley E. Hyman, 'The Marxist Criticism of Literature', *The Antioch Review* 7 (1947), 541–68 (p. 556). The essay reserves some praise for Christopher Caudwell.

[12] William K. Wimsatt, *The Verbal Icon: Studies in the Meaning of Poetry* [1954] (London: Methuen, 1970), p. 269.

in Our Time: Vision, Revision, and British Writing of the 1930s (2003).[13] The critical habit of arguing either for or against the compatibility of literature and politics has a long history. Orwell claimed that Henry Miller's works marked 'an unexpected swing of the pendulum' back in the direction of the good writing of the 1920s.[14] Instead of offering another swing of the pendulum between 'demon theory' and 'apologetics', this book has described the ground on which certain of the decade's artistic problems arose.[15] It has argued that the difficulties which left-wing writers of the 1930s encountered in harnessing their works to political causes were the consequence of historically specific assumptions about the nature of literary language, rather than the result of any properties inherent in poetic discourse as such.

The period's grandiose hopes for poetry and its confessions of incapacity cannot be prised apart quite as tidily as many critical accounts tacitly assume. Introducing one of Upward's last volumes of stories, the late Frank Kermode remarked that the 1930s were by no means a time of simple questions or easy ideological solutions. He observed that 'we have still not fully understood the Thirties, that critical decade in politics and the arts, which tried to face the problems, to them terrible and urgent, which we comfortably push out of sight and out of mind'.[16] I have argued that the failure to 'understand' the 1930s is not just the result of critical negligence, but that it is contingent on the difficulties which thirties authors themselves encountered in trying to make sense of the aesthetic problems they were facing. The seriousness of the 1930s' politics of writing cannot be measured by the fictitious standard yard of some decreed orthodoxy. Rather, the moving on from possibility to possibility—as well as the disorderliness and openness of this process—is characteristic of thirties writing across a broad political spectrum. It has been the aim of this book to bring into focus these diverse and apparently conflicting impulses—the wary anticipation of poetic disappointment and the refusal to settle into a kind of comfortable failure.

[13] Julian Symons, *The Thirties: A Dream Revolved* (London: Cresset Press, 1960); *Recharting the Thirties*, ed. by Patrick Quinn (Selinsgrove: Susquehanna University Press, 1996); *Rewriting the Thirties: Modernism and After*, ed. by Steven Matthews and Keith Williams (London: Longman, 1997); *And in Our Time: Vision, Revision, and British Writing of the 1930s*, ed. by Antony Shuttleworth (Lewisburg, PA: Bucknell University Press, 2003). See also, in a similar vein, *The 1930s: A Challenge to Orthodoxy*, ed. by John Lucas (Brighton: Harvester Press, 1978); and *Class, Culture and Social Change: A New View of the 1930s*, ed. by Frank Gloversmith (Brighton: Harvester Press, 1980).

[14] Orwell, 'Inside the Whale', p. 106.

[15] A. Walton Litz, 'Review: Revising the Thirties', *The Sewanee Review*, 87 (1979), 660–66 (p. 666).

[16] Frank Kermode, 'Introduction', in Edward Upward, *An Unmentionable Man* (London: Enitharmon, 1994), pp. 7–10 (p. 10).

Bibliography

Adorno, Theodor W., 'Art, Society, Aesthetics', in *Aesthetic Theory* [1970], ed. by Gretel Adorno and Rolf Tiedemann, trans. by Robert Hullot-Kentor (London: Continuum, 1997), pp. 1–20

—— 'Commitment' [1962], in *Notes to Literature*, ed. by Rolf Tiedemann, trans. by Shierry Weber Nicholsen, 2 vols (New York: Columbia University Press, 1992), II, pp. 76–94

Agar, Eileen, *A Look at My Life* (London: Methuen, 1988)

Alpers, Paul, 'Empson on Pastoral', *New Literary History*, 10/1 (1978), 101–23

Alvarez, Al, *The Shaping Spirit: Studies in Modern English and American Poets* (London: Chatto and Windus, 1958)

Aragon, Louis, 'Front Rouge/Red Front' [1931], in *Complete Poems of E. E. Cummings, 1904–62*, ed. by George J. Firmage (New York: Liveright, 1991), pp. 880–97

—— *Pour un réalisme socialiste* (Paris: Denoël et Steele, 1935)

—— *Traité de style* (Paris: Gallimard, 1928)

—— 'Waltz', trans. by Nany Cunard, *Left Review*, 1/1 (October 1934), 3–5

Arblaster, Anthony, 'Edward Upward and the Novel of Politics', in *1936: The Sociology of Literature*, ed. by Francis Barker, 2 vols (Colchester: University of Essex, 1979), II, pp. 179–96

Archer, William, 'Poetry and Beliefs', *Experiment*, 5 (February 1930), 29–34

Armstrong, Isobel, *The Radical Aesthetic* (Oxford: Blackwell, 2000)

Arnold, Matthew, *The Poems of Matthew Arnold, 1849–1867*, ed. by A. T. Quiller-Couch (Oxford: Oxford University Press, 1926)

Arnoux, Alexandre, 'From "Le Cabaret"', trans. by Ralph Parker, *Experiment*, 6 (October 1930), 7–12

Auden, Wystan Hugh, *The English Auden*, ed. by Edward Mendelson (London: Faber and Faber, 1977)

—— 'Introduction', in *The Oxford Book of Light Verse* [1938] (Oxford: Oxford University Press, 1952), pp. vii–xx

—— *Juvenilia, 1922–1928*, ed. by Katherine Bucknell (Princeton: Princeton University Press, 1994)

—— *New Year Letter* (London: Faber and Faber, 1941)

—— *Poems* (London: Faber and Faber, 1936)

—— Review of Illusion and Reality, *New Verse*, 25 (May 1937), 20–22

—— *Spain* (London: Faber and Faber, 1937)

—— and Christopher Isherwood, *Journey to a War* [1939] (London: Faber and Faber, 1973)

—— and Louis MacNeice, *Letters from Iceland* (London: Faber and Faber, 1937)

'Authors Take Sides on the Spanish War', *Left Review Special Issue* (1937), [n.pag.].

Ayer, Alfred Jules, *Language, Truth, and Logic* [1936] (London: Penguin, 2001)

Bataille, Georges, 'The "Old Mole" and the Prefix *Sur* in the Words *Surhomme* and *Surréaliste*' [1929–30], in *Visions of Excess: Selected Writings, 1927–1939*, ed. and trans. by Allan Stoekl (Minneapolis: University of Minnesota Press, 1985), pp. 32–44

Belgion, Montgomery, 'What Is Criticism?', *The Criterion*, 10 (October 1930), 118–39

Benedict, Ruth, *The Chrysanthemum and the Sword: Patterns of Japanese Culture* [1946] (New York: Mariner, 2005)

Benjamin, Walter, 'The Author as Producer', trans. by Edmund Jephcott, in *Selected Writings*, ed. by Michael Jennings, Howard Eiland, and Gary Smith (Cambridge, MA: Harvard University Press, 1996–2003), II (1999), pp. 768–82

—— 'Surrealism: The Last Snapshot of the European Intelligentsia' [1929], in *One-Way Street and Other Writings*, trans. by Edmund Jephcott and Kingsley Shorter (London: NLB, 1979), pp. 225–39

Bergonzi, Bernard, *Reading the Thirties: Texts and Contexts* (Basingstoke: Macmillan, 1978)

Bernard, Philippa, *No End to Snowdrops: A Biography of Kathleen Raine* (London: Shepheard-Walwyn, 2009)

Bloch, Ernst, *The Principle of Hope* [1938–47], trans. by Paul Knight, Neville Plaice, and Stephen Plaice, 3 vols (Oxford: Blackwell, 1986)

Bluemel, Kristin, *George Orwell and the Radical Eccentrics: Intermodernism in Literary London* (Basingstoke: Palgrave Macmillan, 2004)

——, ed., *Intermodernism: Literary Culture in Mid-Twentieth-Century Britain* (Edinburgh: Edinburgh University Press, 2009)

Blunt, Anthony, 'Rationalist Art and Anti-rationalist Art', *Left Review*, 2/10 (July 1936), iv–vi

Bowman, Deborah, 'Argufying and the Generation Gap', in *Some Versions of Empson*, ed. by Matthew Bevis (Oxford: Oxford University Press, 2007), pp. 21–41

Boym, Svetlana, *Death in Quotation Marks: Cultural Myths of the Modern Poet* (Cambridge, MA: Harvard University Press, 1991)

Breton, André, 'Légitime défense', *La Révolution surréaliste*, 8 (1926), 30–36

—— 'Limits not Frontiers of Surrealism', in *Surrealism*, ed. by Herbert Read (London: Faber and Faber, 1936), pp. 94–115

—— 'Manifesto of Surrealism' [1924], in *Manifestoes of Surrealism*, trans. by Richard Seaver and Helen R. Lane (Ann Arbor: University of Michigan Press, 1972), pp. 1–46

—— *Nadja* [1928] (Paris: Gallimard, 2008)

—— *Poems of André Breton: A Bilingual Anthology*, ed. and trans. by Jean-Pierre Cauvin and Mary-Ann Caws (Austin: University of Texas Press, 1982)

—— 'The Political Position of Today's Art' [1935], in *Manifestoes of Surrealism*, trans. by Richard Seaver and Helen R. Lane (Ann Arbor: University of Michigan Press, 1972), pp. 212–33

—— 'The Poverty of Poetry: The Aragon Affair and Public Opinion' [1932], trans. by Richard Howard, in *What is Surrealism? Selected Writings*, ed. by Franklin Rosemont (London: Pluto 1978), pp. 76–82

—— Review of Leon Trotsky's *Lenin*, *La Révolution surréaliste*, 5 (1925), 29
—— 'Situation du surréalisme entre les deux guerres' [1942], in *La Clé des champs* (Paris: Éditions du Sagittaire, 1953), pp. 58–73
—— 'Speech to the Congress of Writers' [1935], in *Manifestoes of Surrealism*, trans. by Richard Seaver and Helen R. Lane (Ann Arbor: University of Michigan Press, 1972), pp. 234–41
—— 'Surrealist Situation of the Object: Situation of the Surrealist Object' [1935], in *Manifestoes of Surrealism*, trans. by Richard Seaver and Helen R. Lane (Ann Arbor: University of Michigan Press, 1972), pp. 255–77
—— *What is Surrealism?* (London: Faber and Faber, 1936)
Bronowski, Jacob, 'D.H. Lawrence', *The New Experiment*, 7 (Spring 1931), 5–13
—— 'Experiment', *transition*, 19–20 (June 1930), 107–12
—— 'Postscript', *Experiment*, 5 (February 1930), 34
—— and J.M. Reeves, 'Towards a Theory of Poetry', *Experiment*, 4 (November 1929), 20–27
—— William Empson, et al. 'Editorial', *The New Experiment*, 7 (Spring 1931), 4
Brooke, Rupert, *Selected Poems* [1917] (London: Sidgwick, 1923)
Brooks, Cleanth, *The Well Wrought Urn: Studies in the Structure of Poetry* (New York: Harcourt Brace, 1975)
Brougher, Valentina G., 'Introduction', in *Vsevolod Ivanov: Fertility and Other Stories*, ed. and trans. by Valentina G. Brougher (Evanston: Northwestern University Press, 1998), pp. xiii–xxxvii
Bucknell, Katherine, 'The Achievement of Edward Upward', in *W. H. Auden: 'The Language of Learning and the Language of Love': Uncollected Writings, New Interpretations*, ed. by Katherine Bucknell and Nicholas Jenkins (Oxford: Clarendon Press, 1994), pp. 165–86
Bukharin, Nikolai, 'Marx's Teaching and its Historical Importance', in *Marxism and Modern Thought*, trans. by Ralph Fox (London: Routledge, 1935), pp. 1–90
—— 'Poetry, Poetics and the Problems of Poetry in the USSR', in *Problems of Soviet Literature: Reports and Speeches at the First Soviet Writers' Conference 1934*, trans. by H. G. Scott (London: Martin Lawrence, 1935), pp. 185–258
Bürger, Peter, *The Theory of the Avant-Garde* [1974], trans. by Michael Shaw (Minneapolis: University of Minnesota Press, 1984)
Buzard, James, 'Mass-Observation, Modernism, and Auto-ethnography', *Modernism/Modernity*, 4/3 (1997), 93–122
Caesar, Adrian, *Dividing Lines: Poetry, Class, and Ideology in the 1930s* (Manchester: Manchester University Press, 1991)
Caudwell, Christopher, *Further Studies in a Dying Culture* (London: The Bodley Head, 1949)
—— *Illusion and Reality: A Study of the Sources of Poetry* (Basingstoke: Macmillan, 1937)
—— *Romance and Realism: A Study in English Bourgeois Literature*, ed. by Samuel Hynes (Princeton: Princeton University Press, 1970)
—— *Studies in a Dying Culture* (London: John Lane, 1938)

Chaney, David, and Michael Pickering, 'Authorship in Documentary: Sociology as an Art Form in Mass Observation', in *Documentary and the Mass Media*, ed. by John Corner (London: Edward Arnold, 1986), pp. 29–46

Coffey, Brian, Review of *A Short Survey of Surrealism*, *The Criterion*, 15 (April 1936), 506–11

Connolly, Cyril, 'Comment', *Horizon*, 1 (1940), 5–6

—— 'Comment', *Horizon*, 1 (1940), 58–71

Connor, Steven, 'British Surrealist Poetry in the 1930s', in *British Poetry, 1900–50: Aspects of Tradition*, ed. by Gary Day and Brian Docherty (London: St. Martin's Press, 1995), pp. 169–92

—— '"A Door Half Open to Surprise": Charles Madge's Imminences', in *Mass-Observation as Poetics and Science*, ed. by Nick Hubble, Margaretta Jolly, and Laura Marcus (= *new formations*, 44 (2001)), 52–62

—— *Theory and Cultural Value* (Oxford: Blackwell, 1992)

Constable, 'I. A. Richards, T. S. Eliot, and the Poetry of Belief', *Essays in Criticism*, 40 (1990), 222–43

Cornford, John, 'Left?', *Cambridge Left*, 1 (Winter 1933–34), 25–29

Cottom, Daniel, *Abyss of Reason: Cultural Movements, Revelations, and Betrayals* (Oxford: Oxford University Press, 1991)

[Cournos, John,] Review of Vsevolod Ivanov's *Dikhanie Pustini* [*The Breath of the Desert*], *Times Literary Supplement*, 19 July 1928, p. 536

Crevel, René, 'Le Patriotisme de l'inconscient', *Le Surréalisme au service de la revolution*, 4 (1932), 6

Croft, Andy, *Red-Letter Days: British Fiction in the 1930s* (London: Lawrence and Wishart, 1990)

Culler, Jonathan, 'Empson's Complex Words', in *Framing the Sign: Criticism and Its Institutions*, ed. by Johnathan Culler (Oxford: Blackwell, 1988), pp. 85–95

—— *The Pursuit of Signs: Semiotics, Literature, Deconstruction* [1981] (London: Routledge, 2002)

—— *Structuralist Poetics: Structuralism, Linguistics and the Study of Literature* [1975] (London: Routledge, 2002)

Cunningham, Valentine, 'The Age of Anxiety and Influence; or, Tradition and the Thirties Talents', in *Rewriting the Thirties: Modernism and After*, ed. by Steven Matthews and Keith Williams (London: Longman, 1997), pp. 5–22

—— *British Writers of the Thirties* (Oxford: Oxford University Press, 1988)

—— 'Neutral?: 1930s Writers and Taking Sides', in *Class, Culture and Social Change: A New View of the 1930s*, ed. by Frank Gloversmith (Brighton: Harvester Press, 1980), pp. 45–69

Davis, Helen, and H. V. Kemp, 'The Rise and Fall of Bourgeois Poetry', *Cambridge Left*, 1 (Summer 1934), 68–77

Dobb, Maurice, *On Marxism Today* (London: Hogarth Press, 1932)

—— *In Soviet Russia, Autumn 1930* (London: Modern Books, 1930)

Durant, Alan, 'Raymond Williams's *Keywords*: Investigating Meanings "Offered, Felt For, Tested, Confirmed, Asserted, Qualified, Changed"', *Critical Quarterly*, 48/4 (2006), 1–26

Eagleton, Terry, *Marxism and Literary Criticism* [1976] (London: Routledge, 2002)
Eliot, Thomas Stearns, *The Complete Poems and Plays* [1969] (London: Faber and Faber, 2004)
—— 'Dante' [1929], in *Selected Essays: 1917–1932* (London: Faber and Faber, 1932), pp. 223–63
—— 'Literature, Science, and Dogma', *The Dial*, 82 (March 1927), 239–42
—— 'A Note on Poetry and Belief', *The Enemy*, 1 (January 1927), 15–17
—— 'Poetry and Propaganda' [1930], in *Literary Opinion in America*, ed. by Morton Dauwen Zabel (New York: Harper, 1951), pp. 97–107
—— *The Sacred Wood* [1920, rev. 1927] (London: Faber and Faber, 1997)
—— '*Ulysses*, Order, and Myth', *The Dial*, 75 (November 1923), 480–83
—— *The Use of Poetry and the Use of Criticism* [1933] (London: Faber and Faber, 1964)
Ellis, Havelock, *The World of Dreams* (London: Constable, 1911)
Empson, William, 'The Ancient Mariner' [1964], in *Argufying: Essays on Literature and Culture*, ed. by John Haffenden (Iowa City: Iowa University Press, 1987), pp. 297–319
—— 'Compacted Doctrines' [1977], in *Argufying: Essays on Literature and Culture* (Iowa City: Iowa University Press, 1987), pp. 170–95
—— *Complete Poems*, ed. by John Haffenden (London: Penguin, 2000)
—— 'Early Auden' [1963], in *Argufying: Essays on Literature and Culture*, ed. by John Haffenden (Iowa City: Iowa University Press, 1987), pp. 375–77
—— 'Foundations of Despair' [1937], in *Argufying: Essays on Literature and Culture*, ed. by John Haffenden (Iowa City: Iowa University Press, 1987), pp. 418–20
—— *The Gathering Storm* (London: Faber and Faber, 1940)
—— 'Honest Man', *Southern Review*, 5 (1940), 711–30
—— 'I. A. Richards and Practical Criticism' [1930], in *Argufying: Essays on Literature and Culture*, ed. by John Haffenden (Iowa City: Iowa University Press, 1987), pp. 193–202
—— 'A London Letter' [1937], in *Argufying: Essays on Literature and Culture*, ed. by John Haffenden (Iowa City: Iowa University Press, 1987), pp. 414–17
—— 'Obscurity and Annotation' [1930], in *Argufying: Essays on Literature and Culture*, ed. by John Haffenden (Iowa City: Iowa University Press, 1987), pp. 70–87
Empson, William, *Poems* (London: Chatto and Windus, 1935)
—— *Selected Letters of William Empson*, ed. by John Haffenden (Oxford: Oxford University Press, 2006)
—— *Seven Types of Ambiguity* [1930] (London: Pimlico, 2004)
—— *Some Versions of Pastoral* [1935] (London: Penguin, 1995)
—— *The Structure of Complex Words* (London: Chatto and Windus, 1951)
—— 'The Use of Poetry' [1935], in *Argufying: Essays on Literature and Culture*, ed. by John Haffenden (Iowa City: Iowa University Press, 1987), pp. 413–14
Engels, Friedrich, *Socialism: Utopian and Scientific* [1880], trans. by Edward Aveling (London: Allen and Unwin, 1892)

Fenton, James, *The Strength of Poetry* (Oxford: Oxford University Press, 2001)
'Fight Hitler We Must', *London Bulletin*, 1 (1940), 18–20
Filreis, Alan, *The Counter-Revolution of the Word: The Conservative Attack on Modern Poetry, 1945–1960* (Chapel Hill: University of North Carolina Press, 2008)
Finney, Brian, 'Laily, Mortmere and All That', *Twentieth-Century Literature*, 22 (1976), 286–302
'Five', 'Wyndham Lewis's *Enemy*', *Experiment*, 3 (May 1929), 2–5
Forster, Edward Morgan, *Aspects of the Novel* [1927] (London: Penguin, 2005)
—— *Four Ways of Looking at a Keyword*, ed. by Sylvia Adamson and Alan Durant (= *Critical Quarterly*, 49/1 (2007))
Frege, Gottlob, 'Über Sinn und Bedeutung', *Zeitschrift für Philosophie und philosophische Kritik*, 100 (1892), 25–50
Freud, Sigmund, 'The Antithetical Meaning of Primal Words' [1910], in *The Standard Edition of the Complete Psychological Works of Sigmund Freud*, 24 vols, ed. and trans. by James Strachey and others (London: Hogarth Press, 1953–74), XI (1964), pp. 153–61
—— *Introductory Lectures on Psycho-Analysis* [1917], trans. by Joan Riviere (London: Allen and Unwin, 1922)
—— *Totem and Taboo: Resemblances Between the Psychic Lives of Savages and Neurotics* [1913], trans. by A. A. Brill (London: Routledge, 1919)
Fry, Paul, 'Hermeneutic Circling: Empson, Rosemund Tuve, and the "Wimsatt Law"', in *Some Versions of Empson*, ed. by Matthew Bevis (Oxford: Oxford University Press, 2007), pp. 201–16
—— *William Empson: Prophet Against Sacrifice* (London: Routledge, 1991)
Fuller, John, 'An Edifice of Meaning', *Encounter*, 45/5 (November 1974), 75–79
Fuller, Roy, *Owls and Afterlives: Oxford Lectures on Poetry* (London: Deutsch, 1971)
Gascoyne, David, *Collected Poems 1988* (Oxford: Oxford University Press, 1988)
—— *Collected Verse Translations*, ed. by Alan Clodd and Robin Skelton (Oxford: Oxford University Press, 1970)
—— *Journal 1936–1937* (London: Enitharmon, 1980)
—— *Journal 1937–1939* (London: Enitharmon, 1978)
—— 'Poetry and Reality' [1936], in *Selected Prose 1934–96*, ed. by Roger Scott (London: Enitharmon, 1998), pp. 74–77
—— *A Short Survey of Surrealism* [1935] (London: Enitharmon, 2000)
—— 'On Spontaneity', *New Verse*, 18 (December 1935), 19
Gide, André, 'The Individual', *Left Review*, 1/11 (August 1935), 447–52
Gorki, Maxim, 'Soviet Literature', in *Problems of Soviet Literature: Reports and Speeches at the First Soviet Writers' Conference 1934*, trans. by H. G. Scott (London: Martin Lawrence, 1935), pp. 27–69
Gramsci, Antonio, *Selections from the Prison Notebooks*, trans. by Quintin Hoare and Geoffrey Nowell-Smith (London: Lawrence and Wishart, 1991)
Grigson, Geoffrey, 'A Letter from England', *Poetry*, 49/2 (November 1936), 101–103

—— Review of *The Year's Poetry 1935*, *New Verse*, 18 (December 1935), 21–22

Haffenden, John, 'Introduction', in William Empson, *Complete Poems* (London: Penguin, 2000), pp. xi–lxv

—— *William Empson: Among the Mandarins* (Oxford: Oxford University Press, 2005)

—— *William Empson: Against the Christians* (Oxford: Oxford University Press, 2006)

Harding, Jason, *The 'Criterion': Cultural Politics and Periodical Networks in Inter-War Britain* (Oxford: Oxford University Press, 2002)

—— '*Experiment* in Cambridge: "A Manifesto of Young England"', *The Cambridge Quarterly*, 27 (1998), 287–309

—— 'The Gifts of China', in *Some Versions of Empson*, ed. by Matthew Bevis (Oxford: Oxford University Press, 2007), pp. 84–103

Harrisson, Tom, 'Mass-Opposition and Tom Harrisson', *Light and Dark*, 2/3 (February 1938), 8–15

—— and Humphrey Jennings, and Charles Madge, 'Anthropology at Home', *New Statesman and Nation*, 2 January 1937, p. 12

—— and Charles Madge, *Britain by Mass-Observation* [1939] (London: The Cresset Library, 1986)

—— and Charles Madge, *First Year's Work by Mass-Observation* (London: Wyman, 1938)

—— and Charles Madge, *Mass-Observation* (London: Frederick Muller, 1937)

Hartman, Geoffrey, *Criticism in the Wilderness: The Study of Literature Today* [1980], (New Haven: Yale University Press, 2007)

Hassan, Ihab, *The Dismemberment of Orpheus: Toward a Postmodern Literature* (Oxford: Oxford University Press, 1971)

Haughton, Hugh, 'Alice and Ulysses Bough: Nonsense in Empson', in *Some Versions of Empson*, ed. by Matthew Bevis (Oxford: Oxford University Press, 2007), pp. 158–81

Hill, Geoffrey, 'The Dream of Reason', *Essays in Criticism*, 14 (1964), 91–101

Hubble, Nick, 'The Intermodern Assumption of the Future: William Empson, Charles Madge and Mass-Observation', in *Intermodernism: Literary Culture in Mid-Twentieth-Century Britain*, ed. by Kristin Bluemel (Edinburgh: Edinburgh University Press, 2009), pp. 171–88

—— 'Intermodern Pastoral: William Empson and George Orwell', in *New Versions of Pastoral: Post-Romantic, Modern, and Contemporary Responses to the Tradition*, ed. by David James and Philip Tew (Madison: Fairleigh Dickinson University Press, 2009), pp. 125–35

—— *Mass-Observation and Everyday Life: Culture, History, Theory* (Basingstoke: Palgrave Macmillan, 2006)

Hulme, Thomas Ernest, *Speculations: Essays on Humanism and the Philosophy of Art*, ed. by Herbert Read (London: Kegan Paul, 1924)

Huyssen, Andreas, *After the Great Divide: Modernism, Mass Culture, Postmodernism* (Basingstoke: Macmillan, 1986)

Hynes, Samuel, *The Auden Generation: Literature and Politics in England in the 1930s* (London: Bodley Head, 1976)
Isherwood, Christopher, *Lions and Shadows* [1938] (London: Methuen, 1985)
—— and Edward Upward, *The Mortmere Stories*, ed. by Katherine Bucknell (London: Enitharmon, 1994)
Jackson, Kevin, *Humphrey Jennings* (London: Picador, 2004)
—— 'Humphrey Jennings: The Poet and the Public', *Contemporary Record*, 7/3 (1993), 663–84
Jackson, T. A., 'Marxism: Pragmatism: Surrealism: A Comment for Herbert Read', *Left Review*, 2/11 (August 1936), 565–7
Jakobson, Roman, 'Linguistics and Poetics', in *Style in Language*, ed. by Thomas A. Sebeok (Cambridge, MA: MIT Press, 1960), pp. 350–77
Jameson, Fredric, 'The Experiments of Time: Providence and Realism', in *The Novel*, 2 vols, ed. by Franco Moretti (Princeton: Princeton University Press, 2003), II, pp. 95–127
—— *Marxism and Form: Twentieth-Century Dialectical Theories of Literature* (Princeton: Princeton University Press, 1971)
—— *The Political Unconscious: Narrative as a Socially Symbolic Act* [1981] (London: Routledge, 2002)
Jameson, Storm, 'Documents', *fact*, 4 (July 1937), 9–18
Jay, Martin, 'Modernism and the Retreat from Form', in *Force Fields: Between Intellectual History and Cultural Critique* (London: Routledge, 1993), pp. 147–57
Jeffery, Tom, *A Short History of Mass-Observation*, rev. ed. (Birmingham: Centre for Contemporary Cultural Studies, 1999)
Jennings, Humphrey, 'Eliot and Auden and Shakespeare', *New Verse*, 18 (December 1935), 4–7
—— 'Plagiarism in Poetry' [1937], in *The Humphrey Jennings Film Reader*, ed. by Kevin Jackson (London: Carcanet, 1993), pp. 247–50
—— Review of *Surrealism*, *Contemporary Poetry and Prose*, 8 (December 1936), 167–68
—— 'Study for a Long Report: "The Boyhood of Byron"', *Contemporary Poetry and Prose*, 8 (December 1937), 146–47
—— 'The Theatre Today' [1935], in *The Humphrey Jennings Film Reader*, ed. by Kevin Jackson (London: Carcanet, 1993), pp. 202–18
—— Charles Madge, and others, *May the Twelfth* [1937] (London: Faber and Faber, 1987)
—— and Charles Madge, 'Poetic Description and Mass-Observation', *New Verse*, 24 (February-March 1937), 1–6
—— and Charles Madge, 'They Speak for Themselves: Mass-Observation and Social Narrative', *Life and Letters To-Day*, 17/9 (Autumn 1937), 37–42
—— and J. M. Reeves, 'A Reconsideration of Herrick' [1931], in *The Humphrey Jennings Film Reader*, ed. by Kevin Jackson (London: Carcanet, 1993), pp. 195–202
Joannou, Maroula, *'Ladies Please Don't Smash These Windows': Women's Writing, Feminist Consciousness and Social Change, 1914–1938* (Oxford: Berg, 1995)

——, ed., *Women Writers of the 1930s: Gender, Politics, and History* (Edinburgh: Edinburgh University Press, 1999)

Jolas, Eugene, and Elliot Paul, 'Proclamation: The Revolution of the Word', *transition*, 16–17 (June 1929), 13

Kermode, Frank, *Continuities* (London: Routledge, 1968)

—— *History and Value: The Clarendon Lectures and the Northcliffe Lectures* (Oxford: Clarendon Press, 1988)

—— 'Introduction', in Edward Upward, *An Unmentionable Man* (London: Enitharmon, 1994), pp. 7–10

—— *Poetry, Narrative, History* (Oxford: Blackwell, 1990)

—— *The Sense of an Ending: Studies in the Theory of Fiction* [1966] (Oxford: Oxford University Press, 2000)

Keywords, ed. by Colin MacCabe (= *Critical Quarterly*, 50/1–2 (2008))

Kohlmann, Benjamin, 'Edward Upward, W. H. Auden, and the Rhetorical Victories of Communism', *Modernism/Modernity*, 20/2 (2013), 287–306

—— ' "A Foot in Mortmere": Christopher Isherwood, Edward Upward, and Allen Chalmers', in *The American Isherwood*, ed. by Jim Berg and Christopher Freeman (Minneapolis: University of Minnesota Press, forthcoming 2014)

Krauss, Rosalind E., *The Originality of the Avant-Garde and Other Modernist Myths* (Cambridge, MA: MIT Press, 1985)

Lautréamont, Comte de, *Les Chants de Maldoror* [1869], trans. by Guy Wernham (New York: New Directions, 1965)

Leavis, F. R., 'Cambridge Poetry', *The Cambridge Review*, 1 March 1929, 317–18

—— *New Bearings in English Poetry: A Study of the Contemporary Situation* (London: Chatto and Windus, 1932)

—— 'T. S. Eliot: A Reply to the Condescending', *The Cambridge Review*, 8 February 1929, 254–56

Lehmann, John, *Autobiography*, 3 vols (London: Longmans, 1955–66)

Leighton, Angela, *On Form: Poetry, Aestheticism, and the Legacy of a Word* (Oxford: Oxford University Press, 2007)

Lenin, V. I., *The State and Revolution* [1918], in *Selected Works*, ed. by Joe Fineberg, 12 vols (London: Lawrence and Wishart, 1936–39), VII (1937), pp. 3–111

—— 'The Tasks of the Proletariat in the Present Revolution' [= 'April Theses'] [1917], in *Selected Works*, ed. by Joe Fineberg, 12 vols (London: Lawrence and Wishart, 1936–39), VI (1936), pp. 21–26

Lenin, V. I., *What Is To Be Done?* [1902], in *Selected Works*, ed. by Joe Fineberg, 12 vols (London: Lawrence and Wishart, 1936–39), II (1936), pp. 25–192

Levitas, Ruth, *The Concept of Utopia* (London: Philip Allan, 1990)

Lewis, Cecil Day, *A Hope for Poetry* [1934] (Oxford: Basil Blackwell, 1936)

—— 'Letter to a Young Revolutionary', in *New Country: Prose and Poetry by the Authors of 'New Signatures'*, ed. by Michael Roberts (London: Hogarth Press, 1933), pp. 25–42

—— 'Revolutionaries and Poetry' [1935], in *Revolution in Writing* (New York: Haskell, 1972), pp. 32–44

—— 'Surrealists Get the Bird', *New Verse*, 19 (February–March 1936), 20–21

——, Charles Madge, et al. 'Answers to an Enquiry', *New Verse*, 11 (October 1934), 2–22
Lewis, Helena, *Dada Turns Red: The Politics of Surrealism* (Edinburgh: Edinburgh University Press, 1990)
Litz, A. Walton, 'Review: Revising the Thirties', *The Sewanee Review*, 87 (1979), pp. 660–66
Liu, Lydia, *Translingual Practice: Literature, National Culture, and Translated Modernity—China, 1900–1937* (Stanford: Stanford University Press, 1995)
Lloyd, A. L., 'Surrealism & Revolutions', *Left Review*, 2/16 (January 1937), 895–98
Longenbach, James, *The Resistance to Poetry* (Chicago: University of Chicago Press, 2004)
Lucas, John, ed., *The 1930s: A Challenge to Orthodoxy* (Brighton: Harvester Press, 1978)
—— *The Radical Twenties: Aspects of Writing, Politics and Culture* (Nottingham: Five Leaves, 1997)
—— 'Standards of Criticism: The *Calendar of Modern Letters* (1925–7)', in *The Oxford Critical and Cultural History of Modernist Magazines*, ed. by Peter Brooker and Andrew Thacker (Oxford: Oxford University Press, 2009), pp. 389–404
Lukács, Georg, 'Art and Objective Truth' [1954], in *Writer and Critic, and Other Essays*, ed. and trans. by Arthur Kahn (London: Merlin Press, 1970), pp. 25–60
MacClancy, Jeremy, 'Brief Encounter: The Meeting, in Mass-Observation, of British Surrealism and Popular Anthropology', *Journal of the Royal Anthropological Institute*, 1/3 (1995), 495–512
MacKay, Marina, '"Doing Business With Totalitaria": British Late Modernism and the Politics of Reputation', *English Literary History*, 73/3 (2006), 729–53
—— *Modernism and World War II* (Cambridge: Cambridge University Press, 2007)
Madge, Charles, 'Magic and Materialism', *Left Review*, 3/1 (February 1937), 31–35
—— 'The Meaning of Surrealism', *New Verse*, 10 (August 1934), 13–15
—— *Of Love, Time and Places: Selected Poems* (London: Anvil Press, 1994)
—— 'Press, Radio, and Social Consciousness', in *The Mind in Chains: Socialism and the Cultural Revolution*, ed. by Cecil Day Lewis (London: Frederick Muller, 1937), pp. 147–63
—— Review of *A Short Survey of Surrealism*, *New Verse*, 18 (December 1935), 20–21
—— 'Surrealism for the English', *New Verse*, 6 (December 1933), 14–18
—— 'Writers Under Two Flags', *Left Review*, 2/5 (February 1936), 228–30
'Manifesto', *transition*, 19–20 (June 1930), 106
Manuilsky, D. Z., *The Communist Parties and the Crisis of Capitalism* [1931] (London: Modern Books)
Marcus, Laura, 'Introduction: The Project of Mass-Observation', in *Mass-Observation as Poetics and Science*, ed. by Nick Hubble, Margaretta Jolly, and Laura Marcus (= *new formations*, 44 (2001)), 5–20

Marks, Peter, 'Making the New: Literary Periodicals and the Construction of Modernism', *Precursors and Aftermaths: Literature in English, 1914–1945*, 2/1 (2004), 14–39

Marx, Karl, *Capital: A Critique of Political Economy* [1867–94], 3 vols, trans. by David Fernbach (London: Penguin, 1976–81)

—— *Economic and Philosophic Manuscripts of 1844*, ed. by Dirk J. Struik, trans. by Martin Milligan (London: Lawrence and Wishart, 1970)

—— *The Eighteenth Brumaire of Louis Bonaparte* [1852], trans. by Cedar and Eden Paul (London: Allen and Unwin, 1926)

Mass-Observation as Poetics and Science, ed. by Nick Hubble, Margaretta Jolly, and Laura Marcus (= *new formations*, 44 (2001))

Matthews, Steven, and Keith Williams, eds, *Rewriting the Thirties: Modernism and After* (London: Longman, 1997)

McCracken, Scott, 'Cambridge Magazines and Unfinished Business: *Experiment* (1928–31), *The Venture* (1928–30), and *Cambridge Left* (1933–4)', in *The Oxford Critical and Cultural History of Modernist Magazines*, ed. by Peter Brooker and Andrew Thacker (Oxford: Oxford University Press, 2009), 598–622

McDonald, Peter, 'Believing in the Thirties', in *Rewriting the Thirties: Modernism and After*, ed. by Steven Matthews and Keith Williams (London: Longman, 1997), pp. 71–90

—— *Louis MacNeice: The Poet in His Contexts* (Oxford: Clarendon Press, 1991)

—— *Serious Poetry: Form and Authority from Yeats to Hill* (Oxford: Clarendon Press, 2002)

McGann, Jerome, *The Beauty of Inflections: Literary Investigations in Historical Method and Theory* (Oxford: Clarendon Press, 1985)

Mellor, Leo, *Reading the Ruins: Modernism, Bombsites and British Culture* (Cambridge: Cambridge University Press, 2011)

Mendelson, Edward, *Early Auden* (London: Faber and Faber, 1981)

Mengham, Rod, 'Bourgeois News: Humphrey Jennings and Charles Madge', in *Mass-Observation as Poetics and Science*, ed. by Nick Hubble, Margaretta Jolly, and Laura Marcus (= *new formations*, 44 (2001)), 26–33

—— '"National Papers Please Reprint": Surrealist Magazines in Britain', in *The Oxford Critical and Cultural History of Modernist Magazines*, ed. by Peter Brooker and Andrew Thacker (Oxford: Oxford University Press, 2009), pp. 688–703

Mengham, Rod, 'Smithereens: *The Railway Accident* and *The Orators*', *Ideas and Production*, 4 (1985), 25–43

—— 'The Thirties: Politics, Authority, Perspective', in *The Cambridge History of Twentieth-Century Literature*, ed. by Laura Marcus and Peter Nicholls (Cambridge: Cambridge University Press, 2004), pp. 359–78

Meyerowitz, Joel, and Colin Westerbeck, *Bystander: A History of Street Photography* (London: Thames and Hudson, 1994)

Miller, Tyrus, 'Documentary/Modernism: Convergence and Complementarity in the 1930s', *Modernism/Modernity*, 9/2 (2002), 225–41

—— *Late Modernism: Politics, Fiction, and the Arts Between the World Wars* (Berkeley: University of California Press, 1999)

Milton, John, *Paradise Lost*, ed. by Alastair Fowler (London: Longman, 1998)
Montefiore, Jan, *Men and Women Writers of the 1930s: The Dangerous Flood of History* (London: Routledge, 1996)
Morris, William, *News from Nowhere*, ed. by David Leopold (Oxford: Oxford University Press, 2009)
Murry, John Middleton, *The Necessity of Communism* (London: Cape, 1932)
Nicholls, Peter, *Modernisms: A Literary Guide* (Basingstoke: Macmillan, 1994)
—— 'Surrealism in England', in *The Cambridge History of Twentieth-Century English Literature*, ed. by Laura Marcus and Peter Nicholls (Cambridge: Cambridge University Press, 2004), 393–416
Ogden, Charles Kay, and I. A. Richards, *The Meaning of Meaning: A Study of the Influence of Language upon Thought and of the Science of Symbolism* [1923] (London: Paul Trench, 1927)
Orwell, George, 'Inside the Whale' [1940], in *The Complete Works of George Orwell*, 20 vols (London: Seckler and Warburg, 1986–98), XII: *A Patriot After All, 1940–1941*, ed. by Peter Davison (1998), pp. 86–115
—— 'The Lion and the Unicorn: Socialism and the English Genius' [1941], in *The Complete Works of George Orwell*, 20 vols (London: Seckler and Warburg, 1986–98), XII: *A Patriot After All, 1940–1941*, ed. by Peter Davison (1998), pp. 391–434
—— 'The Prevention of Literature' [1946], in *The Complete Works of George Orwell*, 20 vols (London: Seckler and Warburg, 1986–98), XVII: *I Belong to the Left, 1945*, ed. by Peter Davison (1998), pp. 369–81
'Oxford Collective Poem', *New Verse*, 25 (May 1937), 16–19
Parker, Peter, *Isherwood: A Life* (London: Picador, 2004)
Penrose, Roland, *Visiting Picasso: The Notebooks and Letters of Roland Penrose*, ed. by Elizabeth Cowling (London: Thames & Hudson, 2006)
Phare, Elsie E., 'Ernest Hemingway', *Experiment*, 3 (May 1929), 13–16
—— 'An Essay on the Devotional Poetry of T. S. Eliot', *Experiment*, 6 (October 1930), 27–32
—— *The Poetry of Gerard Manley Hopkins: A Survey and Commentary* (Cambridge: Cambridge University Press, 1933)
—— 'Several White Leopards', *The Granta*, 30 November 1928, p. 197
—— 'Valéry and Gerard Hopkins', *Experiment*, 1 (November 1928), 19–23
Piette, Adam, 'Empson, Piaget, and Child Logic in Wartime', in *Some Versions of Empson*, ed. by Matthew Bevis (Oxford: Oxford University Press, 2007), pp. 42–59
Pound, Ezra, 'The Coward Surrealists', *Contemporary Poetry and Prose*, 7 (November 1936), 136
Price, Kate, 'Finite But Unbounded: *Experiment* Magazine, Cambridge, England, 1928–31', *Jacket Magazine*, 20 (2001) <http://jacketmagazine.com/20/price-expe.html>
Puchner, Martin, *Poetry of the Revolution: Marx, Manifestos, and the Avant-Gardes* (Princeton: Princeton University Press, 2006)

Purcell, Victor, *Chinese Evergreen* (London: Joseph, 1938)
Quinn, Patrick, 'At the Frontier: Edward Upward's *Journey to the Border*', in *Recharting the Thirties*, ed. by Patrick Quinn (Selinsgrove: Susquehanna University Press, 1996), pp. 233–46
——, ed., *Recharting the Thirties* (Selinsgrove: Susquehanna University Press, 1996)
Raine, Kathleen, *The Land Unknown* (London: Hamish Hamilton, 1975)
Ransom, John Crowe, 'Criticism as Pure Speculation', in *The Intent of the Critic*, ed. by Donald A. Stauffer (Princeton: Princeton University Press, 1941), pp. 91–124
—— *The New Criticism* (Norfolk, CT: New Directions, 1941)
Rawson, Claude, *God, Gulliver, and Genocide: Barbarism and the European Imagination, 1492–1945* (Oxford: Oxford University Press, 2001)
Ray, Paul, *The Surrealist Movement in England* (Ithaca: Cornell University Press, 1971)
Read, Herbert, *Art and Society* (London: Heinemann, 1937)
—— *Art Now* [1933] (London: Faber and Faber 1936)
—— 'Books of the Quarter', *The Criterion*, 3 (April 1925), 444–49
—— *The Green Child* [1935] (London: Robin Clark, 1989)
—— 'Surrealism and Politics', *London Bulletin*, 8/9 (1939), 5–6
—— 'What is Revolutionary Art?', in *5 on Revolutionary Art* (London: Wishart, 1935), pp. 11–22
Reavey, George, 'First Essay Towards Pasternak', *Experiment*, 6 (October 1930), 14–17
—— *Nostradam* (Paris: Europa Press, 1935)
Remy, Michel, *Surrealism in Britain* (Aldershot: Ashgate, 1999)
Review of *Some Versions of Pastoral*, *New Verse*, 18 (December 1935), 17–18
Richards, Ivor Armstrong, 'Belief' [1930], in *Complementarities: Uncollected Essays*, ed. by John Paul Russo (Manchester: Carcanet, 1976), pp. 24–36
—— 'Cambridge Poetry', *The Granta*, 8 March 1929, p. 359
—— 'Gerard Hopkins', *The Dial*, 81 (September 1926), 195–203
—— *Mencius on the Mind* [1932], ed. by John Constable (London: Routledge, 2001)
—— 'Notes on the Practice of Interpretation', *The Criterion*, 10 (April 1931), 412–20
Richards, Ivor Armstrong, 'Lawrence as a Poet', *New Verse*, 1 (January 1933), 15–17
—— *Poetries and Sciences* [1935] (London: Routledge, 1970)
—— *Practical Criticism: A Study of Literary Judgment* [1929] (London: Transaction Publishers, 2004)
—— 'Preface to a Dictionary', *Psyche*, 13 (1933), 10–24
—— *Principles of Literary Criticism* [1924] (London: Routledge, 2001)
—— *Science and Poetry* (London: Trubner, 1926)
—— *Selected Letters of I. A. Richards*, ed. by John Constable (Oxford: Oxford University Press, 1990)

Ricks, Christopher, 'Empson's Poetry', in *William Empson: The Man and His Work*, ed. by Roma Gill (London: Routledge, 1974), pp. 145–207

Ricoeur, Paul, *The Rule of Metaphor: The Creation of Meaning in Language* [1975], trans. by Robert Czerny (London: Routledge, 2003)

Rimbaud, Arthur, *Complete Works, Selected Letters: A Bilingual Edition*, ed. and trans. by Wallace Fowlie (Chicago: The University of Chicago Press, 2005)

Roberts, Michael, ed., *New Country: Prose and Poetry by the Authors of 'New Signatures'* (London: Hogarth Press, 1933)

—— , ed., *New Signatures: Poems by Several Hands* (London: Hogarth Press, 1932)

—— 'Preface', in *New Country: Prose and Poetry by the Authors of 'New Signatures'*, ed. by Michael Roberts (London: Hogarth Press, 1933), pp. 9–21

—— 'Preface', in *New Signatures: Poems by Several Hands*, ed. by Michael Roberts (London: Hogarth Press, 1932), pp. 7–20

Roughton, Roger, 'Eyewash, Do You? A Reply to Mr. Pound', *Contemporary Poetry and Prose*, 7 (November 1936), 137–38

—— 'Soluble Noughts and Croses; *or,* California, Here I Come', *Contemporary Poetry and Prose*, 3 (July 1936), 55

—— 'Surrealism and Communism', *Contemporary Poetry and Prose*, 4–5 (August–September 1936), 74–75

Rowse, A. L., *Politics and the Younger Generation* (London: Faber and Faber, 1931)

Russo, John Paul, *I. A. Richards: His Life and Work* (London: Routledge, 1989)

Sale, Roger, *Modern Heroism: Essays on D. H. Lawrence, William Empson, and J. R. R. Tolkien* (Berkeley: University of California Press, 1973)

Sartre, Jean-Paul, 'Black Orpheus' [1947], trans. by John MacCombie, in *'What is Literature?' and Other Essays*, ed. by Steven Ungar (Cambridge, MA: Harvard University Press, 1988), pp. 289–330

Scarfe, Francis, *Auden and After: The Liberation of Poetry, 1930–1941* (London: Routledge, 1942)

Sellers, W. H., 'Edward Upward: An Introduction', *The Dalhousie Review*, 43/2 (1963), 163–74

Shattuck, Roger, 'Having Congress: The Shame of the Thirties', in *The Innocent Eye: On Modern Literature and the Arts* (New York: Farrar, Straus and Giroux, 1984), pp. 3–31

Sheringham, Michael, *Everyday Life: Theories and Practices from Surrealism to the Present* (Oxford: Oxford University Press, 2006)

Shuttleworth, Antony, ed., *And in Our Time: Vision, Revision, and British Writing of the 1930s* (Lewisburg, PA: Bucknell University Press, 2003)

'The Situation in England', in *International Surrealist Bulletin, Issued by the Surrealist Group of England* (London: Zwemmer, 1936), 2–4

Skinner, Quentin, 'The Idea of a Cultural Lexicon', *Essays in Criticism*, 29 (1979), 205–24

Spender, Stephen, 'The Case of Edward Upward', *London Magazine*, 27 (1987), 29–43

—— 'I Join the Communist Party' [1937], in *The Thirties and After: Poetry, Politics, People (1933–75)* (Basingstoke: Macmillan, 1978), pp. 80–82
—— 'Introduction', in *Poems for Spain*, ed. by Stephen Spender and John Lehmann (London: Hogarth Press, 1939), pp. 7–14
—— 'The Left Wing Orthodoxy', *New Verse*, 31–32 (Autumn 1938), 12–16
—— *The New Realism: A Discussion* (London: Hogarth Press, 1939)
—— 'Oxford to Communism', *New Verse*, 26–27 (November 1937), 9–10
—— *Poetry Since 1939* (London: Longmans, 1946)
—— 'Poetry and Revolution', in *New Country: Prose and Poetry by the Authors of 'New Signatures'*, ed. by Michael Roberts (London: Hogarth Press, 1933), pp. 62–67
—— Review of Louis Aragon's 'The Red Front', *New Verse*, 3 (May 1933), 24–25
—— *The Thirties and After: Poetry, Politics, People (1933–75)* (Basingstoke: Macmillan, 1978)
—— *World Within World* [1951] (New York: The Modern Library, 2001)
Stead, Christina, 'The Writers Take Sides', *Left Review*, 1/11 (October 1935), 453–62
Stanford, Derek, *The Freedom of Poetry: Studies in Contemporary Verse* (London: The Falcon Press, 1947)
Strachey, John, *The Theory and Practice of Socialism* (London: Gollancz, 1935)
Sykes Davies, Hugh, 'The Enjoyment of Modern Poetry II: The Problem of Beauty and Sincerity', *The Listener*, 9 August 1933, pp. 217–18
—— 'The Enjoyment of Modern Poetry VI: Reading the Modern Poets', *The Listener*, 20 September 1933, 435–36
—— 'An Epilaugh for Surrealism', *Times Literary Supplement*, 13 January 1978, p. 34
—— 'The League of Nations', *Experiment*, 5 (February 1930), 6–10
—— *Petron* (London: Dent, 1935)
—— Review of Gertrude Stein's *Narration*, *The Criterion*, 15 (July 1936), 752–55
—— 'Sympathies with Surrealism', *New Verse*, 20 (April–May 1936), 15–21
Symons, Arthur, *The Symbolist Movement in Literature* (London: Heinemann, 1899)
Symons, Julian, *The Thirties: A Dream Revolved* (London: Cresset Press, 1960)
Tate, Allen, 'A New Artist', *New Verse*, 3 (May 1933), 21–23
—— 'Tension in Poetry' [1938], in *Reason in Madness: Critical Essays* (New York: Putnam, 1941), pp. 62–81
'A Terrible Battle Fought on the Fifty-Twelfth Day of Rotten Sticks, and Other Documents from the Same Id', *New Verse*, 23 (Christmas 1936), 1–7
Thistlewood, David, *Herbert Read: Formlessness and Form* (London: Routledge, 1984)
Trevelyan, Julian, *Indigo Days* [1957] (Aldershot: Scolar Press, 1996)
Trilling, Lionel, *Matthew Arnold* (London: Allen and Unwin, 1939)
Trotsky, Leon, *Literature and Revolution* [1925], ed. by William Keach, trans. by Rose Strunsky (Chicago: Haymarket, 2005)

Tzara, Tristan, 'Essai sur la situation de la poésie', *Le Surréalisme au service de la revolution*, 4 (1931), 22–24

Upward, Edward, 'The Falling Tower', *Folios of New Writing*, 3 (Spring 1941), pp. 24–29

—— *The Railway Accident and Other Stories* (London: Penguin, 1972)

—— *Remembering the Earlier Auden* (London: Enitharmon, 1998)

—— 'Sketch for a Marxist Interpretation of Literature', in *The Mind in Chains: Socialism and the Cultural Revolution*, ed. by Cecil Day Lewis (London: F. Muller, 1937), pp. 41–55

—— *The Spiral Ascent* [1962–77], 3 vols (London: Quartet Books, 1977–79)

Vaihinger, Hans, *The Philosophy of 'As If': System of the Theoretical, Practical and Religious Fictions of Mankind* [1911], trans. by C. K. Ogden (London: Routledge, 1924)

Vertov, Dziga, 'A Minute of the World' [1944], in *Kino-Eye: The Writings of Dziga Vertov*, ed. by Annette Michelson, trans. by Kevin O'Brien (Berkeley: University of California Press, 1984), pp. 315–16

Voloshinov, V. N., *Marxism and the Philosophy of Language* [1930] (Cambridge, MA: Harvard University Press, 1986)

Vsevolod, Ivanov, 'Mounds', trans. by George Reavey, *Experiment*, 2 (February 1929), 47–48

Wain, John, *Professing Poetry* (Basingstoke: Macmillan, 1977)

Waley, Arthur, ed. and trans., *A Hundred and Seventy Chinese Poems* (London: Constable, 1918)

Warner, Rex, 'Education', in *The Mind in Chains: Socialism and the Cultural Revolution* (London: Frederick Muller, 1937), pp. 19–37

Warner, Sylvia Townsend, 'Red Front!', *Left Review*, 1/7 (April 1935), 255–57

Wellek, René, *A History of Modern Criticism, 1750–1950, Volume 8: French, Italian, and Spanish Criticism, 1900–1950* (New Haven: Yale University Press, 1992)

West, Alick, 'I. A. Richards', in *Crisis and Criticism* [1937] *and Selected Literary Essays* (London: Lawrence and Wishart, 1975), pp. 54–65

—— 'Marx and Romanticism', in *Crisis and Criticism* [1937] *and Selected Literary Essays* (London: Lawrence and Wishart, 1975), pp. 68–72

—— 'Surréalisme in Literature', *Left Review*, 2/10 (July 1936), vi–viii

Williams, Raymond, *Culture* (Glasgow: Fontana, 1981)

—— *Culture and Society, 1780–1950* (London: Chatto and Windus, 1958)

—— *Keywords: A Vocabulary of Culture and Society* [1976] (London: Fontana, 1988)

—— *Marxism and Literature* (Oxford: Oxford University Press, 1977)

—— *The Politics of Modernism: Against the New Conformists* (London: Verso, 1989)

Wimsatt, William K., *The Verbal Icon: Studies in the Meaning of Poetry* [1954] (London: Methuen, 1970)

Wolfson, Susan, 'Empson's Pregnancies', in *Some Versions of Empson*, ed. by Matthew Bevis (Oxford: Oxford University Press, 2007), pp. 264–88

—— *Formal Charges: The Shaping of Poetry in British Romanticism* (Princeton: Princeton University Press, 1997)

Woolf, Virginia, 'The Leaning Tower', in *The Moment and Other Essays* (New York: Harcourt Brace, 1948), pp. 118–54

Yeats, W. B., *The Poems*, ed. by Daniel Albright (London: Dent, 1990)

Young, Alan, *Dada and After: Extremist Modernism and English Literature* (Manchester: Manchester University Press, 1981)

Index